BLACK CLOVER

*Murder in a Small Pennsylvania Town
and a Family's Fight for Justice*

C. Lee Ryder

Mechanicsburg, PA USA

Published by Sunbury Press, Inc.
Mechanicsburg, PA USA

www.sunburypress.com

For information about special discounts for bulk purchases, please contact Sunbury Press Orders Dept. at (855) 338-8359 or orders@sunburypress.com.

To request one of our authors for speaking engagements or book signings, please contact Sunbury Press Publicity Dept. at publicity@sunburypress.com.

FIRST SUNBURY PRESS EDITION: October 2021

Set in Adobe Garamond Pro | Interior design by Crystal Devine | Cover by Lindsey Korytowski | Edited by Lawrence Knorr.

Publisher's Cataloging-in-Publication Data
Names: Ryder, C. Lee, author.
Title: Black clover : murder in a small Pennsylvania town and a family's fight for justice / C. Lee Ryder.
Description: First trade paperback edition. | Mechanicsburg, PA : Sunbury Press, 2021.
Summary : *Black Clover* details a murder committed by an escaped work release inmate, search and recovery of the victim's body, crime scene denial, transfer of the case to another county, and three-year battle for justice. The victim's family found themselves underrepresented as officials ignored evidence, lied, and manipulated the murder case to suit their own agenda.
Identifiers: ISBN : 978-1-62006-542-6 (softcover).
Subjects: MURDER / General | TRUE CRIME / General | FAMILY & RELATIONSHIPS / Death, Grief & Bereavement | CRIMINAL / General | LAW / Criminal Procedure.

Product of the United States of America
0 1 1 2 3 5 8 13 21 34 55

Continue the Enlightenment!

Dedicated to all my readers—
those who appreciate a real, true story and to those
who have suffered at the hand of absolute evil.

In Memory of Carl Wade Ryder
My Brother, My Best Friend

My heart is broken, Carl. I think of you every day, and I thank God for every memory of you. I know I will always be in your heart as you are in mine. In this wilderness world, those years on Mercury's wings that we traveled together passed much too soon. It was not an angel of death that took you full of years but a wicked, untimely, calculating hand.

Destiny made you my brother, my friend—a masterpiece. We shared an unbreakable bond since birth, and I always believed we would leave this world at nearly the same time, but here I remain, heartsick and yearning for good things that should have been. I think of the day when I will see you again in the glory from which we came. Not here to spend so long a day, but home where there is nothing to etch grief, sorrow, and sadness upon our hearts. Carl—so brave to go first—please wait for me at the holy gate. The years will race by, and someday, at last, I will see you, far from the horror that parted us, and we will walk the paths of angels far from this cold, dark face of death.

To God,

Those trying days,
I challenged forces both blameless and vile.
The grueling fires of tribulation have left me
blemished and burnished.
Yet, I still believe in You.

—C. Lee Ryder

CONTENTS

ACKNOWLEDGMENTS

Many thanks to my family and friends who supported this writing, waiting eagerly, yet patiently, for its completion. Thank you to Becky Bennett, who came to my aid and was instrumental in helping me see this book through to completion. Thank you to Vicky Taylor, who covered the story for the *Public Opinion* from beginning to end and has been a friend through it all. Thank you to our neighbors, community, and churches for comfort and support as we live with this ungodly nightmare, grief-stricken, and forever changed.

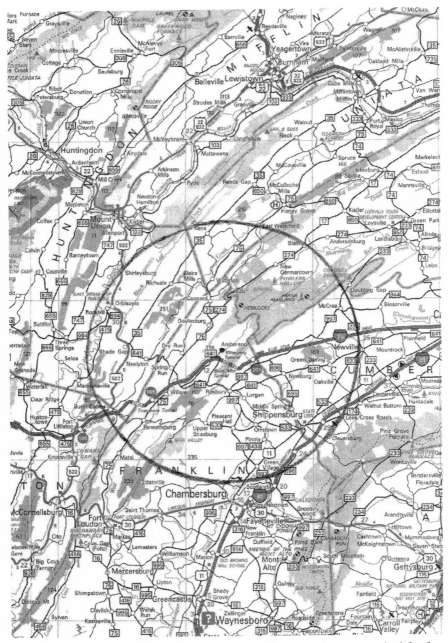

Map of Amberson, Pennsylvania, and the surrounding area that we searched for five days.

INTRODUCTION

I loved my brother Carl to the ends of the earth. Everyone else seemed fond of him too. He was an all-around good guy, six feet four inches tall, with broad shoulders. People would stare up at him into a handsome face with pale green-blue eyes flashing above high cheekbones, in contrast to his thick, dark brown hair with auburn lights. He was the embodiment of a native to the Americas, albeit Scottish, English, and German Palatine.

A man of the woods, he loved the land—the valleys and the mountains, the change of seasons, and, when he could visit, the ocean. To him, life was one big creation-adventure that blended the metaphysical with the physical. He had a perpetual old-soul look in his eyes, even as a young boy—a *knowing*.

He was intelligent, inventive, and talented—a man of character—spiritually grounded with a colorful personality and a good share of kindness. While in high school, he volunteered his time for the newly instituted Franklin County Special Olympics. The kids loved him. As an adult, he was a consummate gentleman. It didn't get past any woman that he viewed her with brotherly reverence and respect. He was good to his fiancée Debbie and had bought her a ring that they had chosen together while shopping in Gettysburg.

He loved his family, and whenever he could, he made it a point to entertain his nieces. At one particularly famous "Uncle Carl weenie roast," Carl had occupied an old, backless wooden chair that he had placed directly *over* the fire while relating a story—until the chair was smoking hot. The little girls laughed about that for days. Uncle Carl had been in the "hot seat." Carrie and Stacey secretly placed plastic spiders and ants on his pillow every chance they got, while Gayle and Jordyn camped in his yard, borrowing tents and flashlights.

He was appreciative when rare good fortune paid a visit. However, the typical trials and tribulations of life, the occasional toil, and heartache made him what he was—strong but aware of both the intangible side of life and the challenges of living in the world. Sensible and earthy, he guarded no dark secrets, nor was there anything dubious lurking in his personality. He always welcomed friends with a "howdy," and they enjoyed his company and admired his innate knowledge of the outdoors. He was a down-to-earth, extraordinary, ordinary guy.

Despite having a laborer's strong, rough hands, he produced some delicate, one-of-a-kind creations, especially woodcarvings. He was a gifted storyteller, enthralling his audience with detailed accounts built to a crescendo, that ended with an astounding twist. His way with words, gestures, and facial expressions drew people to watch him as he spoke. He also wrote poetry but kept most of his rhymes private, occasionally sharing some of them with me.

All our siblings were close, but Carl and I had a special bond as the first two of seven children. It was there before we were born and grew stronger as the years passed and as we faced life's challenges together. We reveled in our unique connection and talked the seasons away, gazing across our little valley encompassed by the ridges of the Appalachian Mountain chain. As we traipsed along the rugged, worn groove of the Tuscarora trail, wending through woods, along streams, and past ghostly ruts of long-abandoned logging roads, we shared our dreams, hopes, and disappointments. Youthful ideas and ambitions ebbed and flowed like the days and nights enveloping Pennsylvania's forested ridges.

One moonless midnight when we were young, the scream of a bobcat pierced the air and held us spellbound as it echoed through the hollows. We pretended that we walked in the wilds before any other man and felt a connection to a time born eons ago and encoded into our genetic bank of recollection. It fed our souls—it was the *best* time of my life. Then time passed.

As I have said, everyone who met Carl liked him—yet he was senselessly murdered on a Saturday night, August 5, 2006. However, his fate was set a little over two years earlier, in June 2004, when Carl made the mistake of hiring Scott North and then had to fire him three weeks later. North's abbreviated employment ultimately cost Carl his life.

Well known by the Franklin County courts, Scott North, the lawless son of a Chambersburg cop, eventually found himself jailed once again, this time for burglarizing a tavern. A judge granted him work release. Then another judge dismissed a gun charge just days before he ran from an unsupervised worksite. It was the beginning of a crime spree with a devastating end that might have been averted.

My family and I would never be the same. Murder desecrated our cherished valley. Some have described Amberson Valley as a piece of heaven if you don't mind traveling twenty miles or more to the nearest store, hospital, or work. The blue-tinted mountains with ridges and hollows cradle the west branch of the Conococheague Creek as it cuts through the bowl of the narrow valley, where a pair of one-room churches stand side by side. But now, malice had found its way into our picturesque surroundings. A storm had erased the color from our world and ushered in a dark, desperate time in which we would scour the byways and hillsides of Amberson, Path Valley, and other areas in adjoining counties in search of Carl's body.

The criminal investigation began with blood found at Carl's house in Franklin County and expanded to Huntingdon County (where Carl's body finally was found, no thanks to the police). It stalled for months as authorities in the two counties shamelessly bungled the case between them. We were compelled to pursue our own investigation, as we had pursued our own search for Carl, because of the astonishing incompetence and negligence of the state police and indifference of county prosecutors. The case inexplicably was handed off to Huntingdon County, despite extensive evidence that the murder occurred at Carl's house in Franklin County, though much of it was mishandled or overlooked by state police. The case languished in Huntingdon for a full year and a half before it was returned to Franklin County.

We came to the shocking realization that "the law" was not on our side. It seemed to us that Franklin County's professed dedication to public safety was nothing more than a smokescreen and that when authorities fail in their duty to protect the public from lawbreakers, *anyone* can become a victim of a violent crime. Nothing can fix or reverse the devastation. Moreover, we learned that crime victims in Franklin County could expect no diligence from police and little justice or recompense from the courts when officials choose to play politics. Victims look to a justice system sanctioned by the state to fight for them, but our stark reality was that those responsible for pursuing justice failed utterly, whether due to incompetence, design, or personal or political allegiances.

Although police and court officials repeatedly admonished us to keep quiet about details of the case, I have written this book to tell the story of our fight for justice—including the heartbreak of the search, the twisted path through the legal system, two funerals years apart (one within days after Carl's death and the other years later after his remains finally were returned), and the wounds that will never heal. I have strived to provide a firsthand, unfiltered account of our ordeal. This nightmare initially caused me to question the goodness of God yet firmly convinced me of the existence of evil. In the end, I cannot claim a hard-won triumph of any sort against injustice, grief, or evil; only battle-scarred wisdom in life forever changed. For those who know such all-encompassing heartache, I hope this book provides some solace. Know that others truly understand what it's like to live with the horrific facts and indelible sorrow of a loved one murdered. Only those who have suffered such atrocity can understand the peculiar feeling of isolation that nags even though you may be among a crowd of well-wishers—isolation born of incomparable psychological and spiritual trauma. May you receive some comfort from the fact that you are not alone.

To tell this story, it has been necessary to mine details, recall particulars, note unbearable facts, dig into public court records, and interview people who have encountered the killer. I have used dialogue from courtroom transcripts and, at other times, paraphrased some conversations. Some quotes come from notes I meticulously kept as events unfolded. The passages at the beginning of each chapter and the very end of the book are taken from the Holy Bible. The book cover is one of our favorite pictures of Carl taken in the mid-1980s.

 CHAPTER 1

MY BROTHER, WHERE ARE YOU?

Fearfulness and trembling are come upon me, and horror hath overwhelmed me. —*King David*

There are some things the soul cannot bear, hurts that render the spirit listless with grief for years on end. Such a thing was about to encompass our lives. What began as a carefree summer developed an undercurrent of featureless dread; a strange sense of unidentified foreshadowing enveloped me. I could not put my finger on the reason, but an uncomfortable apprehension crept in. Then came the loud trill from my cell phone at 4:00 A.M. on Friday, August 11, 2006.

As the noise jangled its way into a restless dream, I reached for the phone, wondering who would be calling at that time of the morning. *Maybe it's a wrong number.* But when I saw Clint's name light up, fear gripped me. Clinton, my youngest brother, had never called before in the wee hours of the morning, and I knew instinctively that I was about to hear something alarming as I pushed the button.

"Hey, when was the last time you talked to Carl?" he asked, sounding terror-stricken. "The cops are here. They caught Scott North in Carl's car."

"Oh my God!" My own words sounded as though they were coming from a stranger's mouth. My heart felt as though wrapped in an icy claw. At the same instant, my blood pressure dropped, hit bottom, and froze. The actual chill lasted only a couple of seconds, but the numbing aftereffects nearly killed me. Now I understood the reason for the strange feeling that had kept me on edge for weeks.

"They wanna know . . . when was the last time you talked to Carl?" he repeated, startling me from a heavy paralysis.

"Last Sunday," I replied. Unfortunately, in shock, I mistakenly provided the wrong day.

"North walked off from work release, and the cops caught him in Huntingdon County," Clint said breathlessly. "And when they found him, he was in Carl's car and had Carl's cell phone and credit cards."

"I'll be over," I said above the pounding of my heart in my eardrums, then hung up.

"Over" meant crossing the mountain, northwestward by Route 641, from the small college town of Shippensburg, where I lived, to the farming valley of Amberson in Franklin County. I replayed Clint's words in my mind, and I instinctively knew that whatever had happened, it was too late to change it. There was no way North could have my brother's car unless he had done something dreadful to him.

I dressed in a frenzy, and as I stumbled through the house, I decided to call Aunt Sue, Dad's youngest sister. Then, with trembling fingers, I attempted several times to punch the right buttons.

When she finally picked up the phone, I managed to break the news.

"Sue, they caught Scott North in Carl's car . . ."

"Oh my God!" she exclaimed.

". . . and we don't know where Carl is . . . please . . . don't go to work."

"Oh my God."

"Don't go to work," I pleaded again. "Just meet me at Carl's."

I was still trying to get out the door when my cell phone rang again at 4:45 A.M. I could scarcely breathe as a Pennsylvania state trooper asked for Debbie's phone number. Debbie was Carl's longtime fiancée. Still panic-stricken, I made another mistake and gave him her old instead of the current number. As I struggled to wrap my mind around whatever crisis was happening, I simply could not answer any questions with clarity.

Minutes later, though, as I gained control of my emotions, I called my sister, Loree, who lived near Shippensburg at the time. I was concerned about waking her whole household, but fortunately, she answered immediately. "I've been wide awake since four," she said.

After I related what Clint had told me, Loree and I agreed that we would wake Mom, who lived nearby, and tell her only that somebody named Scott North had Carl's car. In my heart, though, I knew without a doubt that something horrible had happened to Carl, and the man caught driving Carl's car was nothing but trouble.

My mother, Bonnie, is the oldest daughter of Herbert and Helen Pechart. She grew up in Amberson, along with a sister and two brothers. My father, Norman, was also the oldest child, the son of Norman and Madelyn Ryder, and grew up in Amberson with a brother and three sisters. That week, Dad had been staying in Amberson with my brother, Clint.

Apprehensively, Loree and I entered Mom's front door at about 5:20 in the morning. I couldn't bear to wake her, so Loree did. As Mom sleepily walked into the living room and sat down on the couch, I hesitantly said, "We got a call. The state police caught Scott North driving Carl's car."

"Well, where's Carl?" she asked, both bewildered and frightened.

"I . . . I don't know," I said.

"Well, where's Carl?" she repeated.

"I don't know."

"Well, he wouldn't have killed him," she said more to herself than to us.

"I don't know, Mom. We're going over to Carl's. We'll let you know of anything we find out."

While Loree went home to arrange for someone to stay with her kids, I left with a single thought running continuously through my mind. *My God, I think he killed him. I think he killed Carl.* Beset by the most profound fear I had ever felt in my life, I headed out into the dark and toward Amberson alone.

I don't remember leaving Shippensburg or driving for the first several miles, but I recall that I became aware of a glint of light in the morning sky as I drove up the mountain. At the same time, I felt the tree canopy closing in around me.

Just before 6:00 A.M., I turned left off Amberson Road and onto the long dirt lane to Carl's place. As I parked by his old red barn, I noted a lone patrol car backed into the corner of the wide driveway and stationed directly in front of Carl's truck. From the Chambersburg barracks in Franklin County, Troopers Finkle and Bush had already arrived in response to a request from the Huntingdon barracks to go to Carl's place and try to find out why North had Carl's car, cell phone, and wallet.

"I'm Carl's sister. What's goin' on?" I asked.

"Waiting on other troopers," one officer said curtly while the other remained quiet.

Then I asked, "Well . . . where's Carl?" but was met with more silence.

Since the police made it clear, up front, that they had little to say, I retreated, disheartened, toward the barn. I had a sickening feeling that they were not there to find Carl but to secure the area, so to speak, until other troopers arrived. In the meantime, and as if in slow motion, I glanced down the lane, out across the fields, and to the tree-lined Conococheague Creek that flowed on the far side of the narrow valley. I then looked across the way toward Clint's house and outbuildings, the home place where we all grew up. Fixed against the shaded, blue backdrop of the Kittatinny Mountain, the scene looked like a wooden building block set. The sun had not yet broken over the top of the mountain, and a light fog still hung along its foot as well as at the base of Rising Mountain, behind me. Both mountains cup Amberson valley, jutting southwestward, like two fingers, from the adjoining Tuscarora State Forest. Scotch-Irish settlers gazed upon the same lay of the land in the 1700s when they put down roots in the Native American hunting grounds. Because Carl and Clint's properties were within sight of each other, my brothers would occasionally spy on one another through binoculars—their light-hearted way of nosing into each other's business.

As I stood off by myself, a grim possibility settled on my mind like the heavy dampness of the early morning. *Carl might not be here anymore.* Although the day had barely begun, I already felt that the sun had no right to rise or the earth to turn. Nothing had a right to anything.

Meanwhile, leaning against the barn, shivering, I phoned Clint. "I'm at Carl's. Can you bring me a sweatshirt? I'm cold." Then as I was ending the call, Aunt Sue and her husband, Joe, pulled up. "Sue, we can't find Carl!" I cried out as I ran to their truck. "They caught Scott North in Carl's car, and we don't know where Carl is."

"Do the troopers know anything?" she asked.

"No . . . or at least they're acting like they don't. I don't know what to do." I hugged my arms to myself as we stared at each other in bewilderment and panic.

Clint soon arrived and handed me two men's sweatshirts. For some reason, I found myself focusing on the tags attached to them as if trying to pull some pitiful measure of comfort from the mundane. Then as I pulled one down over my head, I glanced at Clint and thought about how much I loved both my brothers and how special yet different they are. In contrast to Carl, Clint has ginger-colored hair, markedly green eyes, and stands about six foot one . . . he has always reminded me of Christmas.

It was now nearly 7:00 A.M., and the two troopers were *still* sitting in their cruiser and *still* not speaking to us. So, for the time being, I decided to make another call. As I half leaned, half hung on the split rail fence, clinging to it for support, I dialed the Bureau of Records and ID at the State Police Headquarters in Harrisburg, fifty-seven miles away. "I won't be in today," I told the receptionist without offering any further explanation. Little did I know that I would not return to work for weeks to come.

After the short conversation, I continued to stare at my phone, thinking of how desperately I wanted to help Carl. I wanted to call and ask him where he was. I wanted to search his entire property, and if needed, comb the entire valley and mountains. I was ready to scour the whole world to find him. But for the moment, my only option was to stay put and wait for information from the police.

It wasn't much longer before other officers arrived, including a Trooper Brad Ford from the Chambersburg barracks in Franklin County.

"Where's Carl's cell phone?" I asked as we walked toward one another.

"His phone's at the Huntingdon barracks," he replied. "It seems that Scott North tampered with the voice message . . . tried to put a new greeting on it."

Trooper Ford, of average build with brown hair and a trooper cut, didn't strike me as enthusiastic, but because he was the first officer to offer information, I was more than willing to cooperate. After asking for our names, he wanted to know Carl's last known whereabouts and our most recent contact with him. Clint and I both gave the same answer. Carl had just returned from vacation the previous Saturday evening at the Outer Banks, North Carolina, where he had been fishing and installing a stone patio for a buddy, Patrick Hennessy.

While we answered Ford's questions, Loree arrived and parked by the barn, and then Dad's younger brother pulled up. Terry, a big man at six foot four, had played football in his younger days at Shippensburg High School. But that morning, our uncle seemed uncharacteristically diminished and quiet. The police had been at his place before dawn, inquiring about Carl, and he had sent them to Clint. In turn, Clint had called me.

It was still early morning, even as the sun burned the last glistening dew off the ripple grass when Trooper Finkle thought to crawl out of his cruiser. No one in my family paid him much regard until he bellowed across the driveway, "I think Carl is lying somewhere drunk! And he gave North his wallet and his phone and car before he took off with some girl."

Oh my God. You ignorant son of a bitch! I thought to myself.

"There's no way Carl would have done that," I said, offended.

"Stranger things have happened," he barked.

I shook my head.

"You can shake your head," he continued his diatribe, "Carl probably gave North his stuff and took off drunk with some girl."

"Carl does *not* drink," Loree countered.

We all stared at Finkle. He struck us as the type of cop who enjoys instigating a confrontation just for the sake of making an arrest and maybe administering some extra punishment if it would happen to be one of his lucky days. On the other hand, maybe it was his crude way of trying to discover whether it would have been in character or not for Carl to be "lying somewhere drunk" and "with some girl." Either way, there was no reason for his rudeness under the circumstances. No one had been challenging him. Rather, we all bent over backward to cooperate, with Carl's welfare foremost in our minds. We were so petrified that he might be dead we could barely function, let alone fathom abuse from an obnoxious cop.

We continued to hope that one of the other state patrol units that had rolled in throughout the morning would soon deliver miraculous news that Carl had been located alive.

Eventually, I called Debbie, trying to determine the last time either of us had spoken with Carl. I had called him the previous Friday evening, August 4, and she had spoken with Carl on Saturday evening, August 5, before he had arrived home. Frantically then, we counted the days from Saturday and realized that a total of five (Sunday through Thursday) had passed without either of us having spoken with him. Usually, Carl and I were in contact almost every day, as was Debbie. One of us would call the other, and I had planned to phone Carl within the next day or two to hear about his trip to North Carolina. But for some reason, the week had passed with a strange, bedimmed quality, as if some sort of misstep of time had snatched away our habitual connection.

After more conversations with other family members, we all realized that the last time any of us had spoken with Carl had been the prior Saturday evening as well, while Carl was visiting a friend in Chambersburg—a stop he had made on his way home from vacation. A surveillance tape, later obtained by state police, would show that after he had left his friend's house, Carl had stopped at a Sheetz convenience store in Greenvillage, near the Letterkenny Army Depot, to get coffee.

While we continued talking and watching every move the cops made, I decided to turn two empty five-gallon buckets upside down by the barn and put a plank across them so we would have a place to sit. Otherwise, I felt completely useless. Like everyone else, I was desperate for news that Carl was safe, but it was difficult to sit around and wait for something to happen. I struggled with what to do in the meantime. I wanted to look for him everywhere at once, but I had no idea where to start. And I was so filled with anguish that I was unable to come up with a real plan. Furthermore, I didn't want to leave in case the troopers decided to ask more questions, or better yet, relay the news that Carl was actually okay. So, I just stayed put, hoping, praying that he was alive, perhaps injured, and waiting for help.

At some point, we noticed that a few officers began to enter Carl's home, and I wanted to follow right behind. Carl had paid off his property just two months earlier, making his last payment near his birthday in June. Several years earlier, the farmhouse that originally stood on the property burned down. A spark from the wood stove had smoldered all day in a crack in the floor, and when Carl had opened the front door, it created a draft that fed the smoldering wood, which in turn caused the house to burst into flames and burn to the ground. A house trailer replaced the farmhouse, but Carl hated it. Within the past year, he had drawn up a blueprint and started digging a foundation to construct a log and stone cabin. Although I didn't want to think the worst, I began to wonder if his plans might never come to fruition.

I continued to watch the trailer from the driveway, imagining that Carl was inside, just sleeping . . . but I knew better. Earlier, the police had revealed that two troopers had entered the residence during the pre-dawn before they had contacted any of my family. They had also been inside Patrick Hennessy's cabin next to Carl's property. We call it a cabin, but it's a three-bedroom, two-bath log house with a loft, fireplace, and a two-car garage, all set on a full basement. Pat had been living in the Outer Banks and occupied the cabin only on occasion. The police told us that someone had pried out a window screen from Pat's front porch, and the screen was still lying there.

Trooper Ford then asked: "Are Carl and Scott North friends?"

"No, they're not friends," I said quickly, unable to hide my disgust. "Carl doesn't like North, and neither do we. North worked for Carl about two years ago . . . but for only three weeks. That's when Carl fired him for breaking into his house and stealing some of his guns . . . some of his hunting rifles." I was ready to provide more details, but Ford didn't seem interested and moved on to other issues with regard to North.

Not too far into the conversation, though, we began to get the feeling that certain police officers thought of North as harmless, and in Trooper Ford's words, "just a pain in the ass." Minutes later, however, Ford contradicted himself, saying, "We've had to keep an eye on him . . . especially during arrests. We never knew what he might do. North's smart."

As we continued to talk, it became even clearer that he and other troopers were well acquainted with North from prior arrests. In addition to the danger North posed during arrests, they said he was fully aware of working the system. What's more, it sounded as though he had an inflated view of himself. But it never occurred to me that *anyone*, let alone a police officer, would ever consider him "smart." To me, North's arrogance only proved that he was too stupid to know he was stupid.

Ford, now obviously in charge of the case, had information to gather, and with a clipboard in hand, he started to fill out a paper.

"Can you give me Carl's full name and date of birth?" he asked.

"Carl Wade Ryder. June 24, 1963," I replied.

Silently, he then handed me the form, declaring Carl a missing person, and with shaking hands and breaking heart, I signed my name while my conscience shouted back at me, *My God, he's not missing. I think he's dead. Where is he? We need to save him!*

After supplying Carl's information, I wandered toward the front yard, and this time I called his cell phone even though Ford said it was at the Huntingdon barracks. It rang a couple of times, and I wondered whether anyone heard it ringing. Then I hung up. I considered calling his home phone as well but instantly realized I would hear it ring from where I was standing. I wanted to ask him where he was and why he would not answer. I then called a family friend and retired judge of the 33rd Magisterial District, Jim Campbell, to tell him what was going on and how long Carl had been missing. Jim replied, "It doesn't sound good, Cindy."

As I struggled to understand what might have happened, I developed a theory or at least a strong suspicion that North had shot Carl. I believed North was a coward and would have to have done something drastic to achieve the upper hand. The only way he could have gained an advantage over Carl's size and strength would have been through some type of ambush. Surprise, along with a deadly weapon, was the edge he would have needed. Then he merely had to have the gun ready, hide out of sight, and pull the trigger at the right moment. It would be a simple plan that also afforded access to a car, money, and—as a bonus—revenge.

I was almost sure North wanted payback. Two years earlier, when Carl discovered North had stolen his guns, he confronted him, held him accountable, and forced him to return the rifles—something North was not accustomed to. I wanted to express these suspicions in more detail to

Ford, but again, Ford didn't seem interested in listening to anything my family or I might have to add.

Around noontime, as I continued to dwell on my suspicion, I asked Aunt Sue and her husband, Joe, to go over to Clint's house and look in his closet. That's where Carl had stored all of his guns, except one particular shotgun after North had burglarized his home. I needed to know whether Carl had later decided to take that shotgun to Clint's or if he had continued to keep it at his place.

The old-time shotgun, a Hopkins and Allen, had belonged to our great-granddad, Roy Ryder, who had won it at the Path Valley Picnic in 1908 when he was seventeen years old. Carl inherited it when our great-grandmother, Grace McVitty Ryder, passed away in 1999 at one hundred and one years. It had sentimental value, and Carl had been delighted to get that old gun. Now I was afraid that North might have shot him with it. Fortunately, Sue and Joe found the gun at Clint's place and brought it back to Carl's within the hour. I was relieved when Joe handed it to me, thinking that my shotgun theory was wrong, and maybe there was still a chance Carl was alive.

As soon as I had inspected it and was about to put it, with the barrel broken open, into my car, Ford quickly approached and told me that I had just been "drawn down on." Apparently, one of the troopers standing in the driveway saw the gun and drew his.

"He's from the city . . . he isn't used to the way people are in the country," Ford attempted to explain.

"I don't care where he's from," I said. "We need to figure out what happened to Carl."

Then Ford decided to divulge some additional information. "I guess I better tell you. We did find a shotgun and a black facemask on the driver's side back floor of Carl's car."

My heart sank, and once again, I returned to my shotgun theory. It also struck me that a mask and shotgun implied robbery plans and probably worse. At the very minimum, a robbery committed with Carl's car could have framed him as a suspect, at least for a while.

I retreated to my makeshift bench, and after some thought, recalled another shotgun that Carl had bought from the estate of a deceased friend. It was a New England Firearms SB (single barrel) with a black wooden stock. It was Ray Cisney's old gun. Ray had bought it at a fundraiser years before, donated by the original owner, who had bought it from a dealer. Carl had kept Ray's shotgun at his own home. Investigators would later verify all these facts about the gun and that it was the one found in Carl's car.

How was any of this possible? I thought about the last time I had seen Carl. We had been working together the evening before he was to leave for the Outer Banks, finishing the installation of a huge picket fence for a customer outside of Shippensburg. Carl had been wearing a light blue T-shirt and denim shorts. With a slight tan, he looked good—lean and strong. And he was in good humor while both of us worked hard. Determined to finish everything on the job before he left, we shoveled the leftover dirt from around the new posts into the bucket of his Bobcat before dumping it into the back of his truck. Then we gathered the empty picket boxes and cleaned up. Carl was really looking forward to the trip, combining two weeks of fishing with laying some stonework at Pat Hennessy's place.

"What time are you leaving?" I asked him before we parted.

"About four in the morning," he replied with anticipation in his voice.

"Okay, I'll see you later."

It *never* crossed my mind that I would never lay eyes on him again. Instead, I was thinking already about the next trip he would make to the Outer Banks, planned for October—and this time, I would be going along. I had never been there and was already excited.

Carl did leave at 4:00 A.M. for vacation.

Three weeks later, at 4:00 A.M., that horrible call came.

CHAPTER 2

MISSING . . .
MISSING ENDANGERED . . .
LIKELY DEAD

The thief cometh not, but for to steal, and to kill, and to destroy.
—The Apostle John

"I'm gonna hate to see my cell phone bill," a trooper standing in the driveway suddenly exclaimed. The state police had been avoiding air communication that day, using their cell phones so that household monitors would not be able to receive their conversations. I couldn't help but feel that his phone bill was trivial compared to our plight, and it didn't diminish our fear that the police might not be taking the situation that seriously.

With thoughts bouncing back and forth since the early morning, I decided to approach Ford in mid-afternoon. "Has anyone opened the trunk of Carl's car?"

"We have to wait on a search warrant," he replied.

Minutes later, however, Ford came back to me with a question about the car. "Would Carl ever haul a dead deer in his trunk?"

"No, he wouldn't haul a deer in his trunk. And he wouldn't be shooting deer anyway," I said.

Carl would never have toted a gun along on vacation, nor would he have shot a deer out of season in the middle of summer. And he wouldn't have hauled one in the trunk of his car.

The question was an odd one, but Ford felt he had to ask because a judge had issued a search warrant by then. Preliminary inspection of the trunk at the Huntingdon barracks revealed what appeared to be blood.

Trooper Ford first described the blood as "not very much" but later claimed there was "a significant amount of blood"—so much so police removed the trunk liner to send it to a forensics lab. At the same time, when investigators questioned North about the blood, Ford said he remarked coolly, "You guys are gonna feel like assholes when you find out it's deer blood."

My heart ached thinking about Carl's car and knowing how much he liked that old thing. It was a pale blue 1991 Ford Crown Victoria that he had bought in 2004 from a woman in Newville. Carl had been installing a fence in the area when he saw it for sale in her front yard. It had a nice, 302-cubic-inch, small-block engine with low mileage. The car was in excellent shape, and the inside of the trunk was like new. When he brought it home, his friends asked jokingly if he had gotten a free cane with it. That didn't bother him in the least. He knew it was a good car.

Carl's other vehicle was a red Ford F-350, 4x4 pickup that he used to haul tools and fencing materials and pull his trailer and Bobcat. As Trooper Ford relayed more details about the blood in Carl's car, I glanced over again at Carl's pickup parked in the driveway next to the field, with the driver's side door hanging open. A trooper had been standing beside it for several hours, and I had been keeping an eye on it. Hesitantly, I approached him.

"Would you like to look inside the truck?" he asked.

"Yes," I said tentatively, surprised that he was willing to allow me to see it.

Standing a short distance from the open door, I first spotted a heavy-duty, metal-cased plug-in drill lying on the passenger-side floorboard. It held a half-inch bit. The truck's steering column had been torn apart, and the ignition switch was hanging by its wires. *That son of a bitch tried to hot-wire Carl's truck*, I thought.

As I continued looking hastily from a safe distance, not interfering with evidence, and afraid the cop would ask me to stop, I noticed the cab had been cleaned out. This was unusual. Carl always kept a shoebox in the center of the seat, holding receipts, a checkbook, and papers for his fencing business. It was gone! He never removed that beat-up old box. On occasion, he would take out his checkbook and whatever papers he needed at the time, but never the box.

"Thank you," I said as I walked away, only to return minutes later when I thought to look through the cap window into the bed, which normally was loaded with tools. Now it held only a bucket of hardware, tie-down straps, and a digging iron. Later that day, police removed Carl's truck by rollback and transported it to the Chambersburg barracks in Franklin County.

Another trooper then asked, "Would you be able to recognize things that are Carl's?"

"Yes," I said. "Yes, I would."

I was allowed to follow him into Carl's home (where several other troopers were already looking around) and to the bedroom, where I numbly identified a pair of Carl's jeans—jeans that he would have taken along to the Outer Banks. They were clean and dropped partially unfolded beside his satchel. Nearby, a pinkish-mauve backpack sat on the floor, tilted against Carl's dresser.

"This isn't Carl's," I said, pointing to the bag. It was later identified as having been stolen from Carl's closest neighbor, Patrick Hennessy, and belonging to one of Pat's kids.

I also noticed an open can of ravioli with a steak knife stuck in it, sitting on the floor at the foot of the bed. The bed had been stripped, and a brand-new pornography magazine lay open on the mattress. I imagined North lying there like a pig, stabbing cold ravioli straight from the can while leering at his porn.

"Sorry about the magazine," the trooper said.

"It's not Carl's," I said. I knew Carl wouldn't spend money on pornography. He just was not the type. Later, when the district attorney released Carl's place to us, we never found any other pornographic material. The magazine turned out to be one of several items North had bought with Carl's money, and the same with the ravioli. In forty-three years of knowing Carl, I had never seen him eating anything like canned pasta, Manwich, or boxed mac and cheese.

In the kitchen, I noticed candles in glass containers sitting on the kitchen counter with cigarette butts in them. Carl didn't smoke, so I knew they weren't his. There were other items scattered across the table and countertops. In the living room, ashes from the wood stove lay in a wide swath across the floor and trailed toward the safe, as though someone had pulled the ash pan out of the stove, spilling ashes.

"He *dragged* the ash pan across the floor!" I said incredulously.

Then I picked up a letter from the floor and started to read. Before I finished, I looked at a trooper who had been standing nearby and remarked, "This isn't Carl's handwriting."

Now I regret not reading the whole thing before commenting about it before the trooper had taken it from me. Written by Scott North and addressed to "Joe," it mentioned "$1,000," and in another paragraph, something about "sitting around waiting." There was no doubt of its value as an incriminating document—a strong indication that North had no intention of leaving without obtaining whatever he was waiting for—whether a car, money, revenge, or all three. Inexplicably, though, throughout the next months and the long ordeal to come, officials would deny us access to the full letter.

The curtains and rod had been partially dislodged from a back window in the living room, and the window had been opened a couple of inches. It was obvious that it had been a point of entry. I turned to Carl's safe—an old safe with a combination lock and brackets for a padlock. Its door was shut, but the padlock (which had been used because the combination lock didn't work) had been cut in two with a hacksaw. I assumed the contents had been stolen and decided not to touch the lock or the safe.

The tools missing from the bed of Carl's truck were piled inside to the left of the front door—and were spattered with blood. Above the tools, along the edge of the door molding, I saw a spare truck key hanging on a small nail. North apparently had not seen it because he had tried to hot-wire the truck. Blood was also spattered on a rifle propped inside the door next to a floor lamp.

"That's Carl's .22," I said.

"That's a .32," said the same trooper, who was now standing near the kitchen.

For an instant, I thought he was purposely identifying the caliber of the gun incorrectly just to see if I would argue and if I really knew my gun calibers. But he thought the gun was a .32. I had always assumed state troopers knew guns because they carry them. But I came to learn that obviously, not all of them do. Carl did not own a .32 rifle. This gun was a bolt-action .22 Savage Model 65.

Carl kept it handy for pesky groundhogs that dug holes all over the property and devoured his pumpkin blossoms. The gun was propped by the door just how he would have placed it, and its gun magazine had been left on the windowsill. North seemingly had not touched it.

As I stepped back outside, I noticed blood on the doorjamb, and a wide swath of blood spattered across the outside of the door—a door that had been solid white. "There's *more* blood!" I exclaimed.

One of the troopers glanced at me and commented, "That could have come from someone nicking their hand while working." I couldn't believe what he had said, and I couldn't make up my mind whether the officers were trying to give us hope . . . or deliberately ignoring the horrible truth.

"North *did* have a small cut on the web of his hand," Ford said after I left the trailer and agreed to follow him into the hayfield next to the driveway. "He said he fell and cut it on the doorjamb."

"Doesn't look like it to me," I said with conviction. "That's high-velocity blood spatter with tails. A nick doesn't cause blood spatter like that." Ford ignored my comments. I figured he was pretty sure I couldn't possibly know a thing about blood spatters. I later did quick online research on blood spatter tails to know which direction the tails indicated the spatter originated.

We walked about ten feet into the field. Ford pointed out a brown sneaker that police had discovered and marked off with four pieces of tension bar used in building chain-link fences.

"Is this Carl's sneaker?" he asked.

"It looks too small," I said. Yet, it was immediately obvious that the sneaker had lain outside, drawing moisture at night and drying in the sun repeatedly for several days and nights, which would have given it a shrunken appearance. Carl wore a size twelve, but at that moment, it just didn't look big enough. Meanwhile, I thought it peculiar that the police could find, and were concerned about, a sneaker in knee-high hay but seemed to deny other strong evidence, like blood.

As the day wore on, Carl's suspected status worsened from *Missing Person* . . . to *Missing Endangered* . . . to *Likely Dead*. This meant that even though we stubbornly resisted the possibility of murder, our hope significantly dwindled. It was beyond heartbreaking to call our parents throughout the day with updates. However, I couldn't bring myself to share that we had found obvious blood spatter and other evidence indicating something bad had happened.

By 5:00 P.M., troopers began leaving one by one, taking along two cardboard boxes of possible evidence. Besides Carl's truck, I saw them remove the sneaker from the field, the letter I found on the floor, ashes from the stove and ash pan, receipts, an answering machine, a phone bill, and the .22 rifle. Naturally, I assumed all evidence would be taken to the Chambersburg barracks in Franklin County.

Before Trooper Ford left for the day, he told me the Huntingdon police barracks had confiscated an address book during North's arrest the night before, along with a face mask, shotgun, Carl's car, credit cards, receipts, cell phone, and wallet. A to-do list, written by North, also had been seized. Ford had a copy of it and, surprisingly, emailed the contents of the list to me at request two weeks later, noting that he had "cleaned up the misspellings." The list included: "activate credit card, pack tools, pack money, pack ammo, look for ID, wipe down cabin, wipe down everything." In his email, Ford also mentioned a confiscated pocket calendar with a notation by North that read, "Wednesday 2, 12-noon GREAT ESCAPE."

The time we spent waiting in Carl's driveway had passed in a torturous blur, and from then on, I would refer to those hours of hell as "that first day." By early evening, as the last trooper was getting ready to leave, I noticed that while the front door had been cordoned off with yellow crime tape, the rest of the property remained unrestricted.

I called out to the officer, "We'd like to start looking for Carl right away . . . here on his property."

"By all means, go ahead," he replied.

Before the trooper was down the driveway, Clint and I decided to start with the barn. Inside, we instantly noticed the ignition switch on Carl's ATV hanging by its wires, just like the truck ignition switch had been hanging. Apparently, North didn't know what to do beyond prying it out. Seeing nothing else out of place, we left the barn and walked across the driveway to the open living room window I had seen earlier. Carl would not have left it open, knowing he would be away for a couple of weeks. We also discovered faint nicks and scratches on the metal frame as if someone had used a tool to pry open the window.

Next, we scoured the property and along the edges of the surrounding fields for any signs the soil had been disturbed—in case North had tried to bury Carl. Every turned pebble looked suspicious, but we found nothing. We returned to the front yard and wandered around slowly, staring at the ground. Suddenly, I spied a sabot from a shotgun cartridge, this one from a pumpkin ball cartridge, lying in the grass near the driveway. Almost immediately, I spotted another just off the deck. A sabot is a white piece of plastic inside the shotgun shell casing that separates the powder from the lead shot. Upon firing, a sabot will fly from the barrel behind the lead. However, the sabot of a pumpkin ball cartridge differs from one that holds pellet shot in that a pumpkin ball is one solid piece of lead and its sabot a slightly cupped piece of plastic rather than the deep cup-shaped, fingered type made for pellet shot. Both sabots were clean and bright, proof that they had not lain in the elements long.

"Why didn't they gather these as evidence?" I asked. "The cops were here all day."

I decided not to contact the barracks about the sabots because I believed that they must not be important if the state police had not collected them. Still, I took them with me and stored them in a plastic bag in my car console.

I made my way over to the old well in the front yard and decided to heave the heavy steel cover onto its edge to look inside. Even though I wanted to find Carl, I was greatly relieved to see nothing in that twenty-foot-deep old hand-dug well but the sandstone casing and approximately four feet of clear water at the bottom.

By 8:00 P.M., it was too late to start looking for Carl outside the valley. Exhaustion and stress, as well as terror and shock, were taking their toll, and the growing realization that the worst may have happened slowly edged its way into my mind, smothering the hope to which I had clung for hours. As the last person to leave that evening, I stopped by the barn to get a long metal pipe. I wedged the ends into the low branches of two trees standing on either side of Carl's driveway to block curious onlookers from coming too close.

We all returned home that evening, feeling ever emptier, still not knowing if Carl were dead or alive.

 CHAPTER 3

TORMENT OF HOPE

For the morning is to them even as the shadow of death: if one know them, they are in the terrors of the shadow of death. —Job

The likelihood of murder crushed my family and me. We couldn't wrap our minds around the thought that a low-life criminal who should have been in prison might have harmed Carl, whom we dearly loved. But by the end of the first day, it hit us hard that he could be dead.

The phone lines were already burning through Amberson and Path Valley, and there was no real sleep for any of us that night. The day's horrifying events kept turning in my mind. Thinking about what to do next, I wandered around my house in a fury and then in a panic, fighting to keep myself intact. I even considered buying a dozen spotlights for friends and family to start looking that night, but I knew it would be difficult enough to find Carl in daylight, let alone in the dark. A search would have to wait.

Around 3:00 A.M., I collapsed on the couch and eventually fell into not so much a sleep as a stupor. Each time I drifted off, a clamor inside my head jolted me back into the nightmare that was our reality. In the black hours before dawn, I dug out a map that showed Franklin County and the five surrounding counties of Fulton, Cumberland, Perry, Juniata, and Huntingdon. I penciled a black dot on the village of Amberson, then drew a circle, marking a fifteen-mile radius from Carl's home. Within the circle was a vast rural area and several small towns such as Spring Run, Dry Run, Willow Hill, Fannettsburg, Burnt Cabins, Shade Gap,

Concord, and Neelyton. My circle also included Blairs Mills, just over the Huntingdon County line, and clipped Shirleysburg to the northwest. The area covered 706.85 square miles, equal to 452,384 acres of territory.

I decided to ignore the southeastern area within the circle. If Scott North had killed Carl and thrown him somewhere, I guessed that he would have gravitated toward territory familiar to him, which would have been the northern part. I once read that most killers who attempt to conceal a body usually will not travel more than ten to fifteen miles from the crime scene. They will discard the victim as soon as possible in any area that offers some type of concealment to avoid getting caught.

The shock of the previous day had not diminished, even a little, by dawn. It didn't even feel like a new day but one continuous nightmare with no way out. Even though the police seemed to be in no hurry to search for Carl (just as they took their time apprehending North after he fled his work-release assignment), my family and I were not going to sit back and rely on them. Clint and I were on the phone by 6:00 A.M., strategizing how we should begin the search. He agreed that we should concentrate on the northern half of the circle I had drawn on the map.

On Saturday, August 12, I was at Cresslers' grocery market in Shippensburg at 7:00 A.M. sharp because the store had a copier available to the public, and I could make copies for 10 cents a page. I printed fifteen copies of the map and wasted no time getting to Amberson.

From Carl's driveway, I again watched as the sun rose above the mist that trailed along the mountainside, and I wondered for the thousandth time, *Where are you, Carl?* I knew him better than the back of my own hand. I knew him so well I could often tell what he was thinking or was about to say by the look on his face. I usually knew what he was doing even when he wasn't around—I knew just by thinking about him. Yet now, I couldn't even begin to guess where he might be. To my great agony, our invisible connection felt severed, and I desperately wanted to go back in time to erase whatever virulent act had torn us apart.

For some of my family who lived miles away, the anguish was almost unbearable as they suffered a long trip home. My sister Christine caught a flight from Florida to Baltimore, rented a car, and drove the remaining two-and-a-half hours of the miserable journey from Maryland to

Pennsylvania. My youngest sister Sarah arrived from Rehoboth Beach, Delaware. Another sister, Natalie, chose to stay with Mom. And on this morning, Loree was also on her way to Amberson.

I started this second day hating everything. From the beginning of creation to my birth, I hated the world. It was all I could do just to breathe, just to take the next step. All of us were so numb that it was beyond our ability to fully grasp the reality of what we were living hour by hour, let alone imagine what lay ahead for us in the days and years to come. A huge, very special piece of our world was missing. Still, panic numbly drove us forward. We needed to get Carl back somehow, some way. Yet thrown headlong and raw into a search of such an immense territory, I knew the odds of finding our brother's body, if he were dead, were against us.

Standing in the driveway, I called Clint. "I'm at Carl's. Are you coming up?"

"I'll be there in a couple of minutes," he answered.

Before our sisters arrived and we all would leave the valley in an organized search, Clint and I wanted to look around Carl's property in hopes of finding clues. At the same time, I needed the space, the privacy to muster some additional strength and energy before we started.

Clint arrived within a matter of minutes, and the inconceivable circumstances hit us again as we began to look around, trying to make sense of the day before. As I wandered across the yard, I noticed a five-by-seven tan rug half-hidden by a bush—a burning bush—so named because its leaves turn brilliant red in fall. The rug lay bunched up, well away from its usual spot inside Carl's front door, as if thrown there. Turning the rug over, I saw that the grass underneath was still green with just a hint of yellow, which meant the rug had not been there more than a few days. *Why didn't the cops collect this since it's obviously out of place?* I wondered.

As soon as we learned that Chris, Sarah, and Loree had arrived at Clint's house, we left to meet them. It was a solemn gathering, not the usual happy reunion of a highly anticipated visit home. I handed out the maps showing main, secondary, and dirt roads while Sarah pulled out a bag of dried ginger. "This helps with nausea," she said almost apologetically before she divvied it up among us.

"We'll all need to go to different areas and keep track of where we've been," I said, "so we don't all go to the same places." Then, as we broke up and started, I phoned Trooper Ford.

"We're looking for Carl. Can you contact the Game Commission and request that they let their field officers know that we're looking for him? The more people that know, the better."

"I can contact them," he said, without mentioning any other search or what the police might be doing.

The five of us departed Clint's lane in two vehicles on the most important and desperate mission of our lives. Later in the day, we were joined by friends, including Michael, Bob, Gillian, Ralph, Marty, Tommy, and his wife Pam, who were searching somewhere in Path Valley. Uncle Terry's friend, Cliff, had arrived from Canada to help as well. (While I'm not aware of every person who aided in the search for Carl, please know that we will always be very, very grateful for those who helped during that difficult time.)

As we left the valley, we began to scout the main roads, stopping the vehicles to inspect berms and traversing old lanes and trails on foot, several yards in and back out. In addition, we scrutinized every pull-off for tire tracks, broken twigs, and skewed branches. It was hard work to scramble through dumpsites, jump ditches, climb banks, and struggle through nasty briars . . . but we did it. All the while, everyone had sufficient signal strength to keep in touch by cell phone (not a given in the south-central Pennsylvania mountains), which helped me maintain a log of the roads and areas each of us had searched. This kept us from getting disorganized in all the turmoil and ensured we didn't waste time visiting the same places. By dusk, the five of us gathered at Clint's place again, so exhausted we could barely move.

The next morning, after another night of scant and tormented sleep, we started over. On the second day of the search—Sunday, August 13—I decided to ask my youngest sister, Sarah, who had turned twenty-four in June, to travel with me because although she wanted to help, she was very afraid. Carl's fiancée, Debbie, also wanted to help, and so she followed me in her vehicle, checking the opposite side of the road from where

Sarah and I were searching. Still, in Amberson, I decided to search a wooded hollow next to Store Lane.

No sooner had we begun to trudge along the shoulder of the narrow road than a patrol car suddenly appeared and stopped.

"I keep seeing your family everywhere," the trooper said, as though he wanted to strike up a casual conversation.

I had no time to chat, though. I gestured toward the hillside and said, "I'm gonna check that steep bank. It parallels the road coming down off the mountain." The embankment runs below Truck Route 641, coming into Amberson, just beyond the overpass of the Pennsylvania Turnpike, which tunnels through the mountains. One can see the face of the hill more easily from the back road before it intersects with the main road.

I mentioned the areas we had searched the day before and then asked, "I don't suppose North has indicated where Carl is?"

"No" was the only remark the trooper made before driving off.

Of course, North hadn't said a word. His story was that what police had found in Carl's trunk was "deer blood."

While Sarah stayed close by and Debbie remained along the road, I jumped the small stream. It seemed incongruous that the brook bubbled along pleasantly while we were in such distress, although I did glance around to see if Redleg was nearby. The old turtle had lived at that spot for years, and I had always enjoyed looking for him. That moment was like taking a quick, desperate breath of "happy" just to get through the next minute of harsh reality.

I clambered halfway up the steep incline without realizing how far I had gone. Suddenly, I started to slide, and when I grabbed a small rotten tree for support, it broke off with a muffled pop, sending me plowing to the bottom through fifteen feet of leaves and sticks. Still holding a piece of the tree and amazingly still on my feet, I eyed the newly exposed trail of black dirt, thankful for my abrupt expulsion from the slope. It was as if *Someone* had pushed me off the hill, telling me my efforts were being wasted, that Carl was not there.

We moved on to another area, but it wasn't long until Sarah, Debbie, and I began to feel apprehensive. It wasn't the thought of North, who may have killed Carl and who was behind bars, that stirred our fear. In fact, in my grieving warrior state, I would have welcomed his presence just for a chance to wipe him from the face of the earth. Instead, our unease stemmed from the possibility of the *unexpected*. Emotional pain and total vulnerability made us wary of every movement and noise. Clint and I would experience the same angst, months later, on Carl's property. The moment an unfamiliar vehicle drove in, the hairs would rise on the back of our necks, like hackles on a dog. It usually turned out to be one of Carl's old friends searching for solace, ending up at his place.

Everywhere we went, we ran into familiar faces combing areas near their homes. In two days of searching, we would cover a lot of territory but realized we also needed a lot of luck or intervention from a Higher Power. Every hour, I begged the Lord to keep Carl somehow alive and that if we had to take him to a hospital, he would heal quickly. We carried water with us always, knowing that Carl would surely be thirsty if he had lain somewhere injured for days.

At the end of another day, we had searched until we could barely go on, and some of us couldn't shake nausea. Before I was willing to stop, though, I called Clint. "I'd like to look around at Carl's place one more time before it gets dark," I said, still longing for some sort of miraculous clue. A short time later, Clint met me, along with several others, at Carl's place. Unfortunately, though, it was late, and stifling fatigue prevented us from continuing. "There won't be any justice," I remarked grimly to Clint before I returned to my car and drove away.

As the sun dropped behind the mountain, I decided to return to the first stop that Sarah, Debbie, and I had made on our way out of the valley early that morning. Mustering a little more strength, I parked near the slate quarry a few hundred yards from the steep hillside I had skidded down, and then I stepped from the car. Suddenly, I noticed a Sheetz coffee cup on the berm.

Carl had often stopped for coffee at the Sheetz convenience store in Greenvillage near Chambersburg. If it was Carl's, I suspected North had thrown it out of Carl's car during one of his stolen rides; Carl wouldn't have tossed the cup—he loved the outdoors and had never been one to litter. What's more, neighbors had seen North driving Carl's car on this same road, although no one realized it had been North until after his arrest. Then I spotted a red-and-black checkered shirt or jacket, crumpled and stiff, in the culvert near the cup. It fit the description of the one North had worn when he had escaped from his work-release assignment. I immediately contacted the police so they could collect the items. The officer on the line didn't seem interested in the shirt or the cup, which only fed my suspicion that they had little interest in Carl's disappearance. Each snub from the police felt like a mockery of our nightmare. Dismayed yet resolved, I stuck the items in a plastic bag and put them in my car.

For a few moments, I stood by my car and stared into the distance as an erratic heartbeat pounded in my ears. Hope for Carl hung by a frayed thread, but I valued it as if it were a three-strand cord. I climbed the slate bank nearby with little energy and stared down at the thick slivers of gray stone. The evening was dim, and the world had lost its color. Suddenly, an awful realization came over me. While we had been celebrating the birthday of one brother on August 5 at Mom's house, the other might have been suffering at the hands of a murderer. I asked myself how something so evil could have come about. *Would God just let something like this happen? What kind of devil could even be so hateful? Was this some sort of sick joke?* There was no answer in the trill of a lone cricket, and I went home.

On the third day of the search (the fourth day since the police had contacted our family), we briefly expanded our quest northwest to the top of Fannettsburg Mountain, where the corners of Fulton, Huntingdon, and Franklin counties meet. On the same day, other relatives and friends searched the pull-off on Timmons Mountain, overlooking Path Valley and the back roads and lanes of the entire Path Valley area in Franklin County.

As if nature's elements were not pitiless enough already, a muggy mid-summer drizzle set in, which upset us even more. Wherever Carl was, I didn't want him to be suffering in the rain. As we pushed on, the hot August stench of an occasional animal carcass on or near the road overwhelmed us. Every time we encountered the "dead smell," we had to force ourselves to look for the source, even though we didn't want to in the worst way. It felt as though darkness and wickedness were everywhere.

Just as we had to pay attention to the smell, it was imperative that we also watch for buzzards. At first, it seemed a shameful thing, like some sort of aberration of thought—a trespass against what should be in one's mind—but desperation overcame the reluctance, and we continued. At one point, following that same "dead smell," Clint and his friends Michael, Tommy, and Pam located a huge dumpsite spread down a steep slope along German Valley Road, which runs from Shirleysburg. While one of them grew distraught and refused to go near, the others pushed themselves to look but found nothing. Searching took every ounce of nerve and energy. We were overcome with exhaustion, not to mention distraught and discouraged.

By the end of the third day, our search party had covered every main road and back road from Amberson to Fannettsburg, and from Amberson through state lands, past Fowlers Hollow, through the New Germantown area, and on to Route 274, Big Spring Road, and Burns Valley Road. We then caught Route 75 near Doylesburg in Upper Path Valley and searched farther northeast past Concord. Still, I heard nothing from the state police, nor was I given any indication that they intended to help us with the search. They were fully aware that we had been diligently looking, which, I believe, is what eventually compelled them to bring out the cadaver dogs the next day, searching along dirt roads in state forestlands at the head of Amberson, as well as at Carl's place, but without finding anything.

The Tuscarora State Forest covers 91,165 acres. The larger tract starts in Franklin County at the head of Amberson Valley and expands into the southwest end of Perry County—an area that would take weeks, if not months, to cover. In any case, the police were beginning to investigate some areas along the dirt roads and were likewise searching the pull-off at the top of Timmons Mountain, where our friends had been earlier. The word was, they were looking for a second body—a relative of North's—but it turned out to be just another rumor. The fact was, the relative was currently in jail.

The grapevine overflowed with gossip, hearsay, and tales, large and small. Residents told us of all kinds of things they had heard—reports that traced back to bizarre speculations from bored souls who couldn't resist becoming part of the tragedy. Hurt enough; we determined to ignore any outrageous suggestions or ridiculous chatter that reached us and instead remain focused. Meanwhile, no true leads or reliable information came our way, yet loyal friends and neighbors continued to offer help in the search, and we gladly accepted.

That night, as I lay tormented and wide-awake, I went over the places we had covered and wondered if we would ever find Carl. For the past few nights, thoughts of a house—a green-colored house on Allison Road in Blairs Mills—kept coming to mind. I was familiar with the place owned by Mitch Coons, a childhood friend of Carl's, who had grown up in Amberson but had moved right after high school to this house in Blairs Mills.

Although Blairs Mills, founded along the Tuscarora Creek, was once a bustling village in the 1800s with a railway, gristmills, and timber industry, it was now just a rural spot, nestled in rather spooky wooded hills. I had always felt edgy in that area and had not been near it in years. Nevertheless, because the house had become a persistent nightly image, I decided to include the area in our search the next day.

By the fourth day, our scattered scouting had become more concentrated as we gravitated toward the areas of Doylesburg and Concord, and especially Blairs Mills. So many people wanted to find Carl so badly that it seemed as though a shared intuition, as well as a deep love for Carl, had drawn several of us to that area. We also felt growing anger that a repeat offender might have murdered Carl. Numerous people asked how Scott North, with his extensive criminal record, ever gained *permission to step outside of jail for a work-release assignment?*

Naturally, I kept in constant touch with the state police regarding North, hoping for new information. I remember pleading with Trooper Ford during one call that day, "Will you ask him [North] again where he put Carl?"

"Uhh . . . North has requested an attorney," Ford replied, "and so we're no longer permitted to question him." Ford added that when they had been able to talk to North, he gave the impression of "feeling important" and appeared unconcerned as he sat drawing pictures in the Huntingdon County Jail. I wished to God that North had never been born.

"Well . . . is there *any* new information that might help us?" I begged.

"You know, you don't need a body to get a conviction," he replied, drawing one of my biggest fears to the fore.

"But we *do* need to get Carl back. How can we *not* look for him?" I said. "We're worried that North might've dumped him in a lake somewhere. How would we ever find him then?"

"Bodies always float," Ford claimed, but with little assurance in his voice.

I knew that wasn't true. An intact body can remain sunken, despite gases from the decomposition that make the body buoyant. From what I have read, it takes four times the victim's weight to keep a corpse submerged, but it can be done if someone is determined to weigh a body down. Likewise, a dismembered body can stay submerged forever with little effort. In fact, Carl and I had unknowingly come disturbingly close to that truth in July 1981, when we found ourselves near the scene of just such a crime.

Carl had just graduated from high school, and we decided to take a drive on a summer afternoon when we chanced upon a deep, water-filled quarry near Williamson. He and I knew it would be spectacular to jump off the rock cliff into the water. So, at the highest point and on a count of three, we leaped into a freefall and plunged into the quarry. We found ourselves further below the surface than we thought we would go. I could barely make out Carl in the dimness, as huge glass-green bubbles—balls of ethereal light—wreathed around us then raced upward. Swimming upward through layers of light-suffused water—deep emerald twilight, mint-green dawn, and finally clear water—until we broke the sunny surface, we basked momentarily in the pure joy of breathing air again.

Then as we trod water, Carl murmured, "What if there's a body in here?"

"Yeah, let's get out of here," I said quickly.

Inexplicably uneasy from the moment we had hit the water, a strange apprehension drove us to swim hurriedly across the quarry to where we could climb out. We left that place without stopping for even a few seconds to dry ourselves.

The following spring, in 1982, the car radio blared the news that investigators had found a body in the Williamson Quarry. Staring at each other in surprise, Carl and I remembered the day that previous summer when we had leaped into the water—just weeks after a local young woman named Debra Ray Witmer had been murdered, dismembered, and dumped into it.

The renowned psychic, Dorothy Allison, from New Jersey had provided compelling clues in locating Debra, yet the ordeal was not over for Debra's poor mother, Nancy Ray. The Pennsylvania State Police somehow lost her remains for over a decade, and Mrs. Ray eventually filed a lawsuit to locate what was left of her daughter. The lawsuit drew attention, and she eventually received a box with only fourteen bones. She passed away in 1999 without knowing who killed her daughter and suspicious that the recovered remains might not actually be Debra's.

In 2006, the same year of our life-changing ordeal, the FBI in Quantico, Virginia, determined that Debra's exhumed remains did match family DNA. Her partial skeleton is now stored in Franklin County on the chance that charges may someday be filed. As of 2021, Debra's brothers still hope for accountability for the crime and welcome any new information pertaining to the case.

With the water worry on our minds, we continued our search that fourth day for Carl, again having unusual access to cell service in the mountainous areas and keeping in touch with one another. But we would need more help than just functioning phones.

As we continued to comb the countryside, another past crime began to haunt me. The psychic Dorothy Allison had also played a key role in providing clues in the search for nineteen-year-old Debbie Kline. In 1976, two career criminals had kidnapped and tortured, then murdered Debbie, and discarded her body near an old dumpsite atop Fannettsburg Mountain. Robert Cox and Kenneth Peiffer, Jr. recounted her murder in the book *Missing Person*. Again, I thought of the torment her family, like ours, must have gone through.

Had Dorothy Allison not passed away in 1999 (the same year as Mrs. Ray), I, too, would have contacted her in a desperate bid for help in locating Carl.

CHAPTER 4

TO THE HOUSE OF GREEN

If, when evil cometh upon us . . . we stand before this house, and in Thy presence . . . and cry unto Thee in our affliction, then Thou wilt hear and help. —Ezra the Priest

Struggling with terrible emotional anguish left less strength to go on with each day that passed, and it was dragging us down fast. We barely noticed that it was already Wednesday, August 16, the fifth day of the search. Fear that we might never find Carl was at the forefront of everyone's mind. We also realized it was unlikely that Carl was still alive, and it was doubtful he had lived long, if at all, beyond the time he had arrived home.

Meanwhile, the routine we had developed was the best we could do. Early each morning, we began a new marathon, dragging ourselves along roads, watching the sky for birds, and noting the smell of the air. The world seemed hostile. The sun burned, and briars tore at our skin. Dirt filled our shoes, and stress sapped our energy. Every site we examined left some sort of wound. Even so, we plowed through anything that got in our way. Unable to eat, I dropped an excessive amount of weight, and chest pains suggested a coronary concern . . . but I gave it little attention.

From his home across the valley that Wednesday morning, Clint noticed two state police cruisers parked at Carl's place. To our knowledge, the police had been there only twice before—that first day on August 11 and again on August 15, when they had brought in the cadaver dogs. Consumed with our search, we briefly wondered why they had suddenly shown up so early that morning but thought no more about it as we went on with our search plan.

In mid-afternoon, though, Sarah and I abruptly stopped searching and drove to Clint's place for some strange reason. Debbie followed, and Clint, Loree, and Chris had inexplicably done the same. Everyone had experienced the same mysterious urge, yet we had not called one another about returning.

While we dispiritedly discussed which areas we should search next, Mom's sister, Lurea, called. "Cind, J.J. just called and said that he heard a body was found near Blairs Mills this morning." J.J. Stake was our cousin.

"Well, that's probably just another rumor going around," I replied. "We were in that area this morning, and I didn't see any cruisers on the road. And they surely would've told us," I added.

I had expected that if someone had found a body, the police would contact us immediately. Upon second thought, I said, "But maybe we should go see for ourselves."

Without another moment's thought, the six of us teamed up in two cars and bolted out of Amberson. As we rushed northeast in a frazzle, I missed the road to Blairs Mills, and at the same moment, a cruiser passed us, coming the other way at a fast clip. A prompt U-turn and heavy foot enabled me to gain ground on the trooper, but I lost it again as he disappeared around a tractor-trailer. It didn't matter, though, because I knew I would soon catch up with him . . . and I *knew* that Carl would be there. Approximately twenty minutes from the time we had hastily left Amberson, we turned onto the narrow winding road leading into Blairs Mills and onto Allison Road.

Suddenly, to my left was the green house that had nagged me at night. Now I knew why. It was a subtle message from my subconscious— the house symbolized the area where Carl would be found. Mitch Coons and others were standing in the yard.

I stopped on the road, and Mitch yelled, "Keep going for about two miles!" Those two miles wound on like a slow road to hell. Suddenly, a cruiser sat blocking both lanes before us, and I pulled up to it as close as I could. A few troopers stood several yards up the road, others occupied the side of the long bank below the road, and even more, cruisers blocked the road from the other direction. I paid special attention to the trooper directly in front of us, who was now preventing us from walking closer to the scene. I had no idea what to expect, but if any sacrifice had to be made as far as glimpsing something awful that could never be unseen, it would have to be made by me. I asked my siblings to stay put near our cars as I approached the trooper alone. I felt as if I were slogging through high water.

"We're Carl's sisters and brother," I said, shaking in my shoes.

"Okay. You can go back up there with your family, and I'll bring someone up to talk with you," he instructed.

I returned, and we huddled in a loose circle, stealing solemn glances at each other. Then, as Huntingdon County Coroner Ronald Morder and a group of troopers from both the Huntingdon and Chambersburg barracks approached, my stomach began to churn.

"There's a male body in a decomposed condition," a trooper began. "It'll be transported to the coroner's office." At the same time, he pulled out a notebook and cordially asked each of us for our name, number, and address.

One by one, we provided our information, but at the next moment, we began to press the troopers for more information—for anything that would convince us that it was *not* Carl's body they had found. We learned that the clothes on the body were torn and bloody and that the victim still wore one shoe. Chances were good that the shoe's mate was the one investigators had found in the field next to Carl's home on that first day. There was no longer any reason for an outlandish suggestion from a trooper that Carl was "lying somewhere drunk."

"Does he have dark hair?" I asked.

"Yes."

We stared at the ground in silence. In those first horrid moments, I felt as though I were looking down from above in an out-of-body state, observing all of us just standing there like little pegs planted on the pavement, rooted in disbelief.

Can this really be real? Will I never see Carl again? Did he really die? Oh God, did he really die and end up here like this?

My family and I had endured six days, plunging back and forth from hope to despair and from despair to hope. Yet amid fresh anguish, there was relief that Carl would not remain forever where North had dumped him along Allison Road. It was so awful, but the search was over. Coroner Ron Morder pronounced Carl dead at 2:45 P.M. that afternoon, Wednesday, August 16, 2006, although it was not his actual date or time of death. Soon, Morder and pathologist Dr. Harry Kamerow would transport Carl's body from that steep, weedy hillside to J.C. Blair Memorial Hospital in Huntingdon for examination the next day. A trooper told us they would begin to search the immediate area for evidence.

Unable to bear that location any longer, we drove numbly to the house that Mitch owned—the green house that had intruded into my thoughts at night. With our cousin Roy and friend Cliff from Canada, Uncle Terry also arrived and stopped on the road in front of Mitch's house. Mustering every bit of strength I had left, I blurted, "The cops are up the road about two miles. We just left." Then I managed to choke out, "It's Carl." Terry shrank further into his seat and drove on, heartbreak written on his face.

For the next hour, we lingered at Mitch's to get our bearings and try to grasp the reality. One after another, we attempted to call our parents and tell them that the police had recovered Carl's body, but not one of us had the cell service we had been blessed with in previous days. We were not able to call until after we had left Blairs Mills. Shock began to give way to the realization that we no longer needed to look for Carl. It was not an easy adjustment for me. In fact, the terrible truth would take days to penetrate my heart and mind truly. It was extremely difficult to give up my last hope and desperate mission so abruptly. At a loss for what to do next, I felt as if my only purpose in life had been stripped away, and suddenly the world was an empty place. It was a certainty—my brother was gone—our brother was gone. We all carried the fresh pain that Carl was murdered.

As we said goodbye to Mitch, I had a fleeting thought of how strange it seemed that the psychic, Dorothy Allison, had the same name as Allison Road. Despite the challenge of finding what amounted to a needle in a haystack, a career criminal's worst act had come to light. As I suspected, he had not bothered to put much distance between himself and the murder scene on Carl's property.

Six days of frenzied searching ended with unbearable pain mixed with tremendous relief that Carl had been found. Whether it was a blessing from heaven, the work of a spiritual force, or due to the goodness of a citizen's heart, for that, at least, I was grateful.

CHAPTER 5

"THERE WASN'T ANY EVIDENCE."

*For we wrestle not against flesh and blood, but . . . against powers,
against the rulers of the darkness of this world, against spiritual
wickedness in high places. —The Apostle Paul*

A young local woman named Angel had discovered Carl's body along
Allison Road in Blairs Mills, Tell Township in Huntingdon County, just
over the Franklin County line. As the crow flies, it is approximately fifteen miles from Amberson. Angel's effort on August 16 freed us of a great
fear that Carl might never be found and possibly saved us a lifetime of
scouring the roads and woods, searching for him. As it turned out, Clint
and a friend, Michael, had been less than a mile from that place the day
before. Friends, Tommy and Pam, had stopped just short of that area.
We all had been in proximity and quite possibly would have found Carl
ourselves.

Now, we were about to learn the distressing details.

Carl had been dumped like a piece of garbage down an embankment
approximately sixty-six feet from the road, in a culvert that cuts across a
petroleum pipeline easement running perpendicular to the road. He lay
face down by a small wild cherry tree with a pine branch thrown over
him to hide his body. The incline was moderately steep and covered with
a mixture of sparse knee-high brush, weeds, moss, and grass that would
get slippery if the ground drew damp. The woods nearby appeared to be
used by locals as a dumping ground for deer carcasses and revealed years
of accumulation of leg bones, skulls, pieces of hides, old buckets, and bits
of rope. With permission from the property owners, Mr. and Mrs. Hill,

the site along the road is marked to this day with a three-foot wooden cross that my family and I bolted to a pine tree.

We had been unaware for several days that Carl was even missing. Eleven days had passed from the night Carl had arrived home (August 5, 2006) until the morning Angel discovered his body. With the cruel facts confronting us and all hope lost, we forced ourselves to move forward emotionally to provide a proper burial. Little did we know that more than three years would pass before the county prosecutors would agree to release Carl's remains.

After they pulled Carl's body from the dumping ground, we left Mitch's place in Blairs Mills and headed directly to Carl's place. Now we understood why Clint had seen cruisers there that morning. When we arrived, we found troopers still there, from both the Chambersburg and Huntingdon barracks.

"What are you doing?" I asked curtly. "Did Carl have any marks on him?"

"There was damage to his neck . . . and his hip was out of socket," a trooper replied.

"Which hip?" I asked in horror.

"I . . . don't know," he responded as he glanced at fellow troopers.

"What was North doing on work release anyway?" I demanded. "How did they catch him in Huntingdon?"

"He was apprehended after he left Whitsel's Pub," a trooper from the Huntingdon barracks replied. "The bartender there knew he was wanted and called us. North was then spotted by Trooper Rhyner."

His account was noticeably lacking in detail, but what immediately stood out to me, and what others would remark on later, was the similarity of our name "Ryder" to that of Trooper Rhyner, who had caught Scott North on the run.

"Until then, we didn't know Chambersburg was looking for an escapee," the trooper from Huntingdon said.

"They *weren't* looking for him," I retorted.

"Well . . . the case is being transferred from Franklin County to Huntingdon, and the state police there will be investigating the murder. But Ford from the Chambersburg barracks [Franklin County] will also remain on the case."

"Why is it being transferred to Huntingdon?" I asked incredulously.

"We don't know what happened, but it didn't happen here [at Carl's home] in Amberson," a trooper from the Chambersburg barracks interjected.

Then, looking directly at me, a trooper from Huntingdon muttered, "We're not too happy about having the case either."

"One thing . . . Huntingdon will have more time to spend on it," a third trooper from Chambersburg added.

I had no idea what that comment meant, but I couldn't believe my ears when they claimed Carl had not been murdered at his own home in Franklin County.

The bizarre news supplanted what little relief we felt for having at last recovered Carl's body. We couldn't fathom why Franklin County officials handed off the case to a county that had nothing to do with the crime, except for the fact that North had dumped Carl's body on the Huntingdon side, just over the Franklin County line. We knew with certainty that North had attacked Carl on his property. Evidence, clearly visible and throughout Carl's home, although ignored by Chambersburg troopers, spoke volumes. That moment, immediately after finding Carl's body and confronting those disingenuous officers, sealed my determination to expose the truth, which was right before their eyes. The fact that I had no experience in a murder investigation would not deter me. Carl did not drive from the Outer Banks, give his car, money, and phone to a person he disliked; eat food and read magazines that he had never touched before; attempt to hot-wire his truck; throw his front rug out in the grass; spatter a tremendous amount of blood across his front door, on his fencing tools, and in his car trunk; and then travel to Blairs Mills, cover himself with a pine branch, and die.

Staring at both groups of troopers in Carl's driveway, I realized what little footing we had been striving to maintain had just been kicked out from under us. County officials had already collaborated via an exchange of phone calls and paperwork when the coroner had removed Carl's body from the hillside. I couldn't help but wonder, *Would Carl still be alive if they had put that much cooperative effort into finding North after he escaped?*

Even then, my first instinct was that it must have been Franklin County District Attorney John (Jack) Nelson who had instigated the unconventional transfer of the case to Huntingdon County. *But why?*

I knew that a crime-scene location invariably determines the case's venue, which means the case should have remained in Franklin County. State police had to have provided DA Nelson with critical details and unmistakable evidence of murder. Then, by rights, due to the seriousness of the crime, the DA should have visited Carl's property and overseen a thorough investigation in Franklin County; it was solely his responsibility to request and follow up on any additional gathering of evidence. Strangely, he did none of this. Even an untrained eye would have recognized Carl's home, along with a mass of physical evidence, as the scene of a bloody attack. It was not just the fact that Huntingdon now had the case. I was appalled that Franklin County was denying the evidence and hence the killer and the crime.

Immediately, I wondered, *if a case can be sent away arbitrarily to another county, what kind of messed-up criminal justice system is the state dealing with daily? Suppose that's the way criminal activity is handled. Why didn't the police in Mifflin County charge North with fleeing and eluding, since that is where he was apprehended, rather than charge him in connection with a high-speed chase that started in Huntingdon County?*

What were they trying to cover up? Who were they attempting to protect?

We knew what time Carl was on his way home, where he was along the way, and that he was going home to go to bed—because of a phone conversation Carl had had with his girlfriend, Debbie. We certainly knew he would not have voluntarily gone anywhere with Scott North, nor would North have been able to force Carl to go elsewhere to kill him. It simply didn't happen that way.

We left Carl's property to gather our thoughts at Clint's place, and while we were sitting around the kitchen table, my cell phone rang. When I answered, Huntingdon County District Attorney Robert Stewart introduced himself and explained that Trooper Ford had provided my number.

"I have the case," Stewart said.

"I want North dead! I want the death penalty! I want to watch him die!"

"That's doubtful," Stewart replied, "but I can guarantee that Scott North will never see the light of day."

"He'd better not!" I said. "But what I don't understand is why *you* have the case. North didn't kill Carl in Huntingdon County . . . it happened at Carl's place," I insisted. "Carl came home from vacation, and that worthless bastard killed him!"

The next thing that came out of the DA's mouth defied comprehension.

"Well . . . there wasn't any evidence to prove a crime scene," he asserted. A heavy silence followed.

It was a ludicrous claim, especially since he, like DA Nelson, had never examined the scene.

"The crime scene is at Carl's!" I repeated. "There's blood on a lot of things!"

"I recommend that you get Carl's estate settled," Stewart interrupted, changing the subject.

"What?!" I asked. "What do you mean?" Carl's body had been found just hours before, and we were still dealing with the awful realization of his murder. Now, this man was talking about settling his estate.

"Do you have an attorney yet?" he asked.

"What? Well, no," I said, astonished that he had asked such a peculiar question. *Why do we even need an attorney?* I wondered. I just wanted this nightmare to go away and to have Carl back—alive!

"Who do you think you might get as your attorney?" he pressed.

"I don't know." Then I changed the subject back again. "He deserves to die!"

"Who do you think you have in mind as your attorney?" Stewart asked for the third time.

"Bushman!" I finally spat out the first name that came to mind.

"Oh," Stewart paused, "He's a good friend of mine. You tell him I said not to charge you anything, and . . . we'll be in touch." Then he hung up.

The bizarre conversation left me more confused than ever. *What prosecutor offers up free services from another attorney? Why did Stewart even call? Why does he have our case?* I wondered, staring at the phone after Stewart hung up.

I then contacted Trooper Ford.

"Now that we've found Carl, what does North have to say?" I asked.

"He's written a six-page account, and he's fashioned it to appear as if it was all unintentional—just plain bad luck—some sort of unfortunate mishap between two old friends. He said he went there to ask Carl to help him. Then Carl gave him his car, cell phone, and credit cards . . . and then Carl took off with some woman. North also said that he had plans to go to South Carolina to live with a former cell buddy."

"What's *his* name?" I asked.

"Joe," Ford replied, without providing a last name. "North made a phone call to him, and this guy told him that he was stupid for escaping and to go back. It seems North had a plan, so he says, to open a tattoo parlor. But he needed a car to get there."

The "former cell buddy" was likely the same "Joe" addressed in the letter I had picked up from Carl's floor.

"Why didn't he take off then? He had a car after he killed Carl," I said.

"He didn't have enough money," Ford said.

The "unfortunate mishap" story was the first of many tales North would concoct. I didn't believe a lack of money prevented him from heading to South Carolina. North had stolen several bank cards belonging to Carl and had been using them. Carl's account held thousands of dollars, and North had been helping himself to my brother's hard-earned cash. I felt it was more likely North was reluctant to leave the familiar ground and probably would not have known what to do in South Carolina.

Ford continued to stick to his claim that there was no crime scene and no sign of a struggle inside Carl's home. I agreed with him on the second part because a struggle never occurred. It was an ambush that left telltale bloody signs everywhere.

"How come you guys are insisting there's no crime scene?" I asked.

"There's just nothing there. We don't know what happened, but it didn't happen there," Ford reiterated the remark a trooper had made earlier that day.

Then taking me by surprise, he asked, "Do you have an attorney?"

"Stewart asked that too . . . Bushman, I guess."

"Oh . . . he's a friend of mine," Ford said.

That's strange, I thought with increasing misgivings. *Stewart also said that.*

"Well, who's the lead investigator in Huntingdon?" I asked, collecting information in dribbles.

"Trooper Stauffer, and he'll probably be contacting you. And Vivian Ritchey is the Huntingdon County Victim/Witness coordinator. You might want to call her." As he rattled off the phone number, I scribbled it on a scrap of paper.

Right before ending the call, Ford added, "Hey, remember now, we don't want you guys talking about this case."

Really? Why can't we talk about the murder of our brother? I wondered.

The pressure to choose a personal attorney seemed to be motivated by some purpose other than concern for us. Why would it be to the cops' and DA's advantage to know if we had legal counsel and who it was? Might they be concerned if we were to retain an attorney who would challenge actions that went "beyond the norm"? The change of venue defied common sense and even legality and implied an element of corruption. A loved one falling victim to murder is any family's worst nightmare, but ours was made even worse when we began to realize the case might be twisted by politics. Moreover, the suggestion by Stewart to settle Carl's assets as soon as possible was puzzling.

It was not only my family who was trying to make sense of the actions of the authorities. The abrupt transfer of the case to Huntingdon, the pressure to identify an attorney, the odd request to settle Carl's estate, and the warning to keep quiet caught the attention of many people. Our family friend and retired judge, Jim Campbell, remarked on how "unusual [it was] that a case would be transferred to another county other than where the murder took place." He said he had never heard of such a thing. We worried that it could jeopardize Carl's right to justice and whether they would even charge North with murder.

And so, we found ourselves paralyzed by indecision and inexperience, consumed with grief, and appalled at how the investigation had taken such an odd turn. We had a frightening dilemma on our hands with no resolution in sight, which added to our stress.

That evening, I fell into a stupor on the couch, brooding over the intransigence of the police. Suddenly, I jumped fully awake to a vision of a smirking black devil face staring at me, and I saw my left arm and hand had shriveled up to nothing but bone. I rolled off the couch and trudged wearily up the stairs, thinking of the face of murder and of my withered arm symbolizing the officials' attempt to disarm and render us powerless to demand truth and justice.

As events unfolded, we began to scrutinize everyone involved from the very beginning—which was the moment North had gotten his plea bargain, work release, and easy escape from his work site. While we questioned the laxity of prosecutors, police, and cogs of the work program, we also combed through Scott North's past and soon learned more than a few disturbing facts about him. From all indications, those in charge should have considered North a high-risk offender rather than someone suitable for employment. To exacerbate the matter, the county had placed him with an inattentive employer who left him unsupervised.

Before North's incarceration in 2006, the Pennsylvania Criminal Justice Advisory Board had set a goal to shrink the county and state inmate population by implementing money-saving early releases and revamped work programs. Following suit, the Franklin County Prison Board changed its release and work programs—around the time it hired John Wetzel as warden. Eligibility for early release and work release became more lenient. The county's website that existed in 2006 touted the program as placing "good candidates" in the workforce and they continued increasing the workforce after Carl's murder. With fully a third of the county's inmates placed on work release, Wetzel boasted, "There are few jails in the country that can claim that." (*Public Opinion*, Chambersburg, PA. January 9, 2009, "Change in Franklin County's Criminal Justice System Means More Money for the County.")

Meanwhile, the county prison system also claimed that while screening inmates for work release, *public safety would remain a priority*, making it even more difficult to understand how North, a repeat felony offender, got permission to participate in a work program.

Work release, supposedly limited to those who demonstrate "good behavior," also requires supervision while on the worksite. On July 5, 2006, Judge Carol Van Horn had ordered "intense supervision" as part of his burglary sentence in North's case. (Court of Common Pleas of Franklin County, Criminal Docket #CP-28-CR-00001890-2005,

Commonwealth of Pennsylvania v. Scott Nathan North.) No program
is infallible, but there is no excuse for the county's egregious failure to
ensure the supervision of North. A York County attorney, with whom
I shared an account of the crime, described work release as "all about
the money." Franklin County's work-release program strayed far from its
original intention to make *public safety* a priority.

Link by link, a chain of opportunities unfolded, which enabled North
to escape, to burglarize, and to commit murder, yet no county or state official made a statement, offered an apology, or showed any concern for us as
a family. All the while, the remiss employer continued to participate in the
work program, and inmates continued to work there after North's escape.

Though it was a huge embarrassment to the highly touted Franklin
County work program to have an inmate walk off and murder a citizen,
we never dreamed state police would disavow a crime scene and district attorneys would so readily collaborate in shifting the murder case away from
where it happened. It made us suspect that Huntingdon County District
Attorney Robert Stewart's "guarantee" of life in prison was only the beginning of a long string of meaningless assurances and empty promises.

Gossip and speculation were rife. Locals familiar with North and the
officials offered three theories for why Franklin County denied the crime
scene and unloaded the case. The main opinion was simple favoritism.
Some people had seen certain Franklin County judges, District Attorney
Jack Nelson, and the killer's father, Ralph "Scotty" North, belly up to the
same bars, including the members-only Chambersburg Club (C Club)
and other watering holes. "Scotty" had retired as a Chambersburg Borough cop in 2000. The county also employed several of North's relatives
in local law enforcement and at the courthouse.

Another suspected motive for the transfer was that the county would
have had to set aside money for a trial and suffer bad publicity for dropping a gun charge and granting work release to a known felon who had
already served state time.

Or maybe the upcoming elections influenced the quick decision,
and no politician running for reelection would want to explain how an
inmate with a history of escapes, parole violations, and violent incidents
ended up in the work release program and could walk off the job so easily.

No matter how we looked at it, we couldn't find a legitimate reason for denying the murder had occurred in Franklin County and moving the case. They did it because they could—while my family and I suffered, waited, worried, tried to make sense of it all, and prayed for some sort of justice. Along with the rest of my family, I became plagued by nightmares, frightening images that intruded on the little sleep I could get. Most were recurring dreams of three people scheming to kill me. These would go on for years. Several weeks after Carl's death, though, I had a particularly heartbreaking dream, or visit, in which Carl sat in his skid loader in the driveway and said he would like to plant some Christmas trees. Conscious of his murder, even in my dream, I said, "You can do anything you want."

"Yeah, but they put me under the earth," he said solemnly.

One word stood out: *They.* Carl had said, "they." He didn't say, "*He* put me under the earth," referring to North. Rather, *they* had buried him under the weight of their interests and hyped work program. That painful visit has stuck with me more than all the other nightmares put together.

Despite those we came to distrust, reporter Vicky Taylor became a friend. Vicky wrote for the *Public Opinion*, a local newspaper in Chambersburg, and after the discovery of Carl's body, she requested an interview with our family. The police had admonished us, not just once, but numerous times "don't be talking about this." But since we viewed them with increasing suspicion, we agreed to meet with her, although apprehensively. Genuine concern shone in Vicky's attentive blue eyes upon our first meeting, and she was well-versed in courthouse politics. She would cover our case over the years, from North's escape to the grim conclusion.

On August 12, 2006, Vicky posted the first article about the crime a day after North was apprehended.

FRANKLIN ESCAPEE CAUGHT AFTER CHASE. State police captured a Franklin County prison escapee following a late-night high-speed chase Thursday that began in Huntingdon County and ended in Mifflin County. Scott Nathan North, 26, of Fannettsburg, was driving a 1991 silver Ford Crown Victoria owned by a 42-year-old Amberson resident when he was captured at 10:30 P.M. Thursday in Granville. . . .

North walked away from a work-release job in Shippensburg on Aug. 2
and had been at large since then. He was serving an 11 to 23-month sentence for a 2005 burglary and theft. (*Public Opinion* newspaper, Chambersburg, Pennsylvania. August 12, 2006. "Franklin Escapee Caught
After Chase," pages 1A-2A.)

Just as we appreciated Vicky, we would have welcomed the help of
PSARC (Pennsylvania Search and Rescue Council), but it was not until
months later that I learned of their existence. A group of well-trained
volunteers, PSARC assists in searching for lost or missing persons anywhere within the Commonwealth, even wilderness areas. They coordi-
nate search missions and provide search-and-rescue education to local
officials and the public. The state police have access to this group yet
failed to mention it to us.

We also learned that state police had received an anonymous tip on
August 3, the day after North's escape, from a citizen who had dropped
him off in Amberson—but no one in Amberson was notified. And although the escape was posted in a local newspaper (*The Shippensburg
News-Chronicle*, Shippensburg, Pennsylvania, August 3, 2006) the day
after North walked away from the worksite, nothing more was printed
regarding North's last known whereabouts, nor did the police bother to
visit the valley or warn anyone that North was on the loose in the community. Why did they never warn the public of this potential danger?
Why did they not tell anyone?

I constantly relived my actions in the week leading up to the night
Carl returned from vacation and blamed myself for not discovering
North's presence. Loree had called me on Thursday evening, August 3.
"Hey, I read in *The News-Chronicle* that Scott North escaped. They have
a mugshot of him and say that he was working in Shippensburg."

"He's creepy," I said. "What kind of idiot would walk off work
release?"

Later that evening, it crossed my mind that maybe I should check
Carl's place. *North knows where Carl lives, and he did steal from him.* In
the meantime, I called the Chambersburg barracks. But second-guessing
myself, I immediately hung up. It was common knowledge among those
in the valley that the state police in Chambersburg were usually reluctant

to travel the thirty minutes to Amberson and Path Valley. Many people had received a cool reception when they called to report an incident or a crime. I feared the cops would view me as a nuisance and assumed they would trivialize my request to check Carl's place; after all, it had been two years since we had had any dealings with North. I even questioned whether I might be overreacting.

However, had I realized the depth of North's depravity and his nerve to show up where he was unwelcome—had I known what the state police already knew—I would have called 911, the barracks, and everyone else I could think of. To this day, I deeply regret putting that phone down, and I remain sick to the soul, wondering whether my call might have made a difference.

After I talked with Loree, my thoughts kept churning. I knew Carl was due home in two days—on Saturday. So, I determined before I went to bed that I would drive over the next evening on Friday, August 4, to check around his property.

As it happened, I didn't drive over to Carl's house; instead, I called Carl on Friday evening after work. "Hey, it's in the paper that Scott North escaped from work release. He was working here in Shippensburg."

"I need to come home," he responded immediately.

"When?"

"I'll probably leave tomorrow morning."

"Okay, call me when you get close to Chambersburg," I said, intending to meet him there and follow him home to Amberson. I knew it was at least a six-hour drive from the Outer Banks, and I figured Carl would call me sometime during the mid-afternoon.

Five minutes later, Carl called back. "I was thinking," he began, "North knows he's not to set foot up there. And he has no way of knowing I'm away . . . so I'm not worried about it."

"All right," I answered, feeling as if I had overreacted. We said goodbye with the understanding that I need not meet Carl the next day.

However, neither one of us had given enough serious thought to the possibilities, nor did we know the extent of North's capacity for violence. From what little we did know about North, we assumed he might hide out in Fannettsburg. Phone records indicated that Carl must have had second thoughts that evening and called Uncle Terry in Amberson, presumably to ask him to check his place; Terry wasn't home. Then Carl called Clint but strangely dialed an old number no longer in use. I don't know why he did so because he knew Clint's current telephone number.

That Friday evening, setting concerns mostly aside, Carl and I had convinced ourselves there was little chance of North showing up at his place. Days later, however, after realizing that the worst had happened to Carl, I would begin to wrestle with guilt that would last for years. I had not taken precautions when I learned that North was on the loose. I had not gone to Carl's property on Thursday or Friday. I started to desperately wish that, even at the risk of my own life, I had found North there before Carl had arrived home.

 C H A P T E R 6

FROM BLACK CLOVER

The voice of thy brother's blood crieth unto Me from the ground.
—God

After Carl's body was removed from the hillside and taken to J.C. Blair Memorial Hospital morgue in Huntingdon, Coroner Ron Morder and pathologist Dr. Harry Kamerow followed standard autopsy procedures. They took photographs, separated his skeleton from his body, and cremated the rest. This added to our pain because it went against our traditions and religious principles. Had he died a natural death, we could have overseen the handling of his body, ensuring our requests, but because my brother had been the victim of a crime, we had no say.

Carl was officially identified after authorities compared radiographs of mandible remains to dental records, the quickest and simplest identification method. The next duty was to pinpoint the cause, mode, and manner of death—three elements are considered before completing a death certificate. In this case, the cause of death would be the instrument used—such as a knife, a gun, or even a hand. The mode would be the pathological agent that resulted in death, such as excessive bleeding, a fractured skull, or asphyxiation. The manner of death would be a classification—natural, accidental, homicide, suicide, or undetermined. We expected the cause, mode, and manner of Carl's death to be promptly established, but each remained indeterminate.

That same day—the day Carl's body was found—after talking on the phone with DA Stewart at Clint's house, Clint and I returned to Carl's place to look for further clues. We went together because, truthfully, neither of us wanted to be there alone. The murder had left us so trau-matized that even the faint sound of the wind in the old pines seemed menacing, as if evil hung in the air ready to pounce.

This time, I noticed the padlock to the shed. Its shackle had been cut in half and tossed on the ground. As I cautiously entered the shed and glanced around, I saw that it was loaded with tools and fencing hardware, as expected. All at once, I spied a shotgun barrel and an electric hacksaw lying on the workbench, along with a small heap of shiny metal shavings. "Look at this!" I called to Clint. "He sawed the barrel off! They never told us it was sawed off!"

Without hesitation this time, I called Ford. "The lock to the shed's been cut, and there's a shotgun barrel on the workbench. By the looks of it, it's newly sawed off, and I know it goes with that shotgun North had when you caught him."

"Someone will be over to get it later in the week," he replied with little apparent interest.

Since the police had never checked the shed, I added, "There's also a five by seven tan rug that's been lying in the yard since that first day. How come no one took it? It used to be inside Carl's front door, but now it's lying in the yard." I glanced toward the yellow barricade tape across the door of the mobile home, wondering what else they had not collected.

"It'll be gathered along with the barrel," Ford assured me. Yet, I couldn't help but feel stung by his indifference.

I went home dead-tired that evening, unable to sleep, staring despond-ently into the darkness, thinking of angels intervening in times of crisis. I thought of Daniel from Judah, who had been sealed in a lion's den by his enemies but was rescued by an angel who had shut the mouths of the lions, ensuring that Daniel remained unharmed. *Where had Carl's angel been? Why hadn't anyone saved Carl?* An ill wind had blown into the valley where evil had done its work. Carl was gone, and there was no good to be found, not even a hint of justice. My family and I had never known such depths. We found ourselves plunged into a dark world far from moral order and normalcy. It occurred to me that the wicked have the advantage in this world, while the good suffer in it, primarily because the wicked are heartless.

On Friday, August 18, 2006, Drs. Steven Symes and Dennis Dirkmaat, from the Applied Forensic Sciences Department and the Science in Anthropology Department at Mercyhurst College in Erie, Pennsylvania (renamed Mercyhurst University in 2012) and several graduate students, arrived at the site in Blairs Mills. Specializing in trauma analysis, they photographed the area, removed surface litter, and sifted soil through a mesh screen. They found a tooth and a hyoid bone (the small bone in the front of the neck between the lower jawbone and larynx). Ford told us they were looking for evidence of a bullet but didn't find any.

I regret not returning to the site in Blairs Mills to meet them, but during their short visit, I had no strength to go back to that horrible place. It was later, through emails, that I came to know Dr. Symes. Once, he courteously asked for a photograph of Carl to demonstrate to his students the importance of remembering that when working with human remains, they are not dealing with just bones; rather, the remains belong to a person, and that person has a family. Desperate for any sort of respect, we appreciated that he included ethics in his classes. We had not received much consideration up to that point from any authority, save three state troopers and the state police commissioner, who had sent cards of condolence.

That Friday afternoon, Dr. Symes met with Dr. Kamerow at J.C. Blair Memorial Hospital and performed a skeletal analysis to confirm trauma, but we would have to wait for any conclusive information. Dr. Symes then took the skeletal remains with him to Erie for further examination, filing his report almost a year later in July 2007, after which Dr. Kamerow generated his report. Part of Kamerow's report would later lead to a strong disagreement between officials and our family.

That week, Trooper Ford, for whatever reason, felt it necessary to inform us that the forensic trip to Blairs Mills had cost the state $6000. We were confused as to why he thought he should share that information. But in any event, we later asked Dr. Symes about the cost, and he was taken aback by the inaccuracy of that claim. He explained that such site visits provide practical experience for students and are funded through the college.

Ford's assertion that it was state-funded made us suspicious that he was trying to divert our attention from the true crime scene and redirect it to Huntingdon County. It didn't work, and the dig at the dumping ground in Blairs Mills ended without producing any revelatory evidence. That was because all the evidence was at Carl's place, where we continued to uncover it independently. We considered the site in Blairs Mills a secondary crime scene—there was never any indication that the murder took place anywhere other than at Carl's home.

While Dr. Symes was at the hospital morgue that Friday, Clint and I spent the day, again looking around at Carl's place, and, again, we came up with more evidence. Several feet from the sidewalk, I noticed a patch of dead grass, approximately six by ten inches. Much of it appeared to be black. I also spotted a three-leaf clover covered with something that had dried, shiny, and black. When I picked it up and peered closely at the edges, the cloverleaves shone blood-red in the late afternoon sun. "Look at this, Clint. I think it's blood, and it's killed the grass."

One more time, I dialed Ford. "I found blood in the grass," I said with exasperation, almost certain by now that the police had little interest in collecting evidence.

"We'll be over to look at it," was his standard reply.

Considering Ford's disinterest, I was surprised when he and Trooper Rush arrived within the hour. "It could be transmission oil," one suggested.

"It's not transmission oil. It's blood!" I insisted as I cordoned off the area with several short boards.

"A soil sample can be taken within the next couple of days," Ford said matter-of-factly. Then he divulged that after Carl had fired North, North told his cousin he would kill Carl and throw his body somewhere. Ford also told us that officials had discovered "you're done" writings in North's cell at the Franklin County Jail that implied he had it in for Carl.

"Again . . . what was he doing on work release?" I asked.

"I tried to get him state time for that last burglary," Ford replied. I learned later that he was referring to a case that Assistant District Attorney Angela Krom had prosecuted.

"This whole thing is outrageous!" I said.

Abruptly the troopers departed, and as we watched their cruiser kick up dust as it traveled down the lane, I mimicked to Clint, "Transmission oil."

"Yeah," Clint sighed irritably, "you can tell it's blood."

By this time, the evening sun had cast shadows along the ground, accentuating the terrain and drawing our attention to a bare spot in the grass, about a foot long and seven inches wide, approximately eight feet from the bloody grass. It was a tire spinout mark, and I wondered aloud, "Do you think they'd bother coming back if we called them *again*?" But darkness was already falling, and I had no real intention of calling.

The next day, a Saturday—three days after Carl's body was found— Clint and I focused our attention on a black rubber tarp, bunched up and partially unfolded, in the grass. It also was obviously out of place, to the left of the deck, and appeared to have been dragged there. I knew Carl had used the tarp to cover a stack of fence boards, which were now exposed. I had seen the tarp to the left of the deck on that first day when we discovered Carl was missing but had not given it another thought. Finding Carl had been my only concern.

As I began to tug the tarp away from where it lay, I could tell that, like the rug, it had not been there long, and as with the rug, the grass underneath had turned yellow-green but had not yet died. Clint helped me flip the bulky material over, and on it, we found a pool of dried blood, a bloody sneaker print, and a bloody palm print—both a lot smaller than Carl's would have been. It was evident that North had rolled Carl onto the tarp after the attack and that the prints belonged to North.

Losing patience, I called Ford again. "There's a black tarp lying to the left of the deck that's covered with a pool of dried blood, a bloody sneaker print, and a bloody handprint."

"I'll have someone from forensics come over," he assured me, and I hung up the phone feeling, and I am not sure why, embarrassed for the state police.

Shaken, Clint and I folded the tarp so that the blood was protected from the elements, and we left it where it was. Unquestionably, it was another piece of the growing evidentiary puzzle proving that North had viciously attacked Carl. Days later, an individual from forensics came to collect a soil sample from the dead grass area, swab the blood on the tarp, and take photographs of both. Yet, they left without taking the tarp. "This is evidence," I said despondently to Clint. "I don't know why they didn't take it. This is evidence." Exasperated, Clint and I refolded the tarp a second time and lugged it to the barn for safekeeping.

Later that month, Dr. Symes, in response to my email inquiry, explained that blood fat (a lipoid substance) is the component in blood that will kill grass; Ford had told us it was the iron content in the blood that had killed the grass. Either way—blood fat or iron content—it takes a lot of blood to kill grass. Carl had suffered a major life-threatening wound that tore through skin, body fat, vessels, and muscle. The blood, approximately sixteen feet from Carl's front door, was crucial evidence, proof of a horrific penetrating injury that ultimately was fatal.

Although I inquired weekly about the forensics results on the blood from the tarp and grass, months passed before Trooper Ford told us that the tests indeed proved it was Carl's blood. I would later wonder if the sample was sent to the lab. However, our inquiries about whether the palm and shoe print had been linked to North went unanswered. We suspect the police never bothered. For certain, they never responded to those questions.

For the next several months, scarcely a day passed in which my family or I didn't ask about the status of the case, and although we were not familiar with the process of a murder investigation, we knew that police should collect *all* evidence and follow up with forensic testing. Furthermore, as the county's chief law enforcement officer, the district attorney should be interested in every trace, sign, and clue; yet we continued to find key evidence uncollected. Listening to their claims that they had gathered plenty of proof, we still had to wonder, *Do they need only some evidence, or are they refusing to collect all the evidence for some other reason?*

Although discouraged by the mediocre investigation, we clung to every sparse bit of encouragement they deigned to offer, whether it was sincere or not. We wanted desperately to have faith in the justice system and to think that someone cared. The idea of seeking outside help to hold these officials accountable and insist they do a better job had not yet crossed our minds, nor did we know where to turn.

I was very angry, not only with the officials but with God. While I was aware of the terrible reality, still I pleaded for it not to be true. In my pain, I ordered God to change things—to move time backward. I questioned Him. I even dared Him to kill me, and in the next moment, begged Him to annihilate the heartless bastard who had killed Carl. I demanded to know why He had not sent an intervening angel to save Carl's life. I stormed, rampaged, and raged and kept reminding God that He had just let Carl die.

With thoughts of justice, revenge, and the death penalty churning, I recalled the murder of one of my favorite professors in Alabama. In October 2003, I had just returned home to Pennsylvania when I learned that an intruder had shot Jack Dempsey and had taken his car and money. Professor Dempsey had studied in Venice, Italy, and, upon his return to the States, taught oil painting techniques. He had also founded the Department of Art at the University of Alabama in Huntsville in 1965. His killer got a life sentence. It did not seem to be enough punishment for taking a life. As I prepared to face the days ahead, I wondered if we could expect the same.

 CHAPTER 7

TO A WHITE CHURCH

If there be therefore any consolation in Christ, if any comfort of love, if any fellowship of the Spirit. . . . —The Apostle Paul

Unraveled souls do not function well. Nevertheless, several days after the recovery of Carl's body, we realized we had to make funeral arrangements, and we needed someone of unshakeable faith and prodigious devotion to help us. Subsequently, my family asked Rev. Dr. Meagan Boozer to perform a service in Carl's memory. She would understand and be able to deal with the grief and outrage devastating our family, friends, and the community.

Meagan's late parents, Bud Messner and Molly Darr, were well-known and talented musicians and beloved radio personalities who owned WCBG radio from 1963 to 1990. They had entertained audiences with *The Bud Messner Show* and Molly's *Molly and Me*. Years prior, Molly had sung on the Grand Ole Opry with musical talents such as Roy Rogers, Lester Flatt, Earl Scruggs, Hank Williams, Roy Acuff, Gene Autry, and Tex Ritter.

We shared with Meagan how much we loved Carl and the things he loved in life. We asked that the service move along at a steady pace with the reading of a Scripture, eulogy, and the singing of a hymn that was familiar to everyone. We also requested that she play a recording of Carl's favorite song.

As I sat in church, I realized this sorrow was mine for good and no good reason. It would be ingrained in my spirit forever. I was raging inside but knew I had to find a quiet place in my mind, at least for the time being. I wanted to do it for Carl. And we needed God and the consoling power of prayer . . . but as for me, I no longer trusted the Almighty. Angry accusations consumed me, questions and blame for Carl's death, with no idea of how or when it would end . . . certainly not by the time of the ceremony. And I had no intention of running from the devil either.

And so, on Saturday, August 26, we held a service in honor and memory of Carl in the white clapboard Presbyterian Church in Amberson. The church, built on a solid foundation of fieldstone from the valley, sits in place of the original Union Church built in 1763; the lumber and site of, according to family history, had been donated by our great-great-great-granddad, Cromwell McVitty. An 1853 framed photograph of the original church hangs upstairs in my house.

Carl had always liked the old one-room church, still in use, with the steeple and bell, horsehair plaster walls, plank floors, and wooden pews. Its double front doors open to a short set of steps inside, landing at the top and a door on the left, and another to the right. Inside each door, aisleways spill along both sides of the long wooden pews that fill the center. Shorter pews butt against each wall, to the left and right of the center section. I remember as a child that the women would congregate in the center pews and the men to the left. A piano sits to the right of the pulpit, an organ to the left. Two large kerosene stoves stand toward the front of the room, one on each side, which we covered with white linen and photographs of Carl.

On many a Sunday, the old church reverberated with the sound of early hymns and the ghosts of whispered prayers from the faithful, who worshipped there for generations. On this day, a feeling of timeless devotion hung in the air despite our sorrow. Who would have thought it would come to this painful hour? Murder had propelled us from ordinary lives into a world of grief, putting one foot in front of the other, fumbling our way through each torturous moment only because we had no other choice. We were the walking wounded, and we knew it. It was not just a wicked dream that had crept into our psyche as we slept. It was not just a glimpse into what hell might be like. It *was* hell. Life's worst nightmare had hit home in all its unbearable wretchedness. Yet, whether I would acknowledge it for myself or not, I knew my family needed church and whatever comfort it could bring.

One by one, on that stifling summer day in August, we trudged up the aisle and collapsed into the front pews, just glad to sit down. The church was full, and extra chairs had been crammed into the back of the room as well as outside to accommodate friends, former classmates, teachers—mourners from the valley and beyond. Pat Hennessy had arrived from the Outer Banks, and other friends had driven down from Canada. People gathered that day for Carl, for us, for themselves, and for God.

As I stared at the green marble urn with the gold buck etched on the front, which Mom and Loree had chosen, it was hard to believe that just three weeks earlier, on a Saturday night, Carl had been taken from us. I couldn't fathom that we had nothing left but ashes. It didn't seem real. My grieving mind ranged through past conversations with Carl . . . to angels . . . to Jesus . . . and, for some odd reason, to olden tales of slaves on ships. Those shackled, terror-stricken souls had also lost something precious—their freedom and old way of life, and thus some had willed themselves to die while still chained on the ship, putting an end to their frightening ocean journey. I understood their preference for death over torment.

It takes unimaginable callousness to dump a person like trash—it's vile, disrespectful, and wicked. Carl had been stripped of his life, and now we were stripped of Carl, robbed of a traditional viewing and a last grieving gaze upon him. We had not been given a chance to say goodbye, nor could we lay his body to rest in a dignified manner. Instead, for five heart-wrenching days, we had to search for him, then stand by as they bagged his body. Now we sat at his service, with only an urn to look at.

I never dreamed that Carl's trip to the Outer Banks would end in such tragedy and that part of him would be reduced to just ashes in a box. Jesus, help us! I just couldn't understand it. Tissues piled up on the pews—such overwhelming grief. In a thoughtful gesture, though, and in consideration for our great sadness, our friend, Pam Cook, had given each family member a spray of flowers after we had been seated. Her thoughtfulness and the beautiful petals helped assuage my sorrow and hopelessness, just enough to get from one miserable moment to the next.

To begin the service, Meagan fulfilled our request and played a recording of Carl's favorite song, a rendition of "Free Bird" by Lynyrd Skynyrd, the original released in 1973 when Carl was just ten years old. It is hauntingly beautiful as piano, guitar, and drums slide into the heart-rending question, "*If I leave here tomorrow, would you still remember me?*" I loved it myself, although I can now no longer bear to hear it.

After the first five minutes, Meagan turned off the recording and jokingly remarked, "You don't think we're going to listen to the whole fifteen minutes, do you?" which was met with a few quiet laughs. Then came Meagan's meaningful life-giving sermon. We hung on to every word of comfort, needing it to stay alive, to take even the next breath. Visitors who didn't know Carl commented that the remembrance I had written, a eulogy which Meagan agreed to read, made them feel as if they had known him all their lives. Even in my anger, I was determined to share Carl's goodness and kindness. For those who knew him from birth, a retelling of humorous moments prompted a few subdued chuckles that broke through the pain and grief.

One specific story sticks in my memory. I was in fourth grade; Carl was in first. While it took me months to adjust, Carl fit into the school routine right away. Soon, he was friends with everyone and had developed a crush on his teacher, Miss Jenkins. By the end of the school year, he wanted to do something special for her, and so one evening, we picked a gallon of wild strawberries from along the lane and packed them into a Gettle's plastic ice cream container.

The next day, he took his seat on the school bus at the front with the container next to him, all pleased with himself. However, the bus came to a sudden stop not long into the ride, and the container slid off the seat. Not only that, the lid flew off. From across the aisle, I sort of felt sorry for him as he kneeled on the bus floor diligently scraping every "schmushed up" dirty berry back into the bucket, determined that nothing would prevent him from giving a gift to his teacher. I hope she washed them well if she had any intention of eating them.

Meagan also played the same piano that Mom had played for church services years earlier, and we sang "Amazing Grace," chosen not only for its age and beauty but because it is one of the most recognizable folk hymns of all time. The lyrics, written by poet and cleric John Newton in the 1700s, promise that regardless of the sins one commits, redemption and forgiveness are possible through God's mercy. Our souls can be saved. We sang it for its meaning and beauty, for us, and those with us. In those moments, however, I couldn't accept that this message could in any way be intended for Carl's murderer. A song, goodwill, and prayer would never be enough to set it right. Beyond the pale of redeeming grace, his salvation lay solely between himself and God.

The harsh reality that Carl was gone hit that day as a permanent fact. Despondently, I turned the story of Jesus and Lazarus over in my mind. The Book of John, the fourth Gospel in the New Testament, tells of how Jesus brought Lazarus back to life after being dead for four days.

Jesus, likewise, spent time in the grave. It had not mattered whether He was a miracle-maker or not. The unholy trinity of power, politics, and payoff of promised silver coin inspired a plot to do away with Him. Officials scourged Him with a flagrum and crucified Him with iron spikes and a lance. Thanks to His friends and followers, though, no one had the opportunity to throw Him away like a piece of garbage after His death. Instead, three days later, he was resurrected. I wanted that for Carl as well—I just didn't know how to call on Jesus to bring him back.

Toward the end of the service, Meagan invited those present to approach her so she could minister to each one individually, but no one moved; no one wanted to go first. Then, finally, our aunt went forward and broke our reserve. At some point, I stepped up, rage churning inside me as I went through the motions for the sake of the funeral. While Meagan's words of conviction and faith poured over me, my eyes burned with the desire for vengeance.

The tolling bell marked the end of worship, and in remembrance of Carl, Uncle Terry pulled the rope forty-three times—one ring for every year that we had been blessed with his life. The old bell rang clear, yet to my ears, it was a sad knell that echoed off the mountainsides. As it resonated through the valley, counting Carl's few years with us, I wondered what the angels thought of the evil that had drawn us to this occasion.

After the final amen, my family slowly filed from the church in a solemn line for committal, passing Center School, the one-room schoolhouse that sits behind the church. Both Mom and Dad attended the school as kids; now, it's occasionally used for voting and as a meeting place for the Amberson Historical Society. The procession to the graveside was just a short walk but was like the deep-water walk I had experienced during those first days of searching for Carl, with each step taking so much effort.

Finally, we came upon a small hole in the ground, and I saw that someone had lined the bottom with pine needles, a symbol of everlasting life. Numbly, I sprinkled some rose petals on the urn to honor my brother.

Some recollections of that day have been obscured by grief, but I will always remember two friends, Marian Stinson and Kathy DePuy, former coworkers of mine from the Game Commission, who willingly braved the drive from Harrisburg and the unfamiliar back roads to attend Carl's service. Marian later remarked that in addition to the beauty of the valley, the most memorable part of the day was the people, especially how highly they thought of Carl and the friendliness of our family. "He was quite a guy," she said. "I wish I had had the opportunity to meet him."

Kathy wished the same. "That was the most touching service I have ever been to," she said. As we talked, I recalled a vivid dream that Kathy had related to me little more than a year earlier. It had stuck with me because it was a bit out of the ordinary. She dreamed that we had met at an old church and had gone inside and sat down. I commented after she described the dream to me, "I hope no one dies." She had this dream around the same time Scott North went to jail for burglarizing the tavern in Fannettsburg. I view it now as another forewarning of wickedness in the works.

After leaving the graveside, we moved to a newer church a short distance down the road, with modern facilities and a recreation hall for the luncheon. Again, the dedicated ladies of the valley had everything ready, but appetites were scarce. Within an hour or so, the gathering began to dissolve until only my family, several friends, and I was left . . . and another day of disbelief ended. It had been an exhausting day—just one of many more to come.

The same week as the funeral, Carl's schoolmate, Ben Gamble, honored Carl in his own way. Nothing less could be expected of Ben, who always entered a flamboyant float in the annual Path Valley Fireman's Parade. That year, during the parade, his float bore a banner: *God Bless Carl Ryder*. It meant a lot to us.

Before the event had begun, though, Jim Campbell (the former magistrate judge and family friend) and longtime announcer of the parade entries offered a prayer. It was an annual tradition for Jim to announce the entrants while I assisted with his entry lists as the parade passed en route to the picnic grounds. Our teamwork spanned nearly twenty years, but I couldn't muster the strength to be there that evening. The following year, we announced the parade entries together one last time, after which we both resigned. The month of August no longer held good memories.

The long tendrils of grief touched even the very young. Two weeks after the service, as I walked in the field above Carl's place, I came upon a curious little arrangement constructed of stones, short boards, and sticks. It appeared that a child had placed it there. I discovered later that a young admirer had built a memorial in private homage to his big buddy. Pat Hennessy's son, Jordan, had loved deep-sea fishing with Carl and felt the huge emptiness created by his absence. Pat also took Carl's death very hard and remarked, "Carl was a good friend. He helped me out a lot. I'm gonna really miss him."

The crushing death would change us forever. With much sadness in her heart, Mom sighed, "I never thought when I was a kid going to Center School that I would end up having a son buried behind it." So many sorrowful hearts are left in death's wake. So much grief was caused for no purpose.

Like a free bird, Carl, you left, and yes, we will forever remember you. Carl, we love you and miss you so much.

CHAPTER 8

INSURMOUNTABLE EVIDENCE

Yea, though I walk through the valley of the shadow of death . . .
—*King David*

I visited Carl's property every day. *Every* day. Always with a heavy heart. Sometimes alone, sometimes not. One morning, I was surprised to see a state police cruiser in the driveway, the yellow tape cut, and Carl's front door wide open. A trooper, along with a game warden carrying a camera, exited. While the trooper resealed the door, the warden gave me a somewhat embarrassed but cordial smile.

"What's goin' on?" I asked.

"Takin' some pictures," the trooper replied.

Dissatisfied with the cryptic answer, I called Ford. "Why is the Game Commission taking pictures?"

I tried to focus as Ford explained that police had found two buck heads in the deep freezer without tags attached during the initial investigation. A trooper informed the Game Commission, Ford said, and "They might confiscate them."

Like hell, I thought and immediately changed the subject.

"Is there anything new with the case?" I asked.

"I don't have anything," he said curtly.

"Well, I found two sabots on the ground that first day. They're *new*. Do you want them for evidence?"

"Just keep them."

I pictured all the evidence I had pointed out or had collected—the sabots, a rug in the yard, a sawed-off gun barrel, metal shavings, a cut shed lock, a bloody tarp, and blood on the grass; all this without yet being inside the residence. *How in the world could the police refuse to acknowledge Carl's home as the scene of his murder,* I thought, *yet feel it necessary to report two frozen deer heads that had been in his freezer for two years?* As far as I know, crime scene photos did not exist, but pictures of two deer heads now did.

An uproar ensued. My family and I felt the authorities had no business concerning themselves with deer heads when they showed so little interest in the murder scene. We would have to explain that one deer was Carl's and the other belonged to a friend; both later proved to be legal kills; the tags were stashed nearby and completed with the proper information. Carl had not stored the tags in the freezer with the heads and had never gotten around to taking the heads to a taxidermist for mounting. I guess he didn't consider the possibility of his being murdered and his family having to explain why he hadn't made tagging heads a priority.

I would later, toward mid-September, be provided an unexpected chance to remove the deer heads. I was determined that no one else would lay hands on them. It was yet another trespass against Carl, and I wondered what more the police thought they could do to him anyway. Someone had already killed him.

The following week, I apprehensively dialed Vivian Ritchey to ask about her responsibilities as a victim/witness coordinator for the Huntingdon County Court. As it turned out, she was a godsend. Even though DA Stewart had not provided her with any information about the case (in fact, he had not even told her he had the case), she immediately set out to discover whatever she could to help us. I will appreciate Vivian forever for treating us with respect and compassion throughout the next year and a half and for calling just to ask how we were doing. When we had a question or needed to talk to her, she never failed to get back to us, although most often, she could relay only the information made available to her. Unfortunately, Stewart didn't offer much in response to our anxious requests about how the case was proceeding. Little did we know, it was not proceeding at all.

A month had passed since Carl's death, and I still felt as if I were looking for him. I couldn't bear the thought that he was gone, and so, I wandered here and there. I remember pondering the story of Elijah the Hebrew, whose spirit was so committed to God that he was taken to Heaven in a whirlwind. Then, I spiraled in the other direction, down into a void, sick to the soul and questioning the purpose of existence. I obsessed over the injustice of it all and questioned why, with all the powers of the heavens, God had not stopped this atrocity before it happened.

On the opposite side of Elijah's righteousness was the path North chose. He made a conscious decision to flee work release and embark on a heedless course that ended in murder. Later, he penned a few letters from the Huntingdon County Jail, copies of which I obtained from Franklin County Courthouse records.

In September 2006, North wrote, "For some reason, thay [sic] are trying to keep me out of Franklin County," he shared with his maternal grandmother, Larena Reeder. Next, he expressed his eagerness to "get upstate and get my time startted [sic]." Then he confidently announced that he was "probably looking at about 4 four years . . . maybe less."

In another letter written several days later, he exulted that he was "ready to get sentenced for this excape [sic] and get upstate," where he intended to "put a bunch of artwork in a book and get it published." He asked Larena to collect his paycheck from the Franklin County Jail because "it would be nice to have a T.V. this time around."

As he anticipated his four-year incarceration and the opportunity to peddle some prison "art," hopefully with a television, he questioned what his grandmother meant when she wrote that she "can't talk." It must have finally dawned on him that officials were monitoring his mail. In either pure stupidity or attempted manipulation, he wrote that he had another letter ready but wasn't going to send it because they were "reading my mail." Police told us they confiscated the letter with a search warrant, but both prosecutors and police have denied us access to this piece of correspondence.

With the case a little more than a month old, DA Stewart, Dr. Kamerow, and Trooper Stauffer visited Carl's property during the second week of September. Kamerow, a short-statured man with a dark complexion, wore a brightly colored poncho and stuck out like a sore thumb. For a few minutes, he wandered the property, then went inside the trailer and asked why there was a "box of bullets" sitting in the living room. I knew Carl would not have left his ammo just sitting there. Most likely, North had pulled it out from Carl's closet and intended to pack it into the car, according to his to-do list that had been confiscated.

"Carl was a hunter," Trooper Stauffer informed Kamerow.

"Well," I interrupted, "actually, Carl did do some hunting during his twenties and thirties. And he hunted two seasons ago . . . he and a friend . . . here on his property. But for the past several years, he mostly just worked." Kamerow then slipped off toward the car without further comment.

Stewart, who appeared to be in his late fifties or early sixties, with salt-and-pepper hair, and a somewhat cowing personality, came off as someone accustomed to intimidating those around him. I ignored this. I didn't consider him a problem, although I still did not see a good reason why the case was being handled by Huntingdon County rather than Franklin. It was strange, though, that Stewart was now visiting Carl's home weeks after the murder, considering that police and Franklin County District Attorney Jack Nelson had refused to recognize it as the scene of the crime.

As he laid a map on the trunk lid of the unmarked cruiser, he traced the county line with his index finger for my benefit, emphasizing the fact that North had dumped Carl's body just across the line on the Huntingdon side. I already knew that. I was there that hellish day. I knew the place right down to the longitude and latitude, the number of miles from Carl's home, and where the county line ran.

Eventually, he said, "This is a slam-dunk case." Then he added, "You don't have anything to worry about."

That was a ray of hope; still, it did nothing to convince me that he should have the case, to begin with. My family and I were hesitant to file a complaint with the state Attorney General's Office asking to have the case returned to Franklin County because if the case were returned, we knew it could end in a plea bargain. But, on the other hand, we desperately needed an official who cared that Carl had been murdered.

Stewart never ventured from the driveway, having stayed just long enough to point out the county line on a map and tell me not to worry. Days later, however, he passed along a message that it would be "a difficult case because there is no crime scene."

I thought back to the day we had left Blairs Mills, heartbroken, and Stewart had called with his guarantee that North would "never see the light of day." Now, just days after his brief visit to the crime scene, with its unmistakable signs of a bloody attack, his "slam-dunk case" had become "a difficult case"—with no crime scene, no cause of death, and no weapon. It seemed that neither county wanted the case nor was interested in establishing a motive (always a crucial element in an investigation). We believed that with two other murder cases already pending in Huntingdon County, a third could not be welcome; we also wondered whether Stewart might be accommodating his fellow DA in minimizing the evidence.

Soon after the visit by the three men, Trooper Stauffer was promoted to corporal, and unfortunately for our family, was transferred. He was one of the very few who had been truly interested in and serious about conducting a proper investigation. His replacement, Trooper Sneath, also showed interest in the case, but he, too, was promoted shortly after that and transferred. We never met him in person until years later.

During all the tumult, Ford would soon inflict another staggering blow by insisting that investigators "can't connect North with the body." As we drowned in grief, North found himself "in the hole" (solitary confinement) for an infraction. We were not privy to what he did, but Trooper Ford told us that North was minimizing his responsibility in a typical fashion and insisting that his misconduct resulted from suffering from unfair charges, unjust imprisonment, and harassment by the guards. At the time, all charges pressed against North by Huntingdon County related to the high-speed chase, while Franklin County filed only an escape charge. A murder charge would be a long time coming.

In the meantime, on Monday, September 11, 2006, one month to the day that we realized Carl was missing, DA Stewart released Carl's trailer to us. According to the officials, there was nothing there they needed. We were shocked at the precipitous action. I then asked again for the rest of Carl's remains but received no answer.

The following Saturday morning, September 16, Clint and I met at Carl's place. Although now allowed to enter his home, we were still hesitant about touching anything, and we had no plans for how we would clean or remove any items. Based on the uncollected evidence we had discovered outside, we were interested in, yet uneasy about, what we might find inside.

Cautiously, we cut the yellow police tape, slowly opened the blood-spattered door, and immediately felt a creepy sensation as we stepped over the threshold onto the very spot where the attack took place. Just inside the door, we stood rooted, our shaky breath assailed by a strong whiff of rotting food.

When I looked down and realized we were standing on subflooring, I stepped to the left. I later learned that police had removed several tiles as evidence. After a pause, I felt drawn to go past the kitchen and down the hall directly to Carl's bedroom. As I opened the door, I instantly spied a round hole in the far wall, about waist high. It was approximately the size of a nickel, and I noticed gouge marks on each side of it, indicating something had been pried from the drywall.

My heart raced as I retraced my steps out of the room and into the hallway, where I spotted a hole in the wall above the bedroom door. I then stepped back inside the bedroom and looked up to see another round hole on the inside wall above the same door. Both holes, in perfect alignment, looked to be the same size as the one across the room on the opposite wall. I knew immediately that all three holes resulted from a pumpkin ball discharged from a 12-gauge shotgun.

I yelled for Clint in a panic, "There's a pumpkin ball hole in the wall!" We had been worrying ourselves sick over what kind of weapon North might have used against Carl, and the holes confirmed our nascent theory. Subsequently, we went about reconstructing our crime-scene scenario based on what we had just discovered—telltale signs of a murderous shotgun blast.

I called Ford. "What was removed from the bedroom wall?" I asked, also hoping to hear why they had not mentioned it to us.

"It was a shotgun slug," Ford replied. "But there's *no* way that slug is what killed Carl. He would've had to have been hanging from the ceiling. We lined it up, and it would've been impossible," he insisted.

Ford's blithe disregard of this key piece of evidence strengthened our suspicion of some sort of plot. I questioned him again a few days later, refusing to let it drop, but he remained adamant that the slug they had removed from the wall had not killed Carl. We knew better. Clint and I lined it up too, and we knew it was possible. Considering the distance the slug had traveled, it would have needed only a slight upward trajectory to penetrate the wall above the bedroom door. On close inspection of the hole above the doorway, I saw what looked like a minuscule amount of blood around the edge. This dismissal of clear evidence was to resurface with a vengeance years later.

A pumpkin ball is a type of shotgun slug. Some slugs are elongated and tapered on one end while a pumpkin ball is round. North had loaded a pumpkin ball into the gun and used it against Carl. For simplicity's sake and in writing this account, I use the term slug.

Although surely the police would have immediately noticed the slug in plain sight, we learned they had not removed it from the wall that first day, August 11, 2006, when all the troopers were there. Rather, they collected it, along with the floor tiles, on the morning of August 16, the day Carl's body was discovered in Blairs Mills. Thus, naïvely, we assumed investigators would immediately submit the slug and tiles to forensics for testing.

As Clint and I continued our probe, I glanced at the foot of Carl's bed and was again sickened by the sight of the can of ravioli with the steak knife protruding from it, as if frozen in time. When I had seen it on that first day, I knew it was not something that Carl would have purchased. Again, I speculated that it was one of North's shopping spree purchases. I stumbled from the bedroom as if trying to break free from a bad dream. However, in the bathroom, I found something disturbing; a large drop of blood, the size of a quarter, dried on top of the vanity. An opened pocketknife lay next to the drop of blood, with the blade sharpened to a razor's edge. We had the jarring realization that one more time, the police had neglected to collect even more evidence—they had not bagged the knife, nor had they swabbed the blood for forensic testing.

I called Ford again. "There's a drop of blood on the bathroom countertop and an opened pocketknife beside it."

"I'll have a trooper pick it up within the next day or so," he responded. *Wow! How many times would I have to point out evidence and ask them
to do their job?*

Police eventually collected the knife, but there was no sign that they
ever disturbed the blood drop on the countertop. We will never know
if that blood belonged to Carl or if it came from the minor cut on the
web of North's hand. Although North claimed his hand injury resulted
from falling in the door, the wound could have occurred in other ways.
Had North stabbed Carl after he had shot him, the knife could have
folded shut on his hand, or his hand may have slipped forward onto the
blade. Another possibility was the recoil from the forearm bracket of a
shotgun—a sawed-off, 12-gauge shotgun has notable recoil, which is a
frequent cause of that type of hand injury. We were also told that North
had shaved his head during his brief reign of freedom. Perhaps he had
used the knife for shaving and may have cut his hand then. Any of these
scenarios were far more likely than North's story of falling and cutting it
on the doorjamb. One thing we know for sure—the police neglected to
consider any one of them, opting instead to let evidence lie untouched in
favor of stories concocted by North.

The amount of overlooked evidence was stunning. Carl's stamp set,
which he had used for his fencing business, lay toppled on the living
room floor. Interchangeable letters, which had been removed from a
stamp, lay loose in the box and had been replaced with a bold-lettered
stamp that read "FUCKING HOSTILE."

Why should I contact Ford again? I thought. I was exhausted and, at
this point, felt defeated by the indifference to so many clues. It appears
the law preferred to believe that it was my brother who left the trailer a
mess with half-eaten food lying around (although Carl had been away
for two weeks in North Carolina). Oddly, though, my frustration with
investigators continued to be tempered with shame and embarrassment
for them. Rather than contact Ford one more time, I carefully placed the
stamp set in a box and stored it at my own home. Much later, I would
tell the prosecutor about it, but it would never become part of the state's
evidence, nor would it matter to any county official in the end.

A Dale Earnhardt picture, spattered with a substantial amount of
blood, hung in the hallway to the right of the front door (stepping in

from the outside). Carl loved Earnhardt, and he had been crushed when he saw the race that took Earnhardt's life. More and heavier blood spatter marked the outside front of the door, indicating that the door was still partially open when Carl came under attack. Had it been closed behind Carl, no blood would have hit the outside surface.

When blood hits a flat plane and continues in the same direction, it tends to form tails, and the tails point in the direction the blood is traveling as it moves across the surface. In this case, the tails of the elongated spatter ran from left to right, revealing the direction that the high-velocity blowback from the entry wound had traveled. To the left of the door, much heavier forward spatter, with tails pointing the opposite direction from the spatter on the door, covered the tools strewn on the floor along the wall and on the floor itself, indicating that the slug had exited Carl's body and traveled to the left across the kitchen and into the bedroom.

On this day, I also found the shoebox that was missing from Carl's truck. It was leaning sideways against a chair in a back room as if hastily tossed there. It still contained unfilled fencing orders from customers who likely wondered why "the fence man" had never shown up.

Having seen the sawed-off lock from Carl's safe that first day with the troopers, I wondered what might also be missing from that strongbox. It appeared that deeds and titles to his property and vehicles were gone, as well as some coins. It was not an especially valuable coin collection, but it was gone all the same. Carl had also been tossing rolls of "fun" money into a large Igloo cooler, saving for something special to buy or do with his girlfriend, Debbie. Unfortunately, most of that money had also disappeared.

The presence of cigarette butts stabbed into Carl's candles suggested North had lain in wait by candlelight as Carl innocently walked through his front door. An occasional wild-eyed glance out a window, watching for my brother, would have provided a heads-up for the burglar/murderer who had made himself at home.

So many pieces of evidence told the story of North's ambush, yet we still had *more* to discover. Terrified that Carl may have suffered, we tried to convince ourselves otherwise, but it was impossible to fool ourselves. Of course, he had suffered. The slaughter was written in blood, inside and out. It covered walls and floors, the front door, tools, a picture, a rubber tarp, and the grass. The wide range made it painfully clear that Carl had died a horrific death.

After such devastating discoveries, I did muster the courage to call Ford one more time that day. "Even though Stewart released the trailer to us, don't you think we should leave it intact in case you need something?" I asked with a small bit of hope.

"No."

I was despondent. I wanted someone, anyone, to admit what was before our eyes and commit to helping us get justice. I knew that when collecting evidence, investigators should *always* assume that everything—everything—at a murder scene is evidence, no matter how insignificant it might seem. The investigator should write detailed notes; photographs should be taken from every angle while not disturbing anything. Working under the district attorney's direction, the police should collect and handle all evidence with latex gloves and store it in plastic bags until the case goes to trial and until any appeals are complete.

No one seemed interested in preserving the scene. I had asked Ford if we should keep the trailer intact, and he had point-blank said, "No."

By now, the trauma had debilitated other family members and me to the point that we had little capacity to make sound decisions or determine how to proceed without legal help. I still couldn't fully grasp the extent of their refusal to acknowledge the evidence. Regrettably, under the weight of such misery, Clint and I decided that whatever we chose to do or not to do, probably would not make a difference anyway.

In the meantime, a week after our first steps through Carl's front door, we returned, along with Debbie, to remove the frozen deer heads and some of Carl's personal items.

I realized the obnoxious smell, now unbearable, was coming from the refrigerator. During the crime spree, the meat had been removed from the freezer and placed in the fridge; pieces of it had been hacked off and fried up. A dirty frying pan sat on the countertop. Somehow, since the time of the murder, the cord to the refrigerator had become unplugged; the roast inside had rotted during the sweltering weeks. So we buried the refrigerator, meat, and all and then stored the deep freezer, TV, and other items at Clint's place. Having no other choice, we also found the energy to remove the mattress where North had lain leering at his porn. But before we burned it, I noticed that a small square piece had been cut from it. We never learned why.

Over the next several weeks, we removed many more of Carl's belongings, and although some were just worthless old papers, they were still difficult to handle because they had belonged to him. I punctuated the arduous task by periodically coming to a standstill and staring around, wondering where Carl stood in the scheme of all things. It struck me as outrageous that crinkled old papers remained while he was gone. Then, I recalled one of Carl's leisurely outings off the shores of the Outer Banks several years earlier. During that summer, in the deeper waters of the Atlantic Ocean and off the side of a fishing boat, he had experienced an unexpected swim with a few sharks. Not one bothered him, yet he would encounter a worse predator lying in wait in his own home one day.

Another day, I thought about the time I had decided to quit my studies in Alabama, where I pursued a master of art degree. Then, an inexplicable urge had sent me home to Pennsylvania. Now, I saw it as a fate, giving me more time with Carl. We would have three more years, and I consider it the greatest gift ever, whether bestowed by a Higher Power, fate, intuition, or providence. Gratitude for that time, however, was mixed with rage. Almost every other thought, good or bad, evolved into blame for the officials, God, or me.

Then came the day Debbie discovered four jail-issued socks lying on the bedroom floor, labeled with North's name in black marker. It was obvious that North had planned to walk off from work release; it hadn't been an impulsive act. Instead, he had taken extra socks, likely wearing both pairs.

At this point, Clint contacted Ford because I had grown weary of calling him every time we ran across more evidence. "We found socks with North's name on them. Do you want them for evidence?" he asked.

"Just keep them," Ford replied.

Despite his indifference, we hastily put the socks in a plastic bag and stashed them. Touching anything that had belonged to North was like touching evil.

As November crept to a close, I contacted Ford one more time. "Do you guys intend to investigate any more inside the trailer?" I asked. "We're thinking about dismantling it."

"No," he replied for the second time. "Go ahead and do whatever you want with it."

We weren't surprised. Unfortunately, naïveté and emotional distress were deciding factors in what we did next. To tear down the mobile home and attempt to erase the awful memories, we first obtained a permit from the township, then had the electricity disconnected and the water shut off. During the next couple of weeks, Debbie and some of Carl's friends helped us take away the remainder of Carl's things. However, the more things we removed, the further away from us he seemed. Even so, after the last piece was carried away, we said a prayer in commemoration. In hindsight, I realize we should not have touched anything. At the time, however, I was gullible and inexperienced, still wanting to believe the police were conducting an honest investigation.

I had been off work for weeks, and it was time to go back. Though I tried to concentrate, I could only sit at my desk and stare at the walls and floor or slide a paper from one spot to another. The next three years would be marked by missed work due to sickness, anxiety, or the rare case-related meeting.

The days shortened with winter's imminent arrival, and all the while, the case stagnated. Almost every week, we would call and ask someone when charges would be filed, when a trial would be scheduled, and why Huntingdon still had the case. We grew cynical about the lack of activity and, at one point, didn't know who was leading the investigation in Huntingdon County. We didn't even have a death certificate. At our request, we finally received one, but to this day, Carl's manner of death is listed as pending. The official autopsy report from Kamerow, at that time, still lay in the future.

Ford had reiterated numerous times that no new evidence had "come to light," and we began to hear an annoying refrain that would continue in the months and years to come. "This isn't CSI. An investigation takes longer than what you see on TV." And when Ford did promise to file murder charges "next month for sure," another, more pressing case always seemed to come up. So we were constantly told: "We have to wait until the DA has all his ducks in a row" or "A couple more weeks, and it will definitely happen."

Naturally, we were naïve and certainly inexperienced with murder, and so we thought warnings such as, "Don't be talking to people" and "Now keep this under your hat" were precautions to help protect the investigation. And so, for a while, we avoided divulging details. But as time went on, those platitudes grew tiresome and slowly bred resentment. Many times, while discussing the investigation among ourselves, "keep this under your hat" became our sarcastic catchphrase.

Stewart began to express apprehension about a defense attorney from Altoona representing North. Nonetheless, he didn't do anything except post a Crime Stoppers notice to the public, requesting that anyone who might have information concerning the murder of Carl Wade Ryder contact his office.

CHAPTER 9

ENABLING A KILLER

He was a murderer from the beginning and abode not in the truth because there is no truth in him. —*The Apostle John*

Amid my grief, I set out to learn everything I could about the body-dumping killer that took Carl's life. It was not a difficult feat—one need only take a quick look at official online court dockets on North to find a lengthy criminal history. The records themselves were dry and lacking in detail but laid out a trail of continuous charges. Moreover, court dates intermingled confusingly because while the courts were processing cases against North, he was out committing an array of other crimes.

Especially disturbing were the numerous instances of leniency. Noted here in *italics*, the courts *dismissed* charges, *lowered* bond signatures declared North *eligible* and *granted work release,* or received a *plea deal.* (Dockets can be found at "The Unified Judicial System of Pennsylvania Web Portal"—ujsportal.pacourts.us.)

Dropping out of school with an eighth-grade education, the courts soon identified Scott North as a juvenile delinquent, and he immediately embarked on an adult criminal career by the time he had turned eighteen. The dockets reflect an array of escalating offenses, nomadic shifting from place to place, and most shockingly, a court-sanctioned path to freedom, time and time again.

The online records open with a stolen property incident in December 1998 at the age of eighteen. Franklin County *released* him on his own recognizance (ROR) and ordered him to appear when called to court. His address was listed as Chambersburg.

Without skipping a beat, he earned two counts of possession with intent to deliver and possession of drug paraphernalia a month later, in January 1999, in Dauphin County. Again, there are no online dockets showing a prosecution.

The following July, the stolen property charge from December 1998 was *dismissed* at a preliminary hearing in Franklin County. North remained in the clear for a while, at least on the official record, but in January 2000, he was charged with felony theft and receiving stolen property in Franklin County. By then, his address had changed to the small community of Upper Strasburg. Jailed with an initial monetary bond of $50,000, later reduced to $3,500 unsecured bail, and then *dropped* to a bond signature (ROR), he was *released* within the month, at which time he moved in with his grandmother, Larena, in Blairs Mills. Later that week, police charged him with careless driving and ordered him to pay fines and costs upon a guilty plea. Three days later, they stopped him for speeding. He pleaded guilty again, and his grandmother paid his fines and costs on a payment plan.

In March 2000, North entered a not guilty plea for the property he stole in January and then promptly disappeared. In May, police picked him up on a bench warrant. He retracted the not guilty plea and entered a guilty plea to felony theft; the court deferred sentencing until June. In June 2000, police arrested him for retail theft in Shippensburg. Again, he entered a guilty plea, and the court ordered payment of fines, costs, and restitution. His address changed to York, Pennsylvania, located an hour and a half east of Chambersburg.

Several days after his arrest for retail theft, the court issued another bench warrant for not showing up for sentencing for the January 2000 theft. They found him later in July, right under their noses in Chambersburg, and charged him with a summary offense—purchasing alcohol by a minor. He pleaded guilty, and the court issued a notice of license suspension. The small town of Newburg in Cumberland County became his new address.

In August 2000, the court sentenced North to four to twenty-four months in Franklin County Jail for the January theft and ordered him to pay fines, costs, and restitution; serve twenty-four months on probation at the expiration of the minimum sentence, and surrender his driver's license because he had used a vehicle during the commission of the crime. Two months later, the court *granted* a *work release*, but officials vacated his automatic parole pending a misconduct incident within the month. While in the slammer, North continued serving time for the theft, and meanwhile, the pre-release supervisor recommended a *reconsideration for work release.*

In December 2000, the stolen property charge from January was *nolle prossed* (not willing to prosecute/dropped charges). Authorities had not dropped the charge earlier in May when North pleaded guilty to the theft charge, although it was part of the same crime spree. In January 2001, the court ordered seventeen-month *parole supervision*, in addition to fines, costs, and restitution, that he seek employment, and maintain a residence, oddly enough, out of state in Hagerstown, Maryland.

By the next month, February 2001, police arrested North for harassment, striking, shoving, and kicking in Guilford Township, Franklin County. The courts leveled a separate summary charge on the same day for the purchase of alcohol. North pleaded guilty to both charges, and the court issued another notice of license suspension. He returned to Blairs Mills.

Ten days later, a Gagnon hearing (a hearing that, by law, must be held before revoking parole) determined that a parole violation had occurred, and the court ordered him to serve the balance of his sentence and again *made him eligible for work release.*

Although North was listed for re-sentencing for the parole violation, District Attorney Jack Nelson *did not address it.* Three months later, in May 2001, North was *released* from jail and ordered to seek employment, pay fines, costs, and restitution, and maintain a residence, this time in Chambersburg.

June 2001 was filled with a brew of criminal activity. Miles away across the state, North was apprehended by the Pittsburgh Police Department and jailed in the Fayette County Prison with a $10,000 monetary bond for felony burglary, theft, and receiving stolen property that he had committed in Letterkenny Township, Franklin County. Eleven days later, he was transported back to Franklin County, where his *bail was downgraded* to ROR, and he was *released.* It was as if nothing—nothing—could keep him in jail.

In July, a Gagnon hearing established another parole violation, and the court again listed North for re-sentencing at the district attorney's call. This violation stemmed from the burglary the month before. Once again, he was *not re-sentenced* but was ordered to serve the remainder of his original sentence simply. At the same time, he was made *eligible for work release* and was to be *considered for re-parole* after serving six months.

According to the dockets, Judge Carol Van Horn granted North permission to leave the jail for *work release* on August 1, 2001, and again on August 24, 2001. However, in late August, he pleaded guilty to the June burglary.

Finally, in September 2001, Judge John Walker sentenced him to six to thirty months for burglary and tacked fines, costs, and restitution. He placed North under the supervision of the State Board of Probation and Parole for eleven months, with his residence listed as Camp Hill State Prison. Upon completing his minimum sentence, he was required to participate in a drug and alcohol program and again ordered to surrender his driver's license to the Clerk of Courts for revocation. The court would *consider a work release*. It *dismissed* the felony theft and stolen property charges and garnished his wages at the Camp Hill State Prison.

The public was safe for a while, but North was back in York by December 2002 (a little more than a year later). Police soon arrested him as a fugitive from justice, likely for failing to report to his probation officer. He was committed to the Franklin County Jail with a bail amount of $10,000. Unfortunately, he didn't have a nickel to make bail, but he was *set free* by the next month.

A lull of about one year and nine months (January 2003 to September 2004) shows as a suspicious blank in the criminal records. Given his history, it only indicates he was not caught for any crime . . . not that he didn't commit any.

In June 2004, North was living in Fannettsburg when my brother, Carl, made the fatal mistake of hiring him to help alleviate the workload of a large amount of fencing orders. Unfortunately, Carl had no idea of North's extensive criminal past, nor did he report his guns' theft when North stole them three weeks later.

Three months after his brief employment with Carl, North received a traffic citation in Fannett Township in September 2004; he pleaded guilty, and the court ordered him to pay fines and costs. He then moved to Spring Run and took a job in early 2005, much to the apprehension of the little village. Many residents were aware of earlier crimes he had committed there. As a result, the county garnished his wages, and the $25 biweekly payment went toward fines, costs, and restitution relating to the theft and burglary crimes in 2000 and 2001.

In April 2005, North was charged with felony possession of a firearm, followed by a retail theft in May, both in Franklin County. He suddenly relocated to Everett, Pennsylvania, west of Franklin County, took a job in June. In July, he pleaded guilty to the May retail theft and was ordered to pay fines and costs.

By August 2005, he was back in Franklin County and burglarized the Hill Top Tavern in Fannettsburg. The owner told us that North had unlatched a window during business hours and returned after closing to ransack the tavern and the apartment above. He allegedly stole guns, money, sweatshirts, booze, cigarettes, and guitars. Trooper Ford was assigned to the case, but before he made an arrest, North returned a second time and burglarized the tavern, which resulted in additional burglary, theft, criminal trespass, and criminal mischief charges. However, no firearm charges were leveled against him.

North was committed to the Franklin County Jail in September 2005 for the April weapons charge. Judge John Walker set a $50,000 monetary bond under the condition of *admittance and approval for the pretrial release program* before releasing from jail.

Meanwhile, North repeatedly filed motions for new counsel, conjuring petty faults with his court-appointed (tax-funded) attorneys. In the meantime, a $20,000 bail was set for the tavern burglary. Finally, North's new attorney filed a motion for continuance (rescheduling) of the gun charge hearing, and Judge Carol Van Horn granted the continuance and rescheduled the hearing for December 2005.

North's attorney filed two separate motions on his behalf—that he receive a trial by judge (non-jury trial) for the gun charges and the burglaries. Judge Walker granted the non-jury trials for April and May 2006, respectively, but in April, North requested withdrawal of the non-jury trials, wanting a trial instead by jury for the two separate crimes, which Judge Richard Walsh granted.

May passed with no trial for the gun charge, but in May, under the prosecution of Assistant District Attorney Angela Krom, he faced burglary, criminal trespass, and theft charges, plus several counts of criminal mischief. The court could easily have sentenced him to state prison, but Krom offered a plea deal instead. North pleaded guilty to charges of misdemeanor theft and felony burglary committed against the tavern. A June 2006 sentencing in Van Horn's court was postponed because she was unavailable. The court had still not addressed the felony firearms charge.

On July 5, 2006, Van Horn imposed a sentence of thirty-six months, restrictive intermediate punishment, six months incarceration in the Franklin County Jail, three months' intense supervision, drug and alcohol and mental health evaluation and treatment, restitution, no contact with the victim, credit of forty-seven days for time served for the theft, and *work release eligibility.*

For the second burglary and theft, she sentenced North to confinement of eleven months and fifteen days to twenty-three months with credit of forty-seven days for time served, twenty-four months of probation, participation in the drug and alcohol treatment program, no contact with the victim, firearms restrictions, restitution, and costs, and *work release eligibility.* In addition, she ordered restitution of $2,246.30 to be paid to the victims. The *plea deal allowed dismissing* the additional counts of first-degree felony burglary, both counts of second-degree felony criminal trespass, a felony theft, and misdemeanor criminal mischief charges.

While North was serving time for the burglary and theft convictions, on Wednesday, July 26, 2006, the April 2005 firearms charge was *dropped* under Judge Walker. And Judge Van Horn, again, *granted work release.* However, the following Monday, July 31, North was hired by Mark Wescott, chief operating officer of AWI (Architectural Woodsmiths, Inc.) in Shippensburg; on his birthday, Wednesday, August 2, 2006, North walked off the unsupervised worksite.

One month to the day of Scott North's sentencing for theft and felony burglary, and ten days after dropping the firearms charge, Scott North shot Carl to death on the night of August 5, 2006.

CHAPTER 10

A TRAIL OF VICTIMS

But know this, that if the goodman of the house had known in what watch the thief would come, he would have watched and would not have suffered his house to be broken up. —*The Apostle Matthew*

I cannot help but wonder if some people are born evil. Prior victims have described Scott North as "spawn." Known to be violent and vindictive, he has set people on edge for years; they feared he would retaliate if they dared to call the law. Some victims tried to wipe him—and thus their traumatic experiences—from their memory. Many of his crimes have never gone on record because they went unreported; at other times, when crimes *were* reported, police didn't arrest him. Those subjected to his menacing glare in court know what I am referring to, and they have had a legitimate reason to fear for their lives.

There has never been anything complex about Scott North. Outwardly friendly but manipulative and predatory, he seemed primed for trouble, needing no trigger to incite him to violence. Rage roiled just under the surface. He knew right from wrong without question but absolutely didn't care—an untreatable and deadly combination.

According to people familiar with his background, North had a chaotic home life in his early years. Placement in a more structured environment in foster care failed to redirect him toward a productive life. Some say his father eventually "washed his hands of him." But whether he had had a bad start in life or a good one, I doubt it would have mattered either way. Nothing could have changed his propensity for evil.

According to a past girlfriend with whom I have spoken, North entertained homicidal fantasies long before he murdered my brother. Perhaps he had decided it was his destiny to destroy. It was almost as if he yearned to kill, after which he reverted to his habitual state: untroubled, confident of few, if any, consequences.

She said he had a tattoo of a goat's head needled onto his chest. In the satanic world, the outline of a horned goat's head forms five points with its horns at the top, ears on the sides, and beard at the bottom, and is supposed to represent an upside-down pentagram. The reversed pentagram shape with the two points projecting upward is reputed to attract sinister forces, overturning the proper order of things—an unbalancing of evil over good. It's a symbol that beckons the sort of chaos and destruction that North seemed to revel in. I'm guessing he still wears the satanic tattoo with pride but, the reality is he proved himself to be a soulless coward—a great nothing with no power.

Despite the string of arrests and fearful victims in North's wake, the courts' attitude toward him was lackadaisical, permitting him to continue his criminal career. Ultimately, at age twenty-six, Scott North crossed the final line and turned killer. After his arrest, his smug arrogance suggested he was proud of the killing—as if it were an accomplishment.

By the time he had murdered Carl, courthouse officials, police, and numerous victims had known him for over a decade. According to the state police, many had been aware of his propensity for violence, including an attack on a counselor during one of his earlier probation periods. Yet, to most officials, he nonetheless seemed a fitting candidate for work release. His violent inclinations certainly were a public safety concern. I wish my family and I had known the level of danger he posed. Had the legal system addressed his crimes as they should have, they would have saved Carl's life.

According to one former girlfriend, North was a vicious bully. In 2001, she refused to participate in North's plan to murder and steal from a man in Hagerstown, Maryland, and no longer wanted anything to do with him. Therefore, he beat her and threw her around until a relative rescued her by tossing him out of the house by his hair. North returned with an ax, pacing back and forth in the driveway, swinging it around until the state police arrived.

After a few cursory questions, one of the troopers drew a few chuckles by announcing, "This is Scotty North's son." Had they bothered to get the whole story from the abused woman instead of making light of the incident and sending North home, the Hagerstown murder plan might have come to light.

"He won them over with his North blood," the woman said afterward.

Other locals also claimed that "North blood" often saved him from arrest. For certain, *something* always seemed to tip the balance in North's favor when he got into trouble. It is no wonder valley residents tiptoed around harm's way instead of calling the police. When police did make a rare arrest, rumor has it that North often sought leniency by declaring that his dad was a cop and his mother never wanted him.

Before the ax incident ended the relationship, he terrorized his girlfriend by holding a gun to her head and telling her she would die. She said she sat with her eyes closed, just waiting to get her head blown off. She supported him financially until the abuse escalated to the level of a murder scheme, the ax threat, and a gun to the head—this one allegedly stolen from the parents of a cousin's girlfriend. It's a wonder he stopped short of outright execution—but perhaps it just didn't suit him at the time.

Although relationships quickly grew turbulent, he initially generated sympathy with manipulative charm and tales of woe. A chain of girlfriends suffered a fusillade of cruelty, abuse, and threats to their lives—after clothing and feeding him, giving him money, paying his child support, and providing a free place to live. They are lucky to be alive.

Everywhere he went, it was as if he were rehearsing for murder. With his phony charisma, compulsive lying, threats, physical attacks, and homicidal cravings, he was the textbook definition of a garden-variety sociopath. He never took responsibility for his actions, always claiming his crimes were the fault of something or someone else. For instance, in a letter to his grandmother, Larena, nine days after Carl's murder (a copy of which I obtained from the Franklin County Courthouse records), he wrote, "The reason I'm writting [sic] now is because I am facing a serious charge for something I didn't do." Then, wallowing in self-pity and casting blame on his latest ex-girlfriend, he continued, "I think some times [sic] that may be the reason my life has gone realy [sic] bad the last few years is because of her. My mind has never been quite what it was since she threw me away."

He had an immature fascination with guns. Stories, both on and off the record, are replete with gun incidents. He never legally owned a firearm but possessed several stolen ones. One exception was an old sawed-off shotgun with a duct-taped stock that his grandmother supposedly had given him. He kept this dilapidated gun just under the edge of the bed, within easy reach, at a girlfriend's house in Path Valley. She reported him to the state police, but they ignored the complaint, even though he was a felon on probation and prohibited from having guns. Weeks later, a police dispatch to the same residence for a domestic incident—one of several—forced the girlfriend to leave but allowed North to stay, even though the house belonged to the girlfriend's mother. I found no record that police confiscated the shotgun.

People feared him. A past victim privately told us that North had lurked around Fannettsburg and stolen a license plate from his truck. He fastened it to his own jalopy and drove out of state for drugs. In court, North glared malevolently at the man who testified against him. Aware of North's pattern of exacting revenge, the victim later remarked that he had never been afraid of anyone, but he was afraid of Scott North.

～～

There are those who would rather steal the fruits of another's hard labor than strive for the satisfaction of their accomplishments. And then there are those few who are callous, vicious, and vengeful enough to kill for it. Scott North worked only sporadically when out of jail, but he wanted to work on the outside as much as possible when in prison. So, in or out, he stole things every chance he got.

Carl, on the other hand, worked hard for everything he had. While in high school, he first labored as a farmhand. After graduation, he cut timber for several years. Later, he worked for Texas Eastern Oil Company, blasting tunnels under roadways for pipeline installations and earning the nickname "Workhorse." All the while, Carl wanted to be his own boss.

In 1996, he established Ryder Fencing and started out digging fence post holes by hand. A year later, he bought equipment that would help make his work easier and faster. Eventually, his business grew to cover a five-county area and included installing fences for companies and private residences and contracting with Lowe's. He also enjoyed constructing the backstop and cages for the Amberson Little League baseball field. *The Blue Book of Fencing* listed Ryder Fencing among top fencers across the country. As a result, "Workhorse" became known as "The Fence Man."

Inundated with fence-installation orders during the summer of 2004, one of his busiest since starting his business, he hired help. It was hard work, and he had continuous turnover. Some employees couldn't take it and quit, or they would find other employment that suited them better. Some liked the job but still left for full-time employment elsewhere. I also helped Carl on evenings and weekends, especially during summer. That winter, he expanded his business to the Outer Banks area, which he thoroughly enjoyed.

The unfortunate decision to hire Scott North in June 2004 began innocently enough. Unfortunately, Carl made two poor decisions that summer. The first was hiring a resident of Spring Run, who was North's cousin. I was leery of him. He seemed shady, but I said nothing because Carl needed the help. It wasn't long, though, before he swiped some blank checks from Carl's checkbook, wrote out large checks to himself, and cashed them at two separate banks. When Carl realized what the man had done, he fired him, and the banks prosecuted him.

The second mistake was hiring one of the man's relatives—Scott North. Carl often overlooked people's shortcomings and was not judgmental when many times he should have been. You couldn't fault him for being goodhearted, but it upped the possibility of his being victimized by a predatory type. He would forget to watch out for the "friendly" face of trouble.

While I was merely cautious of North's cousin, I immediately felt an intense loathing toward North that I couldn't explain. It wasn't that I knew much about him, nor did Carl; it just felt bad. To me, North was like a pernicious runner springing from an old patch of poison ivy—the kind of person one should avoid. I never thought very highly of North's father, the town cop, whose family lived near Spring Run (a few miles from Amberson), and I had heard stories of one horrible uncle. But other than viewing North as lazy and untrustworthy, I had no solid reason to interfere in Carl's business and insist he get rid of him.

During the first week of his employment, North wasted no time taking advantage of Carl's kindness and told a sob story about needing money. When I was helping Carl the following weekend, he told me that he had advanced North's first paycheck and took North along to the Outer Banks to help finish a job at one of Pat Hennessy's properties. Unfortunately, North didn't win any friends there either.

During North's second week of employment, he told Carl that he liked to "bait in and kill animals." My apprehension had been growing, and when I heard this, I jumped at the chance to intervene. "You need to get rid of him," I said. "He's evil. You don't need him around." I knew Carl was thinking about it, and with a nagging sense of trouble brewing, I hoped it would be soon.

That coming week, Carl had a large job to fill for Lowe's, but he first needed to retrieve his truck from the garage after repairs. So, while my other brother, Clint, took Carl to Spring Run to pick up his truck, North remained at Carl's place, feigning enthusiasm for assembling chain-link gates, a project he was working on in Carl's driveway. Once Carl and Clint were out of sight, North jimmied the front door and helped himself to several of Carl's guns, loading them into an old clunker he had bought with the pay that Carl had fronted him. When my brothers returned, North shook Clint's hand before he left. "It was nice meeting you," he said with a false smile and then drove off. That was the thanks Carl got for giving him "a job he badly needed."

When Carl discovered his rifles missing, he was quite upset, having no idea who could have done such a thing. One gun in particular—his first deer rifle—held an extra sentimental value. He had worked on a farm while in high school to make payments on it, and he wanted it back more than all the others.

North stashed the stolen guns at an ex-girlfriend's house in Lower Horse Valley, a rural area west of Roxbury, off Route 641 after topping the Forge Hill. Soon afterward, North's car quit running, and a local woman found herself finagled, as a favor for a friend, into giving North a ride from Lower Horse Valley to the tiny village of Fannettsburg.

Before starting on the trip, North brazenly loaded the guns into her car and then shot from her car window periodically on the way to Fannettsburg. Twenty minutes later, she dropped North and the guns off at Lakeview Inn, where another female acquaintance had been renting a room. Apparently, North had plans to sell one of the guns while in Fannettsburg and keep the rest with him while he stayed at the inn.

Alarmed after dropping North off, the woman driver called the friend who had asked her to help North and gave him heck for not only sticking her with North but also with "a bunch of guns." However, word travels fast through the valleys, and when her male friend realized that North was probably the one who had stolen the rifles from Carl's house two days prior, and that "somebody by the name of Jones was on his way to buy one," he called Carl.

Immediately, Carl went to Lakeview Inn, where he stood near his car in the parking lot and called out North. "I want my guns!" Carl shouted. Then, when North opened the door and stepped out defiantly, Carl added, "If I don't get them back, I'm calling the cops."

North seemed to be proud of his theft, according to a few people who heard him brag about stealing the guns. He also claimed he had already sold one to a man miles away in Waynesboro (on the southeast side of Franklin County). As for the gun that was to be sold to someone in Fannettsburg and the other guns stashed at the inn, Carl confiscated them immediately. Then he spent a good part of the rest of the tension-filled day, accompanied by North, recovering the rifle that had been sold in Waynesboro. Not surprisingly, the buyer there was perturbed that he had bought a stolen gun. Though he was persuaded to return it to Carl, he didn't get his money back from North. During the return drive, North announced that he "oughta just kill the motherf*****." Carl responded, "How come you're blaming it on him when you're the one who's the sneaking thief?"

Back in Fannettsburg, a seething North got out of the car and slammed the door with a snarl. Carl rolled down his window and called out, "I don't need you anymore. You steal. Don't ever set foot on my property again."

North's three-week employment was over. As far as Carl was concerned, North was permanently out of the picture. However, the wheels of North's vindictive mind had most likely already begun to turn. He had seldom been held accountable, nor had many people insisted that he make things right. Apparently, he decided that when opportunity knocked, he would get even with Carl.

Carl didn't report the theft—he was just grateful to have his rifles back. A day later, Carl recounted the incident to me, and out of precaution, he moved his guns—except for a .22 and an old shotgun—to a closet at Clint's place.

A little more than a year later, in September 2005, North finally landed behind bars, this time for burglarizing the Hill Top Tavern (formerly known as The Pines) in Fannettsburg. He had hit the place on two separate occasions, helping himself to guitars and various items in an apartment above the tavern and within the tavern.

I remember telling Carl about North's incarceration one Saturday.

"I heard that North went to jail for burglarizing Hill Top," I said as soon as I got out of my car and approached Carl, who sat in his Bobcat by the barn.

"Good. That's where he belongs," Carl replied.

We never discussed it again. I am haunted, though, by an inner voice that spoke to me the moment Carl said, "That's where he belongs." The message was unmistakable: *He wants to kill Carl.*

I dismissed it as just my imagination because no one in our family, at that point, knew North well enough to know he was a killer. However, that voice had stabbed like a bolt out of the blue, and I just as quickly forgot about it. In hindsight, of course, I view it as an ominous warning.

CHAPTER 11

ON THE RUN

He was hurled to the earth, and his fallen with him. Now they walk among us. —*The Apostle John*

While county officials insisted, even after the murder of my brother, Carl, that North had no history of violence, our family, along with many other victims, disagreed and wanted answers. So why did prosecutors and judges see fit, time after time, to offer plea bargains, drop gun charges, reduce county jail sentences, and grant the privilege of work release? What happened to the "intense supervision" that Judge Van Horn had ordered on July 5, 2006? Assistant District Attorney Angela Krom would eventually inform us that she couldn't get state time for North's burglary at the tavern because "the man got his guitar back." Saved from state prison by returning a guitar seemed a less-than-adequate excuse for failing again to hold a career criminal accountable. Just as exasperating, District Attorney Nelson, for six years (2000-2006), had squandered the opportunity to re-sentence North for numerous probation violations.

The Pennsylvania Crimes Code lists burglary as a *felony offense* and as a *violent crime*, and rightfully so. It stands to reason that anyone brazen enough to burglarize and steal from homes and businesses would not hesitate to hurt someone. He should have been considered an escape risk, if nothing else, because of his juvenile history. As an adult with work release violations, his criminal history, fugitive from justice, physical hostilities, burglaries, gun thefts, and even an alleged theft inside the jail warranted state prison. He had been there before. Yet in August 2006,

North simply picked up where he left off, committing yet another escape and two more burglaries, topped off with a murder. He had proven himself unpredictable and dangerous—as Trooper Ford had said, "[They] never knew what he might do." The police didn't trust him yet made little effort to capture and confine him after he fled work release.

It seemed especially unfathomable, considering that another man had spent over two years in the Franklin County Jail, without counsel, for stealing a pack of hotdogs. The hungry "hotdog man" refused to sleep on a bunk but instead lay on the floor in a cell alone, rolled up in his blanket like a burrito. Warden John Wetzel allowed the much-needed cell space to be wasted (empty bunks for two prisoners) over two years over a $3 pack of wieners. Yet, the courts regularly released Scott North back into the community.

Carl's murder occurred when commissioners and other politicians were campaigning for a new jail, vital to public safety and a solution to overcrowding. Barely a week passed without an article in the local paper featuring Warden Wetzel or Commissioner Robert Thomas advocating for a more secure and modern building. In our view, the danger rested with those running the justice system, not with the building itself. Nevertheless, the new jail opened for business in 2007 on Opportunity Avenue, Chambersburg, Pennsylvania. Yet as years passed, there were never any announcements of policy changes correcting the shortcomings of the work-release program.

Doing my best to set frustration aside, I eventually emailed Commissioner Robert Thomas, who was also the Prison Board president, to ask what changes had been made in the program since the murder of my brother in 2006. Thomas replied but distanced himself, emphasizing that he wanted "to be very clear, WR [work release] eligibility is determined by the judges, not by the commissioners. As a commissioner, I cannot put anyone in jail nor release them."

A representative for the jail also provided a generic response, which Thomas included in his email response, explaining that while it's the court's responsibility at the time of sentencing to determine whether an inmate may be considered for work release, the jail then decides the following: eligibility based on the charges, or actual risk as determined by a risk-assessment tool, or a combination of the two. If a prisoner is deemed inappropriate for the program, they are provided with a treatment plan to move toward the goal of working in the community. The jail representative wrote, "The process of placing an inmate on our work release program has been updated . . . [and] the basic tenets of this process were being followed during the time of Scott North's placement on the work release program."

A probation employee revealed to us that they had recommended against North's work release, but the jail did it anyway.

North started work release on July 31, 2006. First, he worked two full days—long enough to determine how easy it would be to walk off. Then, on the third day, August 2, he strolled unobserved out of AWI (Architectural Woodsmiths, Inc.) on his twenty-sixth birthday.

Located in Shippensburg, AWI was, at the time, an affiliate of Showbest Fixture, Inc., a manufacturer of showcases and display modules for department stores. The architecture of the old factory was typical of the early 1900s era of a booming industry. The red-brick structure, systematically built onto over the years, featured a towering furnace stack and deteriorated wood-framed windows. A set of unused railroad tracks, bedded in a gully, ran behind the building—a rusty trace of railcars that had once delivered lumber to the original manufacturer, Peerless Furniture. In the 1930s, the night watchman (my great-grandfather Carl Barnhart) occasionally allowed hobos from the rails to sleep in the boiler room on cold nights. By dawn, they were gone.

In 1978 after high school graduation, I ran the stockroom for Affiliated Industries (a different company with a different owner) in the same building, which built display cases for stores. Huge wooden beams, butted and bolted together and shored up with enormous wooden posts, supported the interior, while years' worth of wood, sawdust, and paper were wedged and packed between the cast-iron steam registers and pitted brick walls. The timeworn wooden floors were covered with steel plates here and there and supported the main traffic throughout the building. Though, not many people ventured down to the cavernous basement, which wound endlessly in the dark like Minotaur's labyrinth. In the summertime, windows on both floors sat loose in their frames and were propped up with sticks, while doors hung wide open to keep the place tolerable in the heat. During the winter, the windows were covered inside with plastic.

There was a time I remember, during the 1980s, that rats ran free about the place. To eliminate them, management brought in a few cats. But the cats brought in fleas, which infested the premises. Groundhogs and other critters also found a home.

For decades, the factory had been quite industrious, and anyone passing by the 40 Lurgan Avenue address could smell the fumes spewing into the air through the huge paint-coated exhaust fans. However, by the early 1990s, the old factory had become a worn, dirty relic of past industrial vigor.

The year of North's escape, James Shubert of Showbest was the owner of AWI, and the company had been scraping by with a skeleton crew and sporadic job orders. The manager, Mark Wescott, discovered it was cheaper to hire inmates from the county jail than to pay minimum wage to anyone else. Unfortunately, Wescott, a transplant from New York, had a reputation for doling out mistreatment and slights as he meandered through the dusty factory. Consequently, he never endeared himself to the employees.

When North started work on Monday, July 31, Wescott assigned him to the paint shop located on the second floor, and by Wednesday, North knew the routine. On his birthday, August 2, he was able to devise an escape plan as easily as cutting a birthday cake. After Wescott predictably left the building at noon to go home for lunch (about two miles away), North got a substantial head start, sauntering to freedom while other employees dug into their lunchboxes. Lunchtime for employees is half an hour.

North had never punched his timecard before he went to lunch, but at some point, Wescott wrote "12:00 okay per Mark" on North's timecard and then initialed it. After Wescott returned from lunch, he realized North might be missing and sent an employee to look for him. Unfortunately, a second trip was made through the huge building as time

ticked away, totaling one hour and twenty minutes since noon, obliterat-
ing the window of opportunity to nab North nearby. Someone at the
factory eventually contacted probation, who called borough police; they,
in turn, dispatched state Troopers Corbett and Borello, who arrived at
AWI at 2:18 P.M., two hours and eighteen minutes from the presumed
time of escape. They filed an incident report but apparently did not run
a patrol along the most likely routes that North could have taken from
the factory.

On his drive home from work, hours later, Chip Piper offered a ride
to a hitchhiker on PA Route 641 near Roxbury, more than ten miles
from Shippensburg. Chip later told me that he quickly developed an
uneasy feeling as he traveled over the mountain with his passenger and
soon regretted picking up "this guy with the bad vibes." So, at North's
request, when they came to the fork on the mountain, Chip took the
641 truck route toward Amberson Valley instead of continuing over the
steep grade of Timmons Mountain to Path Valley, as he normally would
have. As they descended the mountain near Amberson, North asked to
be dropped off where the road peels off to Amberson, a local landmark
we know as "the fingerboards," named for a large painted billboard ad-
vertisement that stood there years ago.

"Good things happen to people that do good deeds," North remarked
as he shook Chip's hand. Though it was a seemingly nice thing to say,
Chip felt relieved to be rid of him. The next day, however, his apprehension returned when he read the notice of North's escape in the local paper
and realized he had unwittingly assisted a convicted criminal and a scary
one at that. Concerned, he called in an anonymous tip to police, revealing where he had dropped off North—anonymous because he wanted to
protect his family from retaliation. Unfortunately, he had heard of Scott
North's reputation, and what's more, Chip's neighbor had suffered years
of abuse and stalking at the hands of Scott North's uncle, who eventually
went to prison.

Information from neighbors in Amberson helped me piece together
North's subsequent trek. In the late afternoon, Vonnie Piper (no relation
to Chip) had turned off the truck route coming down the mountain into
the low-lying wooded section of Store Lane when she spied a man who

was carrying a red-and-black checkered shirt. He was walking out of the field near the slate quarry and along the woods. North had backtracked on foot from the fingerboards and across the field toward Store Lane instead of following the main drag through the center of the valley.

Another resident coming home from work around 5:00 P.M. saw a dark-haired man emerge from a grassy lane in the wooded hollow. The lane leads only to a primitive hunting shack and an old dumpsite of rusted tin cans and broken bottles. By late evening, at least three more people had seen a man walking at different points along a two-mile stretch of the main road. All three thought it unusual to see a pedestrian on such a rural valley road, but no one realized who he was.

When North reached Drifted Lane leading to Carl's place, he would likely have noticed Carl's red truck parked in the driveway in the distance. As he walked up the lane, woods on the right and a cornfield, as well as a hayfield on the left, afforded him plenty of cover.

North then likely skirted Carl's place to reach Pat Hennessy's unoccupied cabin, where he pried out a screen and entered through the window from the front porch. From a perfect lookout, he could now watch the whole of Drifted Lane and see any approaching visitors. Two days later, on August 4, one of the owners, Diana Hennessy, would disrupt his hideout when she unexpectedly showed up with a friend to retrieve a piece of furniture. Upon entering, the first thing she noticed was that the cabin was not empty. "I smelled him. You can smell empty, and you can smell when someone is there," she later recalled.

She saw two book bags, which belonged to her kids, lying on the floor. She read the name on a jail ID that lay on top of personal items from the cabin in one open book bag. A friend who had accompanied her felt uneasy enough to retrieve a weapon from the vehicle and carry it back inside. "Let's just get out of here," Diana said, thinking that Carl may have permitted one of his employees to use the cabin (although Carl had never previously offered the use of the Hennessys' cabin to anyone.)

It is possible that North, surprised by the visit, was either hiding inside while Diana and her friend were there or had slipped out another door. Either way, unbeknownst to her, it was North who was creeping around the place.

Not knowing whether they would return likely motivated North to vacate the cabin. By this time, he likely realized that Carl had not come home for at least one night and could be gone a while longer. Consequently, he took the book bags and broke into Carl's place by prying up the back window. Once inside, he helped himself.

Saturday, August 5, marked the fourth day of his escape, and still, police made no inquiries locally, nor did they provide any warning. Had they simply informed the public of North's last known whereabouts or asked around the small valley, word would have quickly spread. (In light of North's brief employment with Carl and theft of his guns, my family and I would have checked Carl's place.) Instead, Trooper Ford followed Chip Piper's tip by calling North's grandmother, who lived miles from Amberson—and miles from where Chip had dropped him off.

The police failed to warn the community of North's whereabouts and missed an opportunity to possibly nab him. Instead, they left the community to fend for themselves against a hardened criminal.

Carl didn't have a chance.

 CHAPTER 12

THE MURDER

*Be sober, be vigilant; because your adversary the devil, as a roaring
lion, walketh about, seeking whom he may devour.*
                                                    —*The Apostle Peter*

When we finally understood that prosecuting Carl's murderer would
not be a top priority for the police or the district attorney, my family and
I determined to act.

Loree and I began by piecing together details that we could garner
from the police to build a timeline of the crime. We compiled interview
information from witnesses who had spoken with an investigator. While
Loree also obtained documents from Carl's credit card company, I pored
over phone records of all last conversations with Carl. I extracted the
contents of store surveillance videos from the police, which had been
taped in Franklin, Fulton, and Huntingdon counties. Meanwhile, I asked
about and noted every boast that North made to other inmates about his
criminal exploits. I collected copies of his written correspondence and
noted several "cleaned up" versions of statements to the police, which the
police provided to me. It wasn't difficult to weed out the obvious decep-
tions. Most important, from that first awful day forward, we maintained
a list of all the evidence we had discovered and had reported to the police.
We kept evidence the police had refused to accept or collect at a secure
location at one of our homes. And although it was especially painful and
traumatic, we would not let anyone forget the evidence of blood inside
and outside at Carl's property.

We knew that Carl had left the Outer Banks, North Carolina on Saturday morning, August 5, 2006, heading home to Amberson. At 9:17 A.M., records show he stopped for gas in Kill Devil Hills, North Carolina, and may have eaten breakfast there. A second receipt shows he bought gas again in Newport News, Virginia, at 1:03 that afternoon.

Hours later, he arrived in Chambersburg, where he stopped to visit a friend. He was still at that residence when another friend, Tommy, called him at 8:51 P.M. from my mother's house, where we were celebrating Clint's birthday. A few at the party urged Tommy to tell Carl to stop by. Carl, however, was tired and wanted to get home. So, although I also wanted to talk to Carl that evening, I decided to wait and call him the next day, Sunday.

Carl's girlfriend, Debbie, was the last person to speak with Carl while he was still at his friend's house at 9:29 P.M. By 10:00 P.M., he had left Chambersburg, stopped at the Sheetz convenience store in Greenvillage for coffee, then headed home, where he would arrive approximately thirty minutes later.

At 11:23 P.M., Tommy called Carl again from the party, but there was no answer. Had I still been at Mom's house and learned that Carl had not answered his phone, I would have thought it unusual because Carl always answered his phone no matter what time of day or night.

While at the party, I remember thinking that the celebration was not typical of our usual family fun but was festive on the surface only—as if something had gone awry. Around 10:30 P.M., I suddenly felt an inexplicable weariness—as if the life had been knocked out of me. And so, I left to go home. Just a few minutes later, on my drive through Shippensburg, I felt a nagging urge to change direction and head to Amberson, but it seemed a crazy idea to do so that late at night, and I knew Carl would be going to bed shortly. I considered calling him but again decided to wait until morning.

Mom would later describe a very sad feeling enveloping her as she hosted the party. Through a visceral maternal instinct, she sensed something was wrong and uncharacteristically wished everyone would leave.

The next morning, I awoke from a peculiar dream—one of muted colors. A grandmother—maybe great, great—on the Ryder side of the family sat calmly in her wooden rocking chair waiting for someone. So sure was I that she was waiting for me. I wondered how I was going to die. I was not alarmed, just curious about how it might happen. I awoke feeling depressed, though, and didn't call Carl as I had intended.

Clint also awoke, but from a far more disturbing dream, the same Sunday morning. In his dream, he saw a puppy and naturally walked toward it. But, as he approached the little dog, it transformed into a huge poisonous snake wrapped around a fence post, its ugly flat head poised at the top, ready to bite.

The same morning, our sister Christine was sitting on her back patio in Florida, drinking tea, when she looked toward the woods and saw a vision of Carl standing on a beach, looking out over the ocean. He drew in the briny air with a deep breath and then released it with a contented "Ahhh." Concerned, Chris phoned Loree. "Has anyone seen Carl?" she asked.

"Yeah, we just talked to him last evening on his way home. He's fine," Loree assured her.

Dad's younger sister, our Aunt Virginia, almost 3,000 miles away in the state of Washington, dreamed she drove up a long lane into a parking lot where two men ambushed and shot her as she exited her car. They threw her in the trunk, then dumped her elsewhere. It seemed so terrifyingly real that she has never forgotten it. The dream turned out to have some eerie parallels to the real incident.

There are some unexplainable things in this world, about which we have only limited understanding, but clearly, our dreams, visions, and uneasiness reflected the evil that had crept into our lives. Yet, we had not realized what they meant.

I never did call Carl that weekend. Awash in a fog, I couldn't think clearly, and things were just *weird*. I remember wanting to call him but inexplicably never did. For my entire life, I had talked to Carl almost every day. So why is it that I didn't call him for almost an entire week after I had talked to him on Friday, August 4, especially when I had been so looking forward to catching up with him? I will never be able to explain it.

Through our research and investigation, Clint and I pieced together what we believed happened that night based on familiarity with Carl's routines, crime-scene evidence, and bodily injuries that were determined.

We knew Carl typically pulled his car beyond the driveway into the yard when he had things to unload. However, that night, he left dirty clothes and several tools in the car—his Ford Crown Victoria. A porchlight may have remained lit at Pat's cabin one hundred and twenty yards northwest of Carl's place, which might have drawn his attention when he first arrived home on Saturday night. The light was on when police visited the property six days later—that "first day"—Friday, August 11. It is also possible he saw a light coming from inside his home, even though North had nailed a blanket over the front window and a towel over the window on the door.

At about 10:30 P.M. on August 5, 2016, while my family and friends were still celebrating at the party, Carl parked his car and walked through the grass, up the sidewalk, and across the deck to the front door. His defenses were likely down after a long day of traveling. Nevertheless, whether Carl found the door locked or unlocked, he opened it. The door swung in to the right, and as he stepped over the threshold of his ransacked and burglarized home, a deadly rip from a sawed-off shotgun exploded from the right of the door, which remained open. This was the first of at least two attacks.

As the sudden roar of the gun pierced the silence, the lead plowed through his torso, and at the same time, blood spattered from both the entry and exit wounds in both directions. (Dr. Kamerow's autopsy report would later reveal a deep torso flesh wound.) A pumpkin ball, a solid round piece of lead weighing approximately one-and-a-quarter ounces, with a diameter just shy of three-quarters of an inch, had just been fired from a sawed-off 12-gauge shotgun. Normally equal to the muzzle energy of a .45-70 caliber deer rifle, the velocity was likely somewhat diminished because of the shortened barrel, but the impact was nevertheless devastating. The barrel length also affected the trajectory of the deadly ball of lead, making it unstable and less accurate, but it easily hit its mark at such close range.

Based on our familiarity and knowledge of firearms, and after consulting with a friend, Jim, an experienced gunsmith, we reasoned that the projectile's velocity had diminished considerably after inflicting the long channeling wound, compromising its capacity to travel in a straight line. It continued in a weak upward direction, across the kitchen, and down the hallway, through two pieces of drywall above the bedroom door. By that time, its speed and power had diminished so that its direction was guided by whatever it came up against, causing it to ride along the bedroom ceiling, drawing a perfect lead line such as a pencil would make. After the lead plowed through a thin wooden strip on the ceiling, it slowed considerably and then veered downward at a steep angle with just enough force to lodge visibly in the far bedroom wall, approximately three feet above the floor.

In the split second that it took the deadly ball to land at its final spot, Carl, driven by instinct and terror, fell back out the door. Severely injured and bending forward at the waist, grasping at his wounds slippery with blood, he started to vomit. At the same time, in shock and numbing pain, he stumbled off the deck, trying to escape. But North set out after him. The only thing that allowed Carl to get as far as he did was blind panic trying to save his own life.

It is possible that as North was chasing him down, he shot Carl again, or stomped or jumped on him, battered him with a club, or stabbed him as he lay incapacitated and dying on the ground. (The post-mortem examination indicated that Carl likely suffered additional attacks.) As he lay on the ground, he had a few terrifying seconds to think of his family and friends before he fell unconscious. No doubt, he could also glimpse North's face before the savage attacks took his life.

The two shotgun sabots that we found led us to believe that North used the gun twice. The open knife we discovered adds another possibility. It is also very possible that he used a metal fence post in one of the attacks. The police said they found one in the trunk of Carl's car with the end cut into a "mean-looking point." I doubt police ever sent the fencepost to forensics to test for prints or blood. If they handled it the same way they handled much of the other evidence, it likely was never processed.

North then snatched up Carl's car keys (perhaps from the doorknob, floor, or ground), jumped into the car that Carl had just driven from North Carolina, and pulled it to the right and down a slight grade in the yard. Then he shoved it into reverse and stomped the gas. As he backed it up to where Carl lay bleeding to death in the front yard, the wheels spun, tearing the grass out and leaving an elongated patch of bare earth. Then he slammed the car into park and ran to a stack of fence boards, where he grabbed a black rubber tarp and dragged it to the rear of the car.

As North strained to roll Carl's body onto the tarp, the shift and momentum of Carl's weight threw him off balance. When North pitched forward, his hand and foot slapped onto the tarp to catch himself, thus, leaving bloody prints. The combined weight of Carl and the tarp would have been impossible to load into the trunk. Moreover, the tarp would have been difficult to grasp, especially with slippery, bloody hands. North then abandoned the idea and ditched the tarp by the deck.

Returning to Carl's body, North now needed every ounce of strength, even while adrenaline-fueled, to heave and drag Carl up as far as the lip of the open trunk, just enough to push and roll him inside. When he did, Carl's left shoe came off. Drs. Symes and Kamerow would conclude from the autopsy that Carl suffered four fractured ribs, inflicted while still alive—two on each side—with more in-bending to the left middle ribs, meaning more force was imposed upon the left side than the right. If Carl was not stomped, it is possible that his ribs were broken by his weight slamming down on the edge of the trunk. North likely lifted Carl by standing at Carl's left side as he lay face down, which would be in keeping with how someone would lift an incapacitated body of significant weight.

Carl was still alive, albeit unconscious, when he was loaded, bleeding profusely from an abdominal wound, a probable neck wound (supported by Symes and Kamerow), and broken ribs. North then slammed the lid shut and left Carl to die in a suffocating trunk—alone, broken, and bloody—in total darkness.

At this point, the grass, the back bumper of the car, the inside of the trunk, the tarp, and North himself were all saturated with blood, but it didn't deter him from pitching Carl's sneaker into the field, pocketing his cell phone and wallet, and grabbing his own address book with wet bloody hands. (That book would later become an important piece of evidence, as it held North's print in Carl's blood.)

As Carl lay dying or dead, North returned to Hennessy's cabin, the place of his first break-in and burglary, and there, he showered and hung his bloody clothes on a towel rack. Meanwhile, blood dripped from his clothing and landed on the back of the baseboard register cover, only discovered by Clint and our cousin Roy two winters later. Back at Carl's place, North didn't think, or perhaps he just didn't care to clean up the front door, rug, the rubber tarp, or the car splattered with blood; nor did he remove the plainly visible lead from the bedroom wall. Much more pressing, he had a body to dump.

Donning Carl's clothes, much too large for him, he hauled my brother for the next thirty minutes to a dark and secluded woods. Then he pulled Carl's body from the trunk and dragged him a distance from the road, dislocating Carl's hip. There, in the blackest of night before dawn, North dumped him down a steep bank, alongside animal bones, among trash and debris . . . miles from home . . . face down in a culvert.

CHAPTER 13

BRAZEN THIEVERY AND BALD-FACED LIES

. . . but because he was a thief, and had the bag, and bare what was put therein. —*The Apostle John*

North's actions during the remainder of that murderous Saturday night and throughout the next day are open to speculation, but it was no more than a day later when he was seen openly running the roads with his newly acquired car, money, and shotgun. According to what police told us, he invited two young women from the Path Valley area along on the joyride. Later, they claimed ignorance of the fact that North had stolen the car and had killed someone.

On Monday, August 7, North boldly showed up at an ex-girlfriend's workplace in Chambersburg. Frightened, she called the Chambersburg barracks with a description of the car and reported that he "looked crazy." Unconcerned, they told her to let them know if he returned.

Throughout that day, North remained in the Chambersburg area, driving all over town in a reported and very distinct 1991 light blue Ford Crown Victoria. Video footage from Food Lion on Philadelphia Avenue recorded him dumping a large amount of change into a Coin Star machine in exchange for paper money. Kmart on Wayne Avenue videotaped him the same day at 8:58 P.M., wearing Carl's cap and T-shirt while shopping for a new wardrobe and other items.

On Tuesday, August 8, North fed more change into another coin machine at the Giant Food store in Fulton County—and was again recorded on video. The next day, while shopping at Walmart in Huntingdon County, he bought CDs and other items. By Thursday, August 10, he was back in the Franklin County area. Footage showed he used Carl's credit card at the Waynesboro Walmart at 5:56 P.M. and bought gas at the Route 11 Pitt Stop on Philadelphia Avenue in Chambersburg at 7:24 P.M.

We will never know all the items he bought on his shopping spree because he used cash for some purchases. However, the credit card company documents show he charged more than twenty items totaling over $300, not including gas for the car. Some of the items police found in the car were smudged with blood. In addition, police confiscated a piece of paper on which North had practiced writing Carl's signature.

Besides a black face mask and a Powerline air pistol with CO_2 bottles, North bought a bandana, belt, toothbrush, toothpaste, shampoo, twill pants, T-shirts, jeans, sports shirt, jersey pullover, sneakers, an ankle wrap, a twenty-four-count CD case, and CDs. His purchases also included food, a pornography magazine, and a CD player. What's more, he bought a license plate holder, possibly to replace the factory hardware that he had removed from the front of Carl's car, likely in an attempt to disguise it. Strangely, he also bought a five-quart jug of oil. Carl's car didn't burn oil, but perhaps North thought he needed the oil because he had usually driven oil burners, or maybe he planned to use it as an accelerant to burn the car or trailer. We have never located the jug, and it remains a mystery, even though police supposedly logged most of the listed items into evidence. Years after the murder, when police released Carl's car to us, I discovered several CDs that North had purchased (which I verified with credit card records). I also found several cash receipts that investigators missed.

On the same day—Thursday, August 10—North traveled from Chambersburg to Huntingdon County. He had been running the roads for five days since the murder, living high with new clothes and sneakers, money to burn, and head-banging music when he decided to stop at Whitsel's Pub in Shirleysburg. Unbeknownst to him, the bartender and several patrons knew he was wanted for escape and eyed him tensely while he hung around. They considered tackling him, but something about him set their hair on end. As soon as North left the pub with two six-packs of Budweiser, the bartender called the Huntingdon state police barracks.

At 3:00 P.M., Trooper Warren Rhyner received information that North, an escapee from Franklin County, was driving an LTD-type vehicle in the Huntingdon County area. Later that evening, just south of Mount Union, Rhyner spotted the car heading north on Croghan Pike (U.S. Route 522) near the Shirley Township building. After a brief chase, he was able to stop the car on the bypass. At approximately 10:30 P.M., he approached the car and asked North for identification. North tried to pass himself off as Carl, claiming that he had had plastic surgery. Not convinced, Rhyner ordered North out of the car. But North had other ideas. He restarted the car and stomped the gas, pulling Rhyner down the road a short distance before the trooper could extricate himself. A sixteen-mile, high-speed chase ensued, ending near the Granville Township Fire House in Mifflin County at 10:52 P.M. when police finally disabled the car with stop sticks.

North burst from the car and ran—the new sneakers, which he had bought with Carl's credit card, flew off his feet. Troopers Rhyner and Lipmann continued to tail him in their cruisers and eventually sandwich him between them. Finally, trapped like a rat, North threw his hands in the air, and the troopers placed him under arrest.

As Troopers Rugby and Todd read the Miranda rights, police searched him and found Carl's cell phone and a credit card. They transported him by cage car to the J.C. Blair Memorial Hospital, where a blood test showed a blood alcohol content of .008 percent, below Pennsylvania's legal limit of .08 percent. They then took him to the Huntingdon barracks, where they again read Miranda rights and interviewed him on suspicion of other criminal activity. North tried several more times to pass himself off as Carl, but he couldn't remember Carl's birthdate. Meanwhile, a rollback transported Carl's car to the Huntingdon barracks, where a warranted search produced an additional credit card belonging to Carl and a forged receipt listing numerous items purchased from the Waynesboro Walmart. A keyring with five keys, as well as $65.52 in cash, was also recovered.

In the early hours of Friday, August 11, 2006, escapee Scott North found himself incarcerated in the Huntingdon County Jail. He gave a written statement—full of lies—that I obtained from courthouse records.

First, he concocted a story that he had walked away from work release and hitchhiked over the next couple of days to his "former boss's house," where Carl allowed him to spend the night because they were "friends." Then, he claimed that Carl had asked him to watch over the place because he was getting ready to leave for vacation and had been "having problems with people messing around his property." He also claimed that Carl didn't know how long he would be gone and that he left with a woman who had picked him up.

North said Carl had left him his driver's license so he could use his credit card at Walmart and gave North the use of his car, telling him "not to get caught" or "locked up." He claimed Carl said, "Don't get too wild with the credit card," as he further embellished his story.

"A shotgun found in the car was not mine or associated with me at all. It was in there when I gained access to the car," he wrote, his syntax sounding suspiciously practiced. As time passed, he spun new stories.

The truth was, North walked away from his work-release assignment in Shippensburg and was in Amberson by late afternoon the same day, while Carl was still in the Outer Banks, nowhere close to his home. The only problem Carl ever had with people on his property had occurred two years earlier with just *one person*—North—when he had stolen Carl's guns. Carl would never have offered the use of his credit card and car, nor would he have voluntarily parted with his wallet. Who would part with their own identity? No woman picked Carl up, and he certainly would not have been carrying a shotgun in his car.

Following the chase and capture, state police in Huntingdon County charged North with fleeing and eluding, resisting arrest, false ID, speeding, reckless driving, driving with a suspended license, and flight to avoid apprehension, trial, or punishment—while the state police in Franklin County filed an arrest warrant for the August 2 escape only. Because North was a fugitive and police suspected foul play in Carl's disappearance, the Huntingdon County district justice set bail at $50,000 real money, which meant a bail bondsman would not be permitted to arrange bail for a fee. North would have to come up with the full cash amount to be released. We warily considered that possibility but decided there was little chance anyone would pay fifty grand to get him out of jail.

CHAPTER 14

BEFORE THE BENCH

And moreover, I saw under the sun the place of judgment, that wickedness was there; and the place of righteousness, that iniquity was there. —King Solomon

Weeks after North's capture, the search for Carl's body, and the transfer of the murder case to Huntingdon County, District Attorney Stewart had not yet provided any information to Vivian Ritchey (the Huntingdon County Victim/Witness coordinator), rendering her unable to inform us of any scheduled matters. Meanwhile, Mark Wescott, the manager at AWI (Architectural Woodsmiths, Inc.), was subpoenaed to appear at North's preliminary hearing in Judge Michael Colyer's District Court (Huntingdon County) on August 31, 2006. The hearing was to determine if the Commonwealth had enough evidence to establish a *prima facie* case (enough evidence to prosecute) on the car chase charges. Unfortunately, we were not aware of the hearing until after it was over. Afterward, I requested a transcript from the Huntingdon County Courthouse, which detailed what took place.

While DA Robert Stewart represented the Commonwealth, Steven Passarello served as North's court-appointed attorney and began by entering a "not guilty" plea to all charges. Then he requested the removal of North's handcuffs to enable him to write questions. District Attorney Stewart and Trooper Rhyner objected, but the judge decided to remove the cuffs once Passarello assumed the risk. Meanwhile, North's ankles remained shackled.

In response to Stewart's questioning, Wescott stated that he was employed as the chief operating officer at Architectural Woodsmiths, then identified North in the courtroom and confirmed that he had been assigned to the paint department. Wescott explained that since AWI was "shorthanded" and there was no supervisor assigned to that section, he "spent a good portion of the day" working with North on Tuesday, August 1, and did "the same thing the following morning [Wednesday, August 2]." Regarding that Wednesday, Wescott also said he "was right there with [North]" from "5:00 A.M. until 8:00 A.M." in "the same spray booth." In addition, Wescott claimed there was a "designated area" for lunches and breaks, and North was scheduled to eat from "12:00 to 12:30."

Wescott said that when North failed to report to the paint shop at 12:30, one of the supervisors called him [Wescott] at "approximately quarter to 1:00" to tell him that North was missing. Wescott directed the supervisor to "search the building one more time." When North couldn't be found, Wescott called the probation officer.

Stewart asked Wescott to submit copies of North's timecard, an employment application with North's purported signature, and a copy of the documents provided by the probation officer listing the rules employers are required to follow regarding supervising pre-release inmates. He moved for the admission of all three documents, and after a few more questions, turned away from Wescott.

Passarello, on cross, first asked Wescott about his conversation with police on the day of escape and soon moved on to establish that North had worked "two days and a partial." Passarello also asked and verified that on Wednesday, August 2, North had "punched in at 4:47 A.M."

"What is this '12 o'clock okay per Mark'?" Passarello then asked.

"Scott did not punch out. We knew that he left his work area at 5 minutes to 12:00 to wash up, and we thought that the proper thing to do would be to pay him until noon," Wescott said, acknowledging that he had approved and signed North's timecard in lieu of North punching out and that he had assumed that North had gone "to wash up."

"You actually did not contact law enforcement? Is that my understanding of your testimony?" Passarello asked.

"I contacted . . . the probation officer," Wescott replied, at "quarter to 1:00."

Passarello finished up with questions pertaining to work release rules, and with no more questions from Stewart, Wescott was excused.

From Wescott's testimony, I realized that Scott North had been left alone in a place with no security cameras—consequently, no one had seen him slip away unhindered. But at what time did he escape? Other than North's pocket calendar, which Huntingdon police had confiscated on the night of his arrest, and which included his boast—"Wednesday 2, 12 noon GREAT ESCAPE"—no one at AWI knew the exact time that North had walked away.

Wescott had said, "We knew that he left his work area at five minutes to 12:00 to wash up, and we thought that the proper thing to do would be to pay [North] until noon." But does "knowing" that North left his work area also mean that someone *saw* North at 11:55 A.M. when he supposedly went to wash his hands? And whether someone saw North or not at that exact time, *why* did Wescott sign and approve the timecard when North had not punched out nor back in?

When Wescott returned from his lunch break at his home approximately two miles away, he and another employee wandered around the huge old building twice before reporting the walkaway sometime later. And as far as a designated lunch and break area, inmates sat anywhere they chose in the old factory, according to several employees who worked for AWI at that time. There was no evidence of even a casual adherence to rules of supervision, let alone a controlled lunch area.

Moreover, in a police interview on the day of the escape, Wescott said he didn't know what North looked like (according to the incident report). However, during the preliminary hearing in Huntingdon County, Wescott testified that he had picked up North at 4:30 A.M. on August 2 at the Franklin County Jail in his own vehicle and transported North to work. He also said he had personally worked with North for several hours on both Tuesday and Wednesday. So, if Wescott's testimony in court is true, why did he claim that he didn't know what North looked like on the day of the escape (August 2, 2006)?

In mishandling North, Wescott had proven himself unfit as a manager to participate in the work program. Yet, even after North's escape and Carl's murder, Franklin County permitted him to continue in the program as if nothing had happened.

Months later, while researching the work release program, I discovered that several Franklin County records were grossly out of date. For example, according to the documents, the County had placed North during those three days with a company that no longer existed because it had gone out of business a decade and a half earlier. Moreover, the company owner, whose name the County still used in its records, had retired years earlier.

After Wescott was dismissed from the hearing, Trooper Warren Rhyner of the Huntingdon barracks took the stand. We considered him a hero for risking his life to catch North when no one from the Chambersburg barracks seemed to be making any real effort.

Trooper Rhyner described his encounter with North, beginning on Thursday, August 10, eight days after North had walked away from AWI. At about 3:00 P.M., Rhyner was told that a Franklin County escapee, Scott North, was driving a "gray or silver LTD type vehicle." After spotting the car at about 10:30 P.M., south of Mount Union, heading north on U.S. Route 522 near the Shirley Township building, he turned around to tail the LTD.

When North noticed a trooper behind him with activated emergency lights, he fled at a high rate of speed until he became trapped behind traffic on the 522 bypass. It was only then that he chose to pull over. Rhyner testified, "Mr. North gave me a driver's license bearing the name of Carl Ryder. I observed to Mr. North that the picture on the driver's license did not look much like him. He offered to me that he had plastic surgery. I told [him] to wait in the car, and I would be back in a few minutes. And at that point, I waited for more officers to arrive at the scene, as I was going to take Mr. North into custody."

Rhyner said that after Corporals Lipmann and McNeal arrived, he returned to the Crown Victoria and ordered North from the car. "[North] asked me why. I said, 'Just get out of the car now.' And he said, 'I can't do that.' He reached for the ignition key, started cranking the engine. It didn't immediately start. I grabbed Mr. North by his left arm, tried to pull him out of the vehicle away from the gear shift lever and the ignition. While I was doing that, the car started, and the engine revved very high, and Mr. North apparently got the car into drive and started pulling me down the road. I eventually lost my grip and then went back to my vehicle and began the pursuit. . . .

Speeds during almost the entirety of the pursuit . . . were right at 100 miles an hour. . . . He went . . . into oncoming traffic. The vehicle was finally stopped at the Granville Firehall. . . . The vehicle got stopped because it had two front flat tires because of a tire deflation device deployed by Corporal Fultz of PSP Lewistown. . . . [North] starts to run. Shoes come flying off his feet. I follow him with my car for a few—maybe 30 or 40 yards. . . . I cut him off with my car. He reversed his direction and went around the right side of the building, and Corporal Lipmann . . . followed him in from there. . . . Mr. North then gave up, put his hands up, and stopped. He was placed under arrest by me and Corporal Lipmann."

In court that day, DA Stewart confirmed that Franklin County had charged North with escape, and a criminal history report showed North was a convicted felon. Stewart displayed a set of docket entries from the Franklin County Court, Case Number 1889 of 2005, indicating North's May 8, 2006, guilty plea to felony burglary and the July 5, 2006 sentence of eleven and a half to twenty-three months' confinement. He also produced a certified copy of North's driving history, revealing an October 2005 suspension of driving privileges. Stewart requested the admission of all documents into the record.

On cross, along with several other questions, Passarello asked Trooper Rhyner about his reason for pulling North over.

"Now, the initial reason for the stop, I believe you indicated, was that you had received something from the barracks indicating that there was a person on the loose and that he was driving a car that was silver or gray, is that correct?"

"Yes," Rhyner responded.

Passarello went on to ask if Rhyner's stop had anything to do with the color and model of the car, other distinguishing features of the car, or a description of the driver.

Then Passarello asked, ". . . the only reason you stopped this vehicle was because it was substantially similar to the report that you had?"

Rhyner testified, "That and the fact that when I called in the registration at the barracks, it came back to being registered to Franklin County. . . . And given the fact that we had information that [North] was just leaving Whitsel's Pub. . . . I was on my way down there to arrest him at the time when I saw that vehicle."

After a few other questions, Passarello asked, "Now the statement that Mr. North gave you indicated that Mr. Ryder had given him permission to use his credit card and vehicle, et cetera?"

"Yes," Rhyner answered.

"Is there any reason that you are aware of that the last sentence of his statement is in here regarding the shotgun?" Passarello asked.

"Yes. I asked him about the shotgun specifically," Rhyner replied.

"So, I'm assuming when the vehicle was inventoried, there was a shotgun found in it?" Passarello asked.

"Correct," Rhyner concurred.

Mention of the gun prompted an off-the-record discussion at the judge's bench.

Afterward, Passarello continued.

"Are there any other statements given to you or any other state troopers that you are aware of besides the statement given at the hospital and besides the written statement here?"

"Not to my knowledge," Rhyner replied.

The attorneys held another off-the-record discussion at the judge's bench.

Eventually, Passarello asked, "Prior to you questioning [North] at the barracks with this statement, did you have any information regarding a Carl Ryder?"

"I had asked the barracks to try to make contact with Mr. Ryder, and they were unsuccessful in doing so," Rhyner testified.

"Have you done any further investigation on Mr. North? You personally?" Passarello pressed.

"No. Well . . . I was at the scene of a deceased body, but I was not the primary investigator for that," Rhyner responded.

Upon conclusion of the hearing, Judge Colyer determined that the Commonwealth had established a *prima facie* case for the car chase and hence scheduled a formal arraignment to be held in October 2006, which Huntingdon County later rescheduled for November. In November, however, the arraignment was canceled.

As I finished reading the transcript, the two bench discussions (following the questioning about the shotgun) deepened my suspicions. *Were officials purposely ignoring the evidence? Or could it be that prosecutors didn't want to address an unprocessed yet potentially strong piece of evidence slated for an eventual murder case?* Whatever the reason, all went quiet in Huntingdon.

About three months later, on November 17, 2006, North was transported to Franklin County, where he waived the escape arraignment and pleaded not guilty in Judge Van Horn's court, then returned to the Huntingdon County Jail.

Throughout 2007, the Franklin County Sheriff's Department satisfied several orders to transport North from Huntingdon to Franklin County. Some were for disciplinary hearings regarding violation of work release rules in August 2006; others stemmed from the 2005 burglary, and some pertained to the escape itself.

In February 2007, North's attorney filed a motion requesting more time to prepare a defense for the escape charge, and a briefing determined that the escape was linked with North's latest (2006) parole violation for walking off work release. Subsequently, the hearing found him in violation for failing to return to the Franklin County Jail. Before his resentencing for the parole violation, he withdrew his admission to the violation and filed a petition, arguing under the Post-Conviction Collateral Relief Act that he should not have had jail time. In addition, he claimed he was coerced into his guilty plea for the August 2005 tavern burglary. The court dismissed this petition, describing it as frivolous and lacking fact. Instead, for the 2005 tavern burglary, North was re-sentenced to two to five years in state prison and one to five years for much older probation violations stemming from 2000. When North subsequently appealed to the Pennsylvania Superior Court, the appeal was dismissed.

In May 2007, Vicky Taylor, *Public Opinion,* referred to the 2000 probation violations in the following article:

HEARING REQUESTED IN ODD CASE. The man accused of escaping from Franklin County Prison who was then caught in Huntingdon County in August driving another man's car and trying to use his driver's license changed his mind about a probation violation issue this week, opting for a hearing instead of sentencing.

Scott Nathan North, 26, was scheduled to be resentenced on a *2000 theft charge probation violation* [emphasis added] Wednesday, but at the last minute, he withdrew his waiver of a violation hearing and asked Douglas W. Herman to reinstate his right to that hearing.

North was serving an 11½ to 23-month sentence at the Franklin County Prison on a burglary charge when he walked away from a work-release job in Shippensburg on Aug. 2 and made his way to the Amberson home of Carl Ryder, who was on vacation at the Outer Banks, N.C. Four [correction: three] days later, Ryder returned home and immediately disappeared. . . .

On Aug. 10, North was captured in Huntingdon County, driving Ryder's car and attempting to pass himself off as the older man who had once been his employer. However, when he was first stopped by a state trooper as he left a Mount Union bar, he gave the trooper Ryder's driver's license for identification, and when the trooper commented on the difference in looks, he claimed to have had plastic surgery.

Told to get out of the car, North instead led the trooper on a high-speed chase into Mifflin County.

On Aug. 16, Ryder's body was found in a ditch beside a rural Huntingdon County road. . . .

Huntingdon County District Attorney Robert Stewart III said his investigation into Ryder's death continues, although he has refused to discuss the case, including the cause of death and the identity of any possible suspects.

Franklin County District Attorney Jack Nelson said this week that Stewart has not recently discussed the case with him. (*Public Opinion* newspaper, www.publicopiniononline.com. Chambersburg, PA. May 17, 2007, "Hearing Requested in Odd Case.")

After not being notified of the date for the preliminary hearing for the charges stemming from the car chase in Huntingdon (we blamed Stewart for the secretiveness), my family and I were determined to stay abreast of all court activity involving North. Nine months after the murder, however, no progress had been made in our case, and I pleaded again for some sort of legal action. Finally, Stewart sent word through Vivian Ritchey that they were getting ready to charge North with criminal homicide—but we had heard that before. Trooper Ford also continued to offer the excuse that Stewart had to get "all his ducks in a row" before the DA could attempt to tackle a murder prosecution.

Nevertheless, Stewart seemed to be very busy with the upcoming election, and we wondered again, *Why has this case been assigned to Huntingdon County? And how can Franklin County still refuse to acknowledge the crime scene?*

While we urged that somebody do something, Vicky Taylor, *Public Opinion*, continued to inquire about the case. Finally, while interviewing Franklin County Judge Richard Walsh about another matter that spring, she took the opportunity to ask him what he thought of the Scott North murder case. As soon as Vicky brought up the question, however, the judge abruptly said he couldn't talk about it.

"But why can't you comment," Vicky asked, "especially since the case has been assigned to Huntington and not Franklin County?"

"You never know," he shrugged. "It might just come back."

"To Franklin County?"

"You never can tell."

The entrance to Drifted Lane leading to Carl's place.

The cabin near Carl's place that North broke into and stole items from after his escape.

Carl's 1991 Ford LTD in which North was apprehended.

Carl's Ford F350 that North attempted to hotwire.

The barn where North attempted to hotwire Carl's ATV.

The field where North threw Carl's sneaker after he loaded him in the trunk of the car.

The pipeline clearing where Carl's body was discovered.

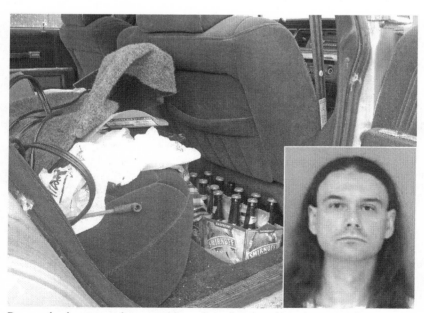

Beer and other items discovered by police after North's arrest in Carl's car.
Inset: Scott North's mugshot.

The green house on Allison Road near the location Carl's body was found.

Our protest against the plea bargain.

The Presbyterian Church where the services were held.

Carl's girlfriend, Debbie at his second funeral in September 2009. (Courtesy Vicky Taylor)

Nieces at the second funeral. (Courtesy Vicky Taylor)

The cross along Allison Road near the site
where Carl's body was found.

Carl with Loree on his graduation day, June 1981.

Carl loved to fish. This was taken in 2005, near the Atlantic Ocean.

CHAPTER 15

JUSTICE DELAYED, JUSTICE DENIED

Therefore, is judgment far from us, neither doth justice overtake us: we wait for light, but behold obscurity; for brightness, but we walk in darkness. —The Prophet Isaiah

I sat staring at the papers on my desk. For months now, I had managed to put one foot in front of the other and struggle through one hour after another. Weeks after the murder, I had returned to work, and nothing much had changed. I still dreaded waking up in the morning and immediately wished for the end of each day. I managed to drive, one mile after another—a daily eighty-mile commute—to and from Harrisburg working for the Pennsylvania State Police, yet I could not help but feel betrayed by law enforcement. I was discouraged but mostly angry—my brother deserved so much better. Instead, I had heard only empty promises and pathetic excuses in pursuit of the truth. Yet, not all hope had faded. On this day in May 2007, I was consumed with Stewart's most recent pledge of a soon-to-be-filed murder charge and was on edge, anticipating a call at any moment confirming it.

I constantly glanced at my cell throughout that morning—I don't know how many times—and by mid-afternoon, the phone finally lit up.

I knew the number. It was Trooper Ford.

My heart pounded, and my hand trembled as I pushed the receive button. At the same time, I grabbed a pencil to write down any details.

Then I braced myself for the news. *Finally*, I thought, *we are about to see some activity.*

"I thought you might want to know," Ford got right to the point after saying hello, "Stewart lost the primary election."

"What's that mean?" I asked, feeling an instant let-down.

"Well, since he's the one who's been in charge of the case . . . I just thought you might want to know."

The news was both unexpected and discouraging. I realized, though, what Ford was trying to say. There would eventually be a new district attorney in Huntingdon County—which meant waiting even longer for movement on the case.

Then I began to consider what could happen next. *Will the new DA be different . . . or just like Stewart? Will he take an interest . . . or simply not care? Or . . . maybe, maybe he'll start an honest investigation . . . maybe a prosecution will spring to life. . . . Then again, this guy might not want the case. And what if it's transferred to Franklin County? What will happen then? My God, we don't want a plea bargain. . . .*

I had so many questions, but for that moment, only one answer: Another lengthy delay was certain. I watched political tides toss the case about rather than narrow in on the facts.

I sank further into despair.

~~~

The unseating of an incumbent district attorney, especially one with more than fifteen years in office, is rare, but Stewart apparently had become unpopular in Huntingdon County. Change was in the air, and we heard that he was shocked at the outcome. I was alarmed, and reading between the lines of Ford's ambiguous call, I understood that this unexpected change upset certain agendas, leaving some politicians, particularly in Franklin County, on edge.

When I relayed the news of Stewart's campaign loss to other family members, we decided to cling to Stewart's early assurance that North would never get out of prison. We were even somewhat reassured when, after losing the election, he continued to promise that our case would be "next in line" and he would file charges before he left office. Trooper

Ford also confirmed that Stewart would be charging North with murder "any time now." Therefore, we waited . . . and waited . . . throughout the summer of 2007. Finally, we realized that Stewart was already packing his bags and had time only for wrapping up loose ends and less serious cases. We became more frantic because now the case most likely would languish until a new district attorney took office in January 2008.

Meanwhile, in June 2007, as North remained in prison, I sent a letter of complaint to state Senator Terry Punt's office, criticizing Franklin County's work program, the horrendously late re-sentencing for North's old probation violations, and the dropping of a gun charge. I pointed out that North's record was not good enough to warrant work release. Specifically, the Court, as well as Franklin County Jail, had not only ignored North's history but also neglected to calculate the high probability of escape. On top of that, they had placed him with an employer who had left him unsupervised. I also brought to Senator Punt's attention that since Carl's murder, the County continued to place inmates with the same employer. Considering AWI's degree of incompetence, another tragedy was likely to happen. Therefore, we wanted a reliable and stringent screening of potential work-release inmates. We felt that officials had failed their duty to provide a safe and responsible work program. By ignoring their own public safety priority, they had enabled North to continue his criminal activities freely, thereby subjecting the community to danger.

After receiving the letter, Terry Punt's staff contacted the Franklin County Jail to inquire about the incident, which is more than anyone else had done up to that point. In response, Warden John Wetzel shrugged off accountability by commenting that my family and I were "just looking for someone to blame."

Punt's office showed more concern and interest than did Lieutenant Governor Catherine Baker Knoll. Worried sick about the stalled case and the wayward work program, I also sent a letter of complaint to Baker Knoll, who presided over the state Board of Pardons. Because the Board's mission statement claimed it was committed to public safety and addressing the needs of crime victims, I thought the Lieutenant Governor would at least acknowledge our grievance.

She didn't.

That same month, Governor Ed Rendell nominated John Wetzel to serve on the state Board of Pardons. After Wetzel's demonstrated indifference toward us, as well as his marginal concern for public safety and crime victims, it seemed an inappropriate appointment.

In addition to sending the letters, I decided to look at the work-release programs in other states, specifically regarding escapes. My research into ten cases found that inmates who had been approved for work release and later escaped had been serving time for misdemeanors only—none had committed serious crimes such as North's felony burglary. Moreover, if a pre-release inmate committed even the slightest infraction while on the job, officials had promptly pulled other prisoners from the employers—and then barred the employers from further participation. Yet, in Franklin County, Pennsylvania, having a work release escapee tied to a suspicious death was not enough to end AWI's participation in the work program.

Franklin County's apparent lack of concern for Carl and my family as victims led us to file a lawsuit. Potential monetary compensation was not the motivation—we wanted someone to sanction the inattentive employer and mishandling of the work program. Franklin County officials had ignored public safety, yet not one person who contributed to this catastrophe had shown enough character to apologize. And some of the people whom we had helped to elect to office were ignoring us. We knew we had little chance of holding the County (shielded by state immunity) accountable. Still, we were determined to demand some sort of accountability as well as draw attention to the slipshod work program.

We hired McCarthy Weisberg Cummings, P.C. law firm of Harrisburg, who filed a personal injury lawsuit. Under the Pennsylvania Wrongful Death Act, there is a distinction between a wrongful death action and a survival action. The survival claim, which our attorneys filed, named Scott North and Showbest/AWI as the responsible parties for Carl's death, making it possible to recover damages for his pain and suffering as well as for the loss of his gross-earning power through his estimated working lifespan. (A wrongful death action, on the other hand, would have recovered funeral and estate expenses as well as compensated the family of the decedent.)

A Franklin County deputy served copies of the civil action to Mark Wescott in Franklin County and AWI's main office in Schuylkill County, and it was out of our hands for a while. We then turned our attention back to personal matters, Carl's estate, and such things as selling his boat. It was another difficult day when Clint and I watched his Gypsy disappear down the road. Wistfully, I recalled our annual fair-weather haul and fishing trip to Raystown Lake, the eighty-three-hundred-acre reservoir in Huntingdon County.

In the waning summer of 2007, we learned that Dr. Kamerow, after reviewing Dr. Symes' findings on Carl's skeletal remains, had generated his autopsy report. Although I dreaded reading it, I knew I had to, in hopes of finding answers to some of my questions.

While some of the findings were not a surprise, one that caught my attention was Dr. Kamerow's note of an "avulsion" across Carl's lower abdomen, which he described as inflicted while Carl was still alive. Large and severe, it tore through muscle and blood vessels but with no exit wound in Carl's back. Oddly, he settled on the manner of death as homicide by "blunt force trauma."

This was exasperating, considering that blunt force trauma rarely causes an avulsion because blunt force trauma is characteristically a non-penetrating injury. An avulsion is an injury in which a body structure, such as a muscle, is forcibly torn away, indicating something plowed through the tissue.

I was also puzzled as to why Kamerow would choose "blunt force trauma" as the manner of death when at the same time he had insisted that due to severe decomposition of the body and pending investigative forensic lab results, it would be impossible to determine a conclusive cause of death (instrument used). He reported that the body's condition had not allowed for the discovery of a specific pathway, such as a bullet, would make when traveling through the torso. He also claimed that he could not conclude whether a bullet wound, stab wound, or another type of wound had caused Carl's death, and he went on to say that his report was "the best that could be professionally determined." Again, I wondered, *Why choose "blunt force trauma" as the manner of death after insisting that a "conclusive cause of death is impossible"?*

Kamerow's disconcerting claims only solidified our certainty of a shotgun wound, especially when considering the presence of a round hole in Carl's T-shirt. We had always assumed that the police had sent the T-shirt, as well as the slug, to the state forensics lab. But we had assumed wrong.

Kamerow said in his report that he and Coroner Morder had photographed Carl's clothing and then gave the items to the attending police officers, along with the shoe that had been on his right foot when the police recovered his body. However, it was not until much later we learned that Kamerow had never actually given these items to the police, nor had the police or district attorney submitted the clothing items, or the slug for that matter, for forensic testing.

Somehow, Dr. Symes still had possession of Carl's clothing, including his T-shirt. A year earlier, he had measured the hole in Carl's shirt during the initial autopsy and had described it as an irregular oval with ragged margins, slightly larger than three-quarters of an inch. The size of the hole closely matched the diameter of the shotgun slug. To this day, we don't know the condition of Carl's shorts. The sneaker that was still on his foot matched the sneaker found in the hayfield at his place, and there was an indication of vomit on the sneaker.

Dr. Symes also noted disruption of neck vertebrae and observed that his rib bones appeared light with thin cortical bone for Carl's robust size. It meant that for Carl's large size, he was not a big-boned man. Carl knew that himself. As a teen, he once commented that he could never be a boxer like Cassius Clay because, as he said, "My bones aren't big enough." But, light rib bones or not, Carl was a large-framed man—a genetic endowment from the McVitty side of the family.

Kamerow's deductions added insult to injury. We had received no hint of consideration while the case wallowed in Huntingdon—there was a chance that the case might be transferred back to Franklin County where it might receive even less attention—and now our stress and heartache were compounded by an autopsy specialist who guessed the manner of death as blunt force trauma.

Would we ever find justice?

 CHAPTER 16

EAGER TO GET STARTED

That we henceforth be no more . . . tossed to and fro, and carried about with every wind of doctrine, by the sleight of men, and cunning craftiness, whereby they lie in wait to deceive.
—The Apostle Paul

An incredibly difficult year had passed since I last saw Carl. The first anniversary of the murder came with so many horrific memories. Poor Clint, his birthday ruined forever. Time moved on but with no resolution.

Vicky Taylor wrote another article, this time quoting Huntingdon County District Attorney Stewart:

ONE YEAR LATER: FEW ANSWERS IN THE DEATH OF CARL RYDER. "Solutions of homicides in the real world don't take place like those cases are portrayed on TV," he said. "We can't investigate them, solve them, make an arrest and bring the accused to trial in an hour with time out for commercials."

(*Public Opinion* newspaper, Chambersburg, PA, August 22, 2007. "One Year Later: Few Answers in the Death of Carl Ryder," pages 1-A and 7-A.)

We never insisted that the investigation, arrest, and sentence be completed or resolved in an hour. However, we did expect that there would be a prompt murder charge, in light of so much evidence, and that we wouldn't have to plead with officials to do their jobs. Clearly, it was not an unsolvable or cold case.

Despite Stewart's excuses, we pretty much grew used to the fact that the case would remain in Huntingdon, even after Stewart left office. Although we knew the officials in Franklin County should prosecute the case due to the location of the crime scene, we grew leery of them. Who wouldn't have felt the same way after learning of North's lengthy criminal background, his longstanding trouble with the police as well as court officials, and the many times his charges had been reduced or dropped? History showed that North's victims rarely received full justice, and it was quite possible that a murder charge would unravel into another plea bargain. To add to our growing anxiety that North might get away with murder, Stewart neglected to warn us that he had dropped the seven charges stemming from the car chase. Unfortunately, we learned that after the fact through Vivian Ritchey.

On the other hand, to our surprise, even before Huntingdon County District Attorney George Zanic was sworn into office as Stewart's replacement in January of 2008, he told Vivian that he was anticipating the work on our case and considered it his priority. During the week between the Christmas and New Year holidays, he began to review the available evidence. We were cautiously hopeful.

But a big change hovered just around the corner. After reviewing the initial bits of evidence that Franklin County had collected a year and a half earlier, George Zanic told Vivian that the case simply did not belong with him. She suggested that he personally explain to us why he planned to transfer the case to Franklin County. Taking her advice, during his first official week in office, he dialed my number.

"As much as I want the case," he admitted, "I have to transfer it back to Franklin County. Due to the evidence, it just doesn't belong in Huntingdon."

"What evidence is that?" I asked.

"It's the blood in the yard," Zanic responded, identifying one of the more significant pieces of evidence.

"Well, I agree," I replied, "but no one will listen to us. Anyone who was at the scene could see all the blood and all the other evidence. Of course, there was a lot more blood than what we pointed out in the yard, but they still insisted there was no crime scene. I'm afraid if they get the case, they won't even prosecute. They don't want it—they've never wanted it."

I had a lot more to say and went on to describe all the various ways that the case had been so desultorily handled up to that point and how the evidence had been halfheartedly gathered or completely ignored. I told him how Clint and I had stepped in to protect and store some evidence and how the crime scene had been outright denied by the police and both DAs. Moreover, neither the police nor the DA showed an interest in developing any possible motive. In fact, many other people were willing to state as to the facts surrounding North's theft of Carl's guns during his brief employment with Carl, but neither Huntingdon nor Chambersburg state police were interested in talking with anyone.

I expressed my dismay that a political change had to happen for the truth to be acknowledged and that finally, after more than seventeen months, our case was being transferred to a county where it should have remained in the first place—but where justice now looked even more elusive. Naturally, we held little hope that the DA in Franklin County, Jack Nelson, would be enthusiastic about the transfer.

North started the new year by filing another Post-Conviction Relief petition, arguing against his October 2007 re-sentencing for old probation violations. The court dismissed it as filed too late. North then appealed to the Superior Court, which affirmed the lower court. In the meantime, more Franklin County escape incidents served to underscore the existence of a serious problem with their work program. One prisoner disappeared after leaving the jail for an interview at a Target warehouse facility in Chambersburg. He never showed up for the interview. Another caused a hit-and-run in Greencastle while driving on a suspended license.

A day or two after Zanic called me, Vivian sent a letter to Franklin County, dated January 7, 2008, enclosing our names and contact information in hopes that someone would reach out to us. She had been astonished to learn that Franklin County had never offered us victim or grief support.

On January 10, George Zanic traveled to Franklin County to meet with Jack Nelson and investigating officers. Eleven people were present as Zanic officially transferred the case from Huntingdon to Franklin County.

A trooper later told us that another trooper from Franklin County, who was present at the meeting, demanded to know why Franklin County had given the case to Huntingdon County. His question went unanswered. Ford attended the meeting and afterward assured us that they were "eager to get started" and that "the case will be top priority."

Five weeks later, in mid-February, I contacted Nelson and introduced myself, "I'm calling about the status of the murder case of my brother— Carl Ryder."

"I don't know anything about a case," he said flatly.

Oh my God! I thought as I scrambled to collect myself. How could he be so deceptive and cold-hearted? I thought I was about to lose my mind.

"You mean to tell me that you sat in that meeting discussing this case when it was transferred to your office, and now you say you know nothing about it? You were there! Ford said this case would be 'top priority,' and now you're telling me that you don't know a thing about it? You can't tell me you don't have this case." I gasped as my heart skipped beats. "George Zanic called me himself and told me he was transferring this case, and you were there when it happened . . . on January 10. That was five weeks ago!"

"I haven't looked at it yet."

Nelson's emotionless reply was followed by silence.

I waited a few more seconds and couldn't help but speak again, simply grateful that he had finally acknowledged "it."

"Well, we'd like to meet with you," I said, desperately hoping he would offer to meet with us, or at least indicate how long it would be until he reviewed it.

"I'll have someone call you," he replied and abruptly hung up.

That chilling conversation sank any small hope that Jack Nelson or anyone in Franklin County would be even remotely interested in the case, let alone treat us cordially. We had taken our hints and cues beforehand and expected cavalier treatment, but this unnerved me to no end. My worst fear was coming true. After all we had been through in the previous eighteen months, Nelson now had control, and I felt our battle was just beginning. Worse yet . . . I wasn't sure I had the strength. One more promise fell flat. What were we to think? The murder had been committed one-and-a-half years earlier, leaving overwhelming yet ignored evidence. I viewed their neglect as criminal too.

The renewed worries reinvigorated the vivid nightmares I had been suffering. They always featured a trio of figures, at first seemingly harmless, but then hell-bent on killing me. At times, the threesome became snakes. The tormenting dreams would persist for more than three years and to this day occasionally recur in fragments as leftovers of a nightmarish reality. Likewise, Clint's dreams always featured a creature, seemingly harmless at a distance but morphing into something horrible as he approached and saw it for what it really was.

While our case languished with Nelson, we were disconcerted to learn that Assistant District Attorney Angela Krom would also be involved with it. Previously, we discovered that she, along with Nelson, had allowed North's parole violations to slide. But most devastating was knowing that when the court could have prosecuted and possibly sentenced him to state prison, Krom had offered a plea deal for North's 2005 burglaries—a deal that allowed the dismissal of several felonies. North's burglary sentence had included incarceration in the Franklin County Jail—and *work release eligibility*—a decision that launched this entire catastrophe.

CHAPTER 17

AT LAST—A MURDER CHARGE

Moreover, ye shall take no satisfaction for the life of a murderer,
which is guilty of death: but he shall be surely put to death.
—Moses

"It's ridiculous how long the DA's office has been delaying murder charges," I said irritably while on the phone with a contact person with Jack Nelson's office about the status of the case. "I think Nelson is refusing to do anything because a bunch of North's relatives work there at the courthouse. And I don't give a damn if North's town-cop daddy is Jack's drinking buddy or not. Somebody better do something—now!"

I was at my wit's end, and the secretary (or whoever it was) on the other end of the line knew it. I had long ago given up asking *when* they would charge North with murder but instead demanded to know *if* they would ever charge him. Three months had passed since DA Nelson claimed ignorance of the case. I was sick and tired of waiting. The case had been idling in Nelson's office for over four months, and I didn't hesitate to accuse him and his office of nepotism.

My little tirade must have rattled someone because the next day, Wednesday, May 7, 2008, I received a call from Ford.

"I'm going to charge Scott North with criminal homicide," he announced.

"Good. It's about time."

I didn't believe him, though, sure it was another lie.

Then, out of the blue, a day later, Nelson initiated contact for the first time, stating he was getting ready to file charges.

"I also want to let you know," he said flatly, "that our office will be holding a press conference with the local paper tomorrow." Then he blurted, "But I don't want you talking to the media."

"We want North charged with first-degree murder," I retorted, ignoring his demand. "He killed Carl. He killed him during a burglary. He killed him for money and a car, and out of pure hatefulness. And he planned to do it."

"Well, I don't want any other media contacted," Nelson repeated.

"Well, if the *Public Opinion's* going to be there, I don't see any reason why other media can't also be there. People should know what's going on. You're calling a press conference, and that's what a press conference is for—to let people know what's going on," I said.

"Be that as it may, we don't need any other media," he insisted.

Being commanded to keep their secrets was infuriating. I was no longer a naïve, trusting, I'll-believe-everything-you-tell-me person. They had done nothing up to this point to help the case. Once again, he was all about manipulation.

Honestly, until Nelson called, I had no intention of contacting the media. But right then, I decided to call a TV station and another paper and tell them when and where the announcement would take place.

The next day, May 9, 2008, Assistant DA Angela Krom approved a criminal complaint, and police issued a warrant for North's arrest. Scott North was transported to the Magisterial District Judge's office in Pleasant Hall, where Ford from the Chambersburg barracks and Trooper Sneath from the Huntingdon barracks charged him with PA Crimes Code Section 2501 Criminal Homicide. Bail was set at $200,000, and Vicky Taylor's headline splashed across the *Public Opinion*.

SCOTT NORTH CHARGED WITH CARL RYDER'S MURDER. Almost two years after Amberson resident Carl Ryder's body was found down an embankment along a rural Huntingdon County road, murder charges have been filed in Franklin County in the case.

Scott Nathan North, 27, was arraigned before Magisterial District Judge Brenda Knepper on a criminal homicide charge this morning. Pennsylvania State Police in Chambersburg have called a press conference for this afternoon to talk about their case against the man who, on August 10, 2006, tried to pass himself off as Ryder when he was apprehended by state police following a high-speed chase in Huntingdon County. North is currently serving a state prison sentence on a 2005 burglary charge. (*Public Opinion* newspaper, www.publicopiniononline.com. Chambersburg, PA. May 9, 2008. "Scott North Charged With Carl Ryder's Murder.")

The criminal complaint stated that Scott North had caused Carl's death by violating the "Penal Laws of the Commonwealth of Pennsylvania" at Carl's address of Drifted Lane, Fannett Township, in Franklin County.

One year and nine months after Carl's murder, Franklin County officials finally acknowledged the murder and the actual crime scene. By this time, though, they had already created a serious delay in prosecuting the case, not to mention a deep distrust we now had for them.

Later that day, Angela Krom's announcement to the press was nothing more than an excuse. She claimed that part of the reason it took so long to file charges was that "the investigation spanned two counties and involved multiple law enforcement agencies," yet she neglected to expound on the real reason for involving more than one county and two state police barracks. She also conveniently blamed Huntingdon County District Attorney Robert Stewart, who, she said, had "clamped a lid on the case."

At the conference, Ford took the opportunity to approach our attorneys Weisberg and Cummings of Harrisburg, and remarked that he didn't want them "saying things." They responded that they were not there to "point fingers but know that Franklin County really dropped the ball concerning this case." To the press, our attorneys stated that although "we can never bring Carl back, we can take comfort in knowing that the justice system is moving forward towards a just resolution to this horrible and unfortunate chapter in our lives." While I appreciated that our attorneys imparted heartfelt gratitude on my family's behalf for all the thoughts and prayers we had received from community members, I privately took no comfort at all in the justice system moving forward, except for feeling relief that North had finally been charged.

At a last-minute hearing four days later on May 13, 2008, the court dismissed the escape charge and canceled the date for jury selection. Krom deemed the action necessary considering the criminal homicide charge already filed. She then refiled the escape charge on June 2, 2008, and included the dropped charges from Huntingdon: false identification, fleeing or eluding, burglary, criminal trespass, theft, access device fraud, forgery, and abuse of a corpse, all as one continuous criminal episode. This joinder is required under Commonwealth law and should have been done in August 2006.

Despite police and prosecutors' initial insistence that there was no crime scene and no new or damning evidence, Nelson now declared that *strong evidence* existed.

The *Public Opinion* carried the latest. NEW CHARGES FILED AGAINST NORTH. The new charges, filed Monday with Senior Magisterial District Judge Brenda Knepper, include charges that had been withdrawn earlier, including a Franklin County escape charge and Huntingdon County charges of false identification to a police officer, and fleeing or eluding police. In addition to those charges, the homicide charge and the abuse of a corpse charge, North is also charged with two counts of burglary, two counts of criminal trespass, four counts of theft by unlawful taking, two counts of access device fraud, and two counts of forgery. . . . After Stewart left office, the case was turned over to Franklin County District Attorney Jack Nelson this year. Nelson said his office needed time to review the evidence before filing charges here. At the time, he said the transfer of the case to his office was appropriate because evidence was strong that the murder occurred here. During a press conference the day the homicide charge was filed, police said evidence included blood samples that matched Ryder's DNA taken from the yard in front of Ryder's mobile home.

(*Public Opinion* newspaper, www.publicopiniononline.com. Chambersburg, PA. June 4, 2008. "New Charges Filed Against North.")

Had North escaped by force, use of a weapon, or in conspiracy with another person, a more serious grading of first- or second-degree felony escape could have been applied according to the Pennsylvania statutes. We are convinced of the possibility of an accomplice because we were told that North had received a phone call before he left the worksite, allegedly from an ex-girlfriend. I'm not sure how he could take the call when work-release inmates are forbidden calls at work. Early in the case, police had been searching for a person in a green blazer who "knows something." However, Ford had said, ". . . the escape was separate" and that he "wasn't on that part of the investigation." To this day, elements of the escape remain unexplained.

Soon after the press conference, North admitted during a police interview with Ford that he had loaded Carl into the trunk of Carl's car and dumped him down an embankment along Allison Road at the location where Carl's body was later discovered. However, that was the only part of his admission that was true. In this latest version, North claimed that Carl was already dead when he first arrived at Carl's home, and because North assumed that he would "get the blame," he got rid of him.

A few weeks later, I confronted Nelson and the state police about their sudden, belated acknowledgment of the crime scene, which they quickly tried to justify.

"There just was not enough evidence at first," Ford said.

That was ridiculous! All investigators who had visited Carl's property that first day, on August 11, 2006, and sporadically for weeks afterward each time we called them back to the property, were nose-to-nose with good solid evidence. From the very beginning, the police had all the proof they needed, plus an escape, a burglary, two obvious motives to kill—one of revenge, the other for personal gain. They also had a weapon, at least one spent slug, DNA evidence, prints in blood, a stolen car, and stolen personal items.

A prompt and successful prosecution would have been possible if Nelson had been interested in justice, and if Stewart had refused a case that clearly was not in his jurisdiction, and if other subordinates had not buckled. It would have saved us years of worry and anguish. Instead, it was nothing short of torment and hell.

Now that they had finally charged North with criminal homicide, our next concern was what degree of murder they would level against him. According to The Pennsylvania General Assembly, Title 18, Chapter 25, Section 2501 (a), a "person is guilty of *criminal homicide* if he intentionally, knowingly, recklessly, or negligently causes the death of another human being."

Criminal homicide in Pennsylvania covers three degrees of murder— *first*, *second*, and *third*; and two types of manslaughter.

Murder of the first degree is an intentional killing, committed willfully and deliberately, by plan or decision, or by taking specific action in such a way that the action will kill. It requires proof of express malice.

Malice is the mental state, such as lying in wait, using a deadly weapon, the wickedness of disposition—cruelty—a conscious disregard for a high-risk action that causes death. Premeditation means having a plan or intent. The amount of time needed to formulate an intent to kill depends upon the person and the circumstances.

In Pennsylvania, there are eighteen aggravating circumstances—specific factors of circumstance, at least one of which must be filed within a certain amount of time by the district attorney if seeking the death penalty in a first-degree murder case. We were interested in the aggravating circumstance that describes the murder as especially heinous, atrocious, cruel, depraved, and committed for pecuniary gain.

From our standpoint, a convicted felon who had escaped, burglarized, murdered, stole a car and personal property, dumped a body, spent the victim's money, and then had the audacity to continue to live in the victim's home, deserved a first-degree murder charge with an aggravating circumstance tacked on, especially since evidence of malice and premeditation existed. Our attorneys agreed. It was depraved, cruel, and committed intentionally for the sake of gain and revenge. We wanted a prosecution for first-degree murder, and if not a death sentence, at the very least, we wanted the killer never to draw breath again as a free man.

Murder of the second degree is a homicide committed while perpetrating another felony such as burglary, but it does not carry the potential for a death sentence. Second-degree murder is what Huntingdon County District Attorney Stewart had initially guaranteed us. If we could not have the first-degree murder charge, murder of the second degree was bearable, but we expected no less. Since Stewart had promised it without so much as a crime scene, we expected Nelson and Krom to pursue at least the same.

Murder of the third degree is defined as "all other kinds of murder" and includes voluntary and involuntary manslaughter. It also involves malice but does not require the circumstance of intent.

With a murder charge hanging over his head, North filed a petition *pro se*, requesting a transfer out of Franklin County, complaining that the law library at the jail was inadequate. He also claimed that he had recently received a potentially serious heart condition diagnosis, his needs had been neglected, and his attorney-client confidentiality entitlement was violated. He eventually was transferred to Greensburg State Prison near Pittsburgh.

While North settled back into his already familiar way of life, our family dynamics slowly shifted. My sisters lived out of state, somewhat removed from the local news, but not from the churning grief and loss we suffered. We all remained close, but a quiet sadness and smoldering anger tore at us. We couldn't express our bereavement in a normal manner, whatever normal might be. Ways of dealing with intense sorrow are as individual as a fingerprint, and in due course, we each retreated into our private pain.

Frequently, my anxiety would summon long-forgotten memories of an easier time of life. Recalling those old times, both pleasant and unpleasant, quickly became routine, simply to relieve the misery of the present. I relived our youthful outings, the cool nights when Carl and I traipsed along the Conococheague Creek with the moon hanging in the night sky and the smell of water trickling across damp rocks. I thought about the hot days of sweat and blisters, a result of baling and stacking hay, and Sunday afternoons avoiding the leeches at the far edge of the swimming hole. We had no worries like murder. I reminisced about the fragrance of leaves as they changed with the season, the frozen fields we crossed, stopping in our tracks to listen to a fox bark in the night, and the misery of snow packed in our boots—our toes as well as fingers and faces numb from the cold. I remembered our joy when something good happened and the sinking feeling of disappointment. I recalled the day Carl was so excited that Jim Plunkett, an outstanding quarterback in the NFL with two Super Bowl wins in 1980 and 1984, came to visit Fannett-Metal High School (at that time, the 1984 win still lay in the future for Jim). Jim spoke to him and shook his hand. He talked about it for days. He said Jim Plunkett was a big man. I felt happy for Carl. All were memories of pure bliss compared to the staggering reality that now consumed our lives.

On the evening of June 10, 2008, I stepped out onto my front porch to retrieve the mail. Among the envelopes, I noticed a receipt from the Franklin County Sheriff's office confirming delivery to all appropriate parties of our civil action complaint against AWI and North. I couldn't believe my eyes when I saw that Scott North's uncle, Richard "Dick"

North, had been the one to deliver the papers. He was working as a deputy for the Franklin County Sheriff's Office.

Enraged, I called Sheriff Dane Anthony the next day.

"Dane . . . Dick North delivered our papers. You do know, don't you, that his no-good nephew killed my brother. We don't want those people touching anything of ours," I said, bracing myself for the same indifference and lame excuses we had received from other officials.

But the next minute, I was taken aback by the sheriff's demeanor. With genuine sincerity, Dane immediately apologized and went on to explain that his secretary assigns the delivery tasks, and he didn't realize that Dick had been involved. I was instantly grateful for his explanation, and I felt bad for putting him on the spot. At the same time, I was irate that Dick North, knowing what he was delivering and to whom, had not declined the assignment.

"Is he transporting North back and forth from the jail to the courthouse?" I asked.

"I wouldn't allow that," Dane assured me. Later, he expressed his regret for the incident to our friend, Jim Campbell. Truly, had he known, he never would have allowed our documents to be delivered by a close relative of Carl's killer.

The next week, I received a written apology from Sheriff Anthony. Impressed by his contrition for something he had been unaware of, I felt his character towered above most others' during this horrendous ordeal. He was one of the very few, and his letter renewed a little of my faith in humankind. But only a day or two passed before I heard comments, like one from the owner of Showbest/AWI, Jim Shubert. When Shubert received the complaint documents of our civil action, our attorneys told us he called it a "frivolous suit." Nevertheless, by the end of June 2008, he quit hiring inmates, albeit two years after the murder.

Would a suit have been so frivolous had it been one of his family, a son perhaps, attacked and killed by an unsupervised inmate? In the event of such a violent assault, I would expect any decent employer to feel an immediate obligation to return any other inmates to jail and voluntarily quit the program.

That takes scruples, though.

CHAPTER 18

"WHICH CRIME SCENE . . . ?"

Against whom do ye sport yourselves? . . . are ye not children of transgression, a seed of falsehood. —Isaiah the Prophet

The preliminary hearing, where a judge would decide whether to send a case to trial, weighed heavily on our minds. We hoped that Nelson would breathe some life into the case instead of allowing it to continue withering away of neglect.

The Franklin County Courthouse sits on the square of Chambersburg, having replaced the original courthouse burned by Confederate forces in July 1864 during the Civil War. For those who appreciate Greek Revival architecture, the granite steps leading to the entrance of the red brick facade are graced by six towering columns, although the front entrance is rarely used. A statue of one of our founding fathers, Ben Franklin, tops the cupola on the roof, encompassed by six monstrous chimneys. The inside of the courthouse with its carpentry, fixtures, and high ceilings is in keeping with the craftsmanship of its 1865 construction.

A stodgy brick annex sits behind the old courthouse. Parking is scarce unless you are an employee of the courthouse or are handicapped. The entrance sits along the main street, known as Lincoln Way (U.S. Route 30). On the second floor, a catwalk runs above the alley connecting with the old courthouse. In 2018, county commissioners decided to raise taxes to help pay for a new 68-million-dollar courthouse that connects to the old one.

After a sleepless night, we nervously entered the annex at 8:55 A.M. on Thursday, June 19, 2008, and quietly waited before the walk-through metal detector, worried that we might be late for the 9:00 A.M. hearing by the time we got through security, up the elevators, and across the catwalk to the courtroom.

The county staffs the checkpoint with retirees to inspect possessions and check IDs if necessary. Most are courteous, but it was our luck to have a nasty one that morning. A female voice coming from a chair along the wall barked at us. "The courthouse doesn't open till 9:00. Didn't you see the sign?"

We retreated out the door looking for the sign, wondering why the door was not locked since entry was forbidden before nine o'clock. Vicky Taylor of the *Public Opinion* approached just then. "Don't go in before 9:00. There's a door witch waiting to jump you," I warned her. "The hearing is scheduled to start in a couple of minutes." Vicky entered anyway and spoke briefly with the woman, then returned for us. We went in together. By then, it was nine o'clock on the nose, so we were safe.

Vicky went to Records, and we continued upstairs and across the catwalk to the old heavy wooden door to the courtroom. I turned the knob, half expecting another rebuke. We were surprised to find only Judge Brenda Knepper in the courtroom.

"We're Carl's family," I said, my voice echoing through the empty chamber.

"Come in and sit down," she said.

Having never been in a courtroom, we sat on the wrong side.

"You might want to move to the other side," she suggested kindly.

Relocating to the prosecution's side of the courtroom, we sat there seemingly forever, listening to the silence. Trying to forget the abysmal reason we were there, I admired the judicial trappings of the high-ceilinged old room—the paintings on the soaring walls, stained glass, and long, wooden tipstaffs used years ago to poke jurors awake should they fall asleep.

By 9:20, we were shifting restlessly on the hard wooden benches when Angela Krom and Jack Nelson finally entered, along with several deputies and a chained Scott North, privileged in that he was fitted with the very first shock belt the county had ever purchased. A chain ran from his shackled ankles to the belt. No one from his family appeared. The benches were empty on the defense side of the courtroom. A courthouse staff member told us that was a rarity. Even the worst serial killers normally have some family members who appear.

It felt strange to be in the same room with Carl's killer, so close yet unable to inflict due vengeance. I hated him. Beset with anger and grief, I wondered for the millionth time if it were real. *How could this have happened? My God, what are we doing here?*

Krom seemed inappropriately cheerful. Discreetly referred to by some courthouse personnel as "the princess," she looked the part while smiling and giggling. I decided her conviction rate was likely unimpressive; otherwise, North would have received state time, making it impossible for this to have happened. Her casual demeanor before the start of a preliminary hearing for murder did nothing to inspire our confidence in her.

I had the opportunity to size up North too. He seemed reptilian, with a shaved head—flattened in the back—and protuberant jowls. I could almost see the poison sacks. He sat unmovingly but struck me as manic because of his half-closed, darting eyes—empty and cold. We prayed the hearing would launch a prosecution that would send him to the eternal prison hell he deserved.

In the case of the Commonwealth of Pennsylvania vs. Scott North, he stood before the court in a preliminary hearing charged with criminal homicide, escape, burglary, criminal trespass, theft by unlawful taking, access device fraud, forgery, abuse of a corpse, false ID to law enforcement, and fleeing or attempting to elude a police officer.

Attorneys John Abom and Ari Weitzman, a team certified to defend potential death penalty cases, represented North. They are both excellent attorneys, but under the circumstances, they were our adversaries. No matter how improbable, many defense attorneys consider their clients innocent until proven guilty. This ensures high standards in a non-biased jury trial, requiring the prosecution to prove its case through solid evidence, reliable testimony, and sound argument. Abom and Weitzman were the sort who demanded a high standard of proof against their clients.

Nelson, on the prosecutor's team, in his usual attire of suit and cowboy boots, seated himself and stared straight ahead. Krom called Warden John Wetzel to the stand. He had seated himself in the back of the courtroom against the wall. He let out an occasional booming chuckle as he ambled up the center aisle in worn black sneakers. Debbie and I looked at each other in disbelief at his attitude, given that he should have had full control over his inmate before this ever happened. None of this should have been a laughing matter, whether from Krom or Wetzel. We were, of course, highly sensitive to the courtroom dynamics. While it may have been just another day at work for them, it was devastating to us, and it was the last place we would ever have wanted to be, let alone endure jollity from officials.

Following is a summary of the hearing, based on my observations and transcripts.

THE CAPTURE

Wetzel testified that North was a Franklin County Jail inmate on work release on August 2, 2006, when he was made aware that North had not returned from his work assignment. The company had contacted the prerelease staff who administers the work program "at approximately 1:20 P.M. to notify them that Mr. North was not there." The court excused Wetzel from further testimony.

Trooper Rhyner of the Huntingdon Barracks took the stand. At Krom's prompt, he explained that during his 3:00 to 11:00 evening shift, he received information from Corporal Park regarding a person "wanted in Franklin County for walking away from work release." After receiving a report that North had just left Whitsel's Pub in Shirleysburg, driving an "older model Ford LTD," he spotted "what turned out to be a Crown Victoria, northbound on State Route 522, which has a pretty distinctive headlight configuration and is easily recognizable." He described the initial traffic stop and subsequent 100 mph, 16-mile chase, the stop strips, flying sneakers, and arrest.

On cross-examination, one of North's defense attorneys, Weitzman, questioned Rhyner about the make, model, and color of Carl's car, and if a Ford LTD is similar in appearance to a Crown Victoria, whether silver and blue are similar colors.

Rhyner explained that the "LTD was the predecessor of the Crown Victoria that is Ford's main line" and that "silver could be misconstrued for blue in the dark. A pale blue would be similar to silver."

"Other than a written statement, were there any other statements that Mr. North provided to you or to any other officers to your knowledge regarding your involvement in the case?" Weitzman asked.

"He said more than what's in the written statement if that's what you're asking," Rhyner replied.

"Just asking you generally speaking as far as what PSP protocol is, are you guys required, upon towing the vehicle, to perform an inventory search on every vehicle?" Weitzman pressed.

"Yes," Rhyner replied.

Weitzman probed the stop and search details, looking for an illegal procedure as any defense attorney would.

On redirect, Krom asked Rhyner, "Just one final question. The individual that you had contact with that night had provided to you Carl Ryder's driver's license that subsequently fled the vehicle and fled from you on foot you took into custody, do you see that individual in the courtroom today?"

"I do," Rhyner replied.

"And where is he?" Krom asked.

"Right there dressed in yellow," Rhyner pointed.

"I would ask that the record reflect that he has identified the defendant in the case, Mr. Scottie North," Krom declared.

The short testimony from Wetzel showed the exorbitant amount of time that had elapsed from North's self-proclaimed noon escape until AWI notified the prerelease staff.

Trooper Rhyner demonstrated a good memory, professionalism, a military-like discipline, *and* he had caught North in the dark immediately after learning that an inmate was on the loose. No one from the Chambersburg barracks had bothered to look, not even after being notified of his exact whereabouts the Monday after the murder or while he roamed around Chambersburg the rest of the week, all in daylight hours.

Just to clarify, Carl's car was a pale blue. Original documents for the car from when it was new identified it as blue, and it looked blue to me. As to the "other statements" North had made the night of the stop, we believe they pertained to the shotgun discovered in the car. Oddly, officials continued to avoid discussing the murder weapon, as if mere mention would draw nigh the plague.

Krom's reference to the killer as "Scottie" was startling. It was a nickname used only by those with a long and familiar association with him. Her casual reference reinforced our sense he was not far removed from being "courthouse family." The hearing began to develop a strange feeling.

Weitzman didn't have much to work with. After all, it was not as though North were a law-abiding citizen going about his business with his car and possessions. Even so, as the defense attorney sought the details of the stop and search, North's empty eyes flickered with an occasional glint of what I took to be hope that his attorney may have hit on something that would provide an upper hand.

WINDOWS

Krom called Trooper Finkle from the Chambersburg Barracks to the stand. He said he was working with Trooper Bush in the early morning hours when the Huntingdon Barracks requested a check at Carl's address in Amberson. He described the property as rural with buildings and acreage with no close neighbors.

Finkle testified that he and Trooper Bush "pulled in the parking lot (driveway) and went to the door of the trailer and knocked on the door." They "knocked multiple times" with no response, then "walked around the trailer and observed a window in the rear of the trailer that was open."

"Was this a window that, based on its size, shape, and location, someone could get into?" Krom asked.

"Yes," he said. "I just yelled at the opening of the window, knocked on the side of the trailer, negative results." Finkle described walking about a hundred yards to another property, a wood-sided house with an attached garage and a backyard abutting the mountain where an outdoor light was on. There was "a screen lying on the front porch, and a window had been opened and unlocked," he testified. "I knocked on the door numerous times, negative results."

The other half of North's defense team, Abom, cross-examined Finkle about any appearance of damage to the open window in the back of

Carl's residence, and whether it was "the kind of window, double-hung window, that slides up and down, or is it the kind that cranks out?"

Finkle described the window as having no damage, and as "one that went to the side, slid to the side, I believe."

"And could you tell whether there were any footprints or handprints just from your personal observation that made it appear that somebody climbed into the window?" Abom asked.

"I don't recall," Finkle said.

With approval from their supervisor, Finkle and Bush had forced open the back door to enter Carl's residence. Abom asked Finkle whether he took "special precautions before entering by wearing gloves and booties." Finkle could not recall whether he wore gloves but said he did not wear booties.

When asked why they did not enter the front door, Finkle described it as locked and the back door as "a little weaker."

"Did Trooper Bush, to your recollection, take any precautionary steps to put on booties or gloves or any sort of outer garments to prevent any sort of possible contamination of evidence at the scene?" Abom pressed, but Finkle did not recall.

Abom asked if they made "other observations of other possible pieces of evidence as to a clue as to where Carl Ryder could be found?"

Finkle explained that they "just looked on the chest and the table" and saw an open "notebook" with "stuff written on it, mail with Carl Ryder's name on." Finkle denied touching or moving anything.

Switching residences, Abom asked whether they got "inside the cabin" and whether there were "signs of forced entry."

"Yes, I believe on the window you could see pry marks," Finkle said.

In reply to additional bootie and glove questions, Finkle testified, "[T]he two times that I was in I didn't have booties on. I don't know if after I left if anyone else wore booties."

"And who took over the collection of the evidence? Who supervised the evidence collection team then?" Abom asked, but Finkle said he didn't know.

"Prior to this case, had you ever been involved in investigating burglaries and break-ins to residences?" Abom asked.

"Yes," Finkle said.

Neither the defense nor prosecution had anything further, and Finkle left the stand.

Recalling his aggressive behavior in Carl's driveway that "first day," I was not thrilled to see smart-aleck Finkle again, and his poor recall was vexing. In some instances, it was nil, and in some inaccurate. Carl's window opened up and down instead of sliding to the side as he testified, and there were pry marks on the frame. We never learned whether police processed Carl's window for fingerprints.

His testimony that the porch light was on at the cabin that sits above and to the left of Carl's place confirmed what we had thought initially and stirred a feeling of unease. If it was on when Carl arrived home, it would have drawn his attention. A distraction would have been to North's advantage. It was chilling the extent to which North had made himself at home at Carl's place, even locking the door while he was out running the roads after he had killed him.

The glove and bootie questions indicated Abom was searching for contamination. My gripe had never been contamination of the crime scene. It was their refusal to acknowledge it as a crime scene in the first place.

BLOODY BOOK

Krom called Trooper Butler of the Huntingdon Barracks to the stand. He had been involved in getting a search warrant for Carl's vehicle. The search produced 60 items that police logged into inventory and onto a property record.

At Krom's prompt, Butler described, "a small address book, and inside the address book was a prison ID of Scott North, and the address book had what appeared to be blood on the outside of [it]."

"Also, on that inventory, does there appear a notation for a trunk liner?" Krom asked.

"Yes." Butler described it as "a fibrous type of carpet that's laid in the entire trunk. It's part of the vehicle." He explained that he took it because there was "a significant amount of blood on it."

Butler named additional listed items taken from the car and belonging to Carl: an "M&T check card," "a Bank of America Visa," and a "Walmart receipt."

Krom had nothing further. The other 54 items that police had removed from the car were never described, including the hushed-up matter of the shotgun.

On cross-examination, Abom persisted with questions pertaining to possible contamination. "[W]hen you processed this vehicle, were you wearing gloves and other kinds of protective items so as not to contaminate?"

"Gloves," Butler replied, and when prompted, testified that he was unaware of any other troopers or law enforcement officers being in the vehicle before executing the search.

Abom had no further questions. Krom had no redirect, and the court excused Butler.

The bloody address book that held North's print in Carl's blood, the one Ford had told us North wanted back in the worst way, would later prove to be a source of further contention between the officials and us.

BLUNT FORCE

Krom called Corporal Sneath from the Huntingdon Barracks to the stand. A rather large man with blondish hair and a quiet demeanor, Sneath testified that he, Corporal Brown, and patrol troopers had responded to the scene after discovering Carl's body in Blairs Mills in Huntingdon County.

"Could you describe for us the scene or the location where the body was found?" she asked.

"The body was actually found on a pipeline. This was all woods except for the pipeline itself, which was cleared, and as I said, it was very rural. Farm area, and up the road from it and down the road from it, as I said, there were really no homes or any residences in the area where the body was found," Sneath said.

He described the location of Carl's body as "down the hill, beside a tree with a tree pulled over top of it. It appeared to be as if it was attempted to be concealed. The body was in an advanced state of decay at that time. The clothing was on the body, one shoe was missing from the body."

"At what point did you learn positively whose remains these were?" Krom asked.

Sneath said that Doctor Scanlon out of Lewistown identified the body "as that of Carl Ryder's and was identified by dental records."

"Now, when Doctor Kamerow writes his autopsy report, does he refer to the individual as Carl Ryder?" Krom persisted.

"Yes," Sneath replied.

"And what does Doctor Kamerow list as the cause of death in this case?" Krom asked.

"Blunt force trauma," he said.

"That's all," Krom said confidently.

A smug look crossed North's face as Krom emphasized what we believed was an unsupported and speculative cause of death. At the mention of "blunt force trauma," the back of his neck arched, his chin dropped to his chest, and his lower jaw fell open. He leaned forward, planted his elbows on his knees, and entwined his fingers. A self-congratulatory look crossed his face as he gazed at the floor. He knew they were wrong, and so did we.

At that moment, Abom dropped a stack of papers. North snatched them off the floor with a huge smile. I hoped it was a bad omen that defense records had fallen and hit bottom. Even so, we felt the case would decline from there. Prosecutors had created a hole for North to slither through, undermining their efforts.

Weitzman cross-examined Sneath about the autopsy and hillside crime scene. "At what point in time did you have contact with Doctor Kamerow?"

"I had spoken to Doctor Kamerow numerous times about this case. I remember speaking to him—probably within the last year, I have spoken with him numerous times since then. He did a lot of autopsies in Huntingdon County, and I spoke of this case often," Sneath said.

"Am I correct in saying that the autopsy report actually was not generated until after July of 2007? A year later?" asked Weitzman.

"Yes, sir," answered Sneath.

"Am I correct in also saying that the report reads that Doctor Ka-merow elected to not write the report until he had spoken with you?" Weitzman asked.

"Yes," Sneath concurred.

"The report prepared opines that blunt force trauma occurred; is that correct?" Weitzman asked.

"Yes," Sneath said.

"Can you tell us what blunt force trauma means?" Weitzman persisted.

"Just trauma," Sneath replied.

Krom objected, "This is beyond the scope of his expertise. Doctor Kamerow will have to be examined with respect to that."

The judge upheld the objection.

"Just as a question to the Commonwealth," Weitzman asked, "I sup-pose, are any other witnesses being put on the stand regarding the autopsy?"

"No," Krom replied.

Weitzman turned his attention back to Sneath, "[H]ow did you guys find this decedent . . . when you guys responded to the crime scene?"

"Which crime scene are you talking about?" Krom interjected.

"The crime scene where the body was found," Weitzman said.

"We received a telephone call from an Angel Burdge," Sneath replied.

"Would you be able to find conclusive proof to indicate that the body had, in fact, traveled down rather than being brought down? Could you see—did you check the side of the hill for any kind of marks that would have indicated the body traveled down that path?" Weitzman asked.

"Yes, like the grass, the weeds were laid down like it was drug [sic] down through there," Sneath said.

"That's been photographed?" Weitzman continued.

"Yes," Sneath replied.

With no further questions, the court excused Corporal Sneath.

The court called a fifteen-minute recess, and Nelson moved in his seat. He had sat so still during the proceedings that I had forgotten about him. We remained in the courtroom during the short break discussing Krom's "which crime scene" question. They had acknowledged only the secondary hillside scene for so long, where no evidence existed, that it caught us off guard that she would ask for clarification of which crime scene. I kept my back to North to avoid expending energy fighting the temptation to go after him.

The mention of the autopsy and "blunt force trauma" would remain a murky hole-and-corner that had been foolishly spotlighted. We argued vehemently against it, and it remained a source of disagreement between the prosecutors and us. We viewed Kamerow's report as an erroneous guess caused by the investigators' outrageous failure to provide evidence they had from the beginning. We also saw no reason for Kamerow to speak with police about it a year after the murder when both continued to ignore the shotgun or for Krom to object that it was beyond the trooper's expertise, yet not subpoena an expert to testify. Could it be because North shot Carl with the shotgun, which they had been going out of their way to ignore?

CHAPTER 19

DNA

And if he smite him with an instrument of iron, so that he die, he is a murderer: the murderer shall surely be put to death. —Moses

We returned to the wooden benches in the gallery after the break and listened intently as testimony resumed.

Sneath returned to the witness stand under Abom's questioning. "The autopsy, I know you said that the cause of death when you testified on direct was blunt force trauma. When I looked at the final anatomical diagnosis, it says, cause of death homicidal act. Can you explain how the cause of death is either a homicidal act or blunt force trauma?"

"The blunt force trauma is a homicidal act. All the circumstances listed, Doctor Kamerow listed the cause as homicidal act from the blunt force trauma," Sneath explained.

Abom inferred that it "wasn't simply evidence gleaned from the decedent during the course of the autopsy, but actually the police report and information . . . collected regarding other items of evidence and other statements that were made." He conjectured, "Blunt force trauma conceivably somebody could—I'm not saying it was a car accident here, but somebody could die of blunt force trauma in a car accident, correct?"

Sneath agreed.

"Did the autopsy—did the pathologist make an effort in his report to determine what caused the blunt force trauma?" Abom pressed.

"Efforts were made to determine that," Sneath replied.

"And could you testify to the court here today what caused the blunt force trauma?" Abom asked.

"That is undetermined as to exactly what caused the trauma due to the advanced state of decomposition," Sneath said.

Abom had nothing further. Krom had no redirect, and Corporal Sneath was excused.

Knowing looks passed between us as the alarming autopsy testimony drove the sting of injustice deeper. Ignoring the real murder weapon and using an erroneous cause of death meant little chance of bringing the case to a first- or second-degree murder prosecution and dangerously close to opening the door for lesser charges and a reduced sentence. The "other items of evidence and statements" remained unnamed and didn't seem to interest the prosecutors. We viewed North's previous out-of-court accounts and excuses as lies. Testimony seemed to consist of nothing but speculation, and it did not belong in court. We knew North could claim anything now; any scenario of self-defense, accident, or weapon would do.

CABIN BURGLARY

Krom called Corporal Ford (he had been promoted) to the stand. He was assigned to the case on August 11, 2006, and we had been told that he would remain on the case even though it was transferred to Huntingdon. As Ford described it, it was "sort of a joint investigation" between the Chambersburg and Huntingdon barracks with Sneath as the "other lead investigator," although Ford would later testify that he "pursued the investigation" for what amounted to five days when he was "no longer lead investigator," that is "until the case came back to Franklin County."

"At some point during the investigation did you collect a soil sample from Mr. Ryder's front yard, for lack of a better word?" Krom asked.

"Yes." Ford said he "received a call from one of the family members that had noticed it." He and Trooper Bush went to the scene and there "appeared to be something on the ground that had actually either killed the grass or had dried and turned the grass brown, so we gathered that sample. . . . "[E]ventually, it was sent to the Harrisburg lab. If you want the steps, I will gladly tell you," Ford offered.

"Let's stick to—let's stick to what we have results for, but what other pieces of evidence did you send to the lab to have analyzed for DNA?" Krom asked.

"The trunk liner from Trooper Butler's search warrant was sent for DNA. The address book was sent for DNA analysis and the soil sample." Ford said.

"So then with respect to—let's start with the soil sample. Did the DNA analysis make a positive or a conclusion as to what was contained within that soil sample?" Krom asked.

"Yes. There was a positive identification that blood in the soil sample was, in fact, matched the DNA match of Carl Ryder's DNA," Ford said.

"How about with respect to the address book?" she asked.

"Again, the blood found—the bloodstain found on the page of the address book matched the one they got a DNA—matched the DNA of Carl Ryder," Ford said, continuing to stumble through answers to the questions.

"And with respect to the trunk liner?" she pressed.

"Once again, the blood was profiled, the DNA profile matched Carl Ryder's They were both—once again, the trunk liner DNA, the blood in that matched Carl Ryder's DNA," Ford stammered.

When asked if he found anything unusual about Carl's shoes, Ford said that he viewed Carl's body along Allison Road and noticed a missing shoe and that they had found a second shoe in a field at Carl's place. "The shoes appeared—the shoe found on Carl Ryder—the match seemed to be the shoe that we found at his residence located in the field close to his yard, yes," he replied awkwardly.

"Do you know who the last person was to have contact with Mr. Ryder?" Krom asked.

"Deb (Carl's girlfriend) called him on August 5, '06 at, I believe, 9:29 P.M. There were other calls made after that. The last person I could confirm that spoke with Mr. Ryder was Deborah," Ford replied.

Ford testified that Diana Hennessy had been at the cabin on August 4 and 5, 2006, when she found that certain items had been disturbed. He recalled, "a backpack and the one with the horse on it had the ID of what she believed to be the name of Scott North inside the backpack."

Diana later identified it as one she had purchased for her kids. Police found the backpack in Carl's trailer on August 11, 2006, and entered it into evidence.

Other things were out of place in the cabin. Ford testified, "[A]n air conditioner was running, a fan was on, there was a paper plate with what [Diana] believed to be crumbs on it, breadcrumbs, and it looked like someone had slept on top of one of the beds in the cabin."

"Do you recognize this document?" Krom asked.

"Yes, I do," Ford replied. "That is—it's kind of hard to explain. A Coin Star voucher from the Food Lion located at 410 Philadelphia Avenue on 8/7/06 at 9:28 P.M.

"Basically, how this works," Ford began, "and I didn't know it until I actually started this investigation, inside the Food Lion is a machine, which you can dump change into. They obviously charge you for the use of the machine, but once you put all the change in, it prints out, from what I gather, this voucher and you go to the cashier, and they charge you for that, but then they give you the money, paper money, U.S. Currency."

Ford had obtained surveillance footage from Food Lion and determined that North had operated the Coin Star machine into which he dumped Carl's coins ($87.84) on August 7, 2006. "Yes, I can identify—it's using—him using the Coin Star machine to retrieve that amount of money," he said.

"From your investigation, were you able to determine where Mr. North had obtained these coins?" Krom asked.

"Yes, I mean, obviously, he escaped from prison and had a large amount of change. In Carl Ryder's residence, he had a very large cooler, like a cooler to keep soda and water in, and it was filled with rolled U.S. currency coins," Ford said.

Shifting from the stolen coins to the hillside site, Krom asked Ford about the May 8, 2008, interview with North, whether "during the course of that interview did he have any information with respect to how Mr. Ryder's body came to be located where it was found in Tell Township, Huntingdon County?"

"He related to me that he placed the body where we found it on August 16, 2006," Ford replied.

"Did Mr. North indicate to you when he put the body at its final location?" she asked.

"Other than he did it in the evening hours, that's all I can recall at this point," he said.

"Did he indicate to you *how?*" Krom pressed further.

"When it was dark," he replied.

"Did he indicate to you *how* he came to choose that particular location or why he chose that particular location?" she reworded.

"I don't believe. I don't recall why he picked that location," Ford said.

Krom requested a moment. It seemed an eternity as we watched her attempt to unearth something from her satchel. Nelson eventually glanced sideways in her direction. At long last, without retrieving anything, she stated that she had nothing further. Whatever she was looking for, she had not found. Any smidgeon of momentum that had existed was gone, lending a feel of unpreparedness to the proceeding.

I don't know why Krom used the phrase "for lack of a better word" when she asked about the collection of a soil sample from Carl's front yard. Her wording made it seem that either it was not a soil sample, or it was not a front yard. It seemed to introduce confusion for no reason when both plainly existed—unless it was a personal comment implying that a trailer home could not have a real front yard.

Ford's choppy testimony was devoid of detail. When asked "how" Carl was dumped, his vague reply "when it was dark" suggested an indifference to details as an investigating officer. Not bothering to review the interview information beforehand to recall important details to provide the court is unprofessional. He should have been *sure* he did not know a more specific time of when the dumping occurred and why North chose the location. I would think that when interviewing someone about dumping a body, those would be among the most important questions. Just as appalling, investigators had forensically confirmed only three of thirteen known bloody items, by that time, as having Carl's DNA on them.

On cross-examination, Abom asked Ford whether there was any "physical forensic evidence that ties Mr. North to being inside that cabin?"

"We have evidence from a window of two latent prints on the window," Ford said.

"So, there is two latent prints that you have that come back to Mr. North, and they're on the window of the cabin?" Abom pressed.

"We have two latent prints on the window that are currently at the Harrisburg laboratory. I don't know whose prints they are," Ford said.

"So, it's clear to the judge, while you might have some latent fingerprints, they're not established they're Mr. North's fingerprints; is that correct?" Abom asked.

"That's correct," Ford said.

"Back to my original question. Any forensic evidence to establish that Mr. North was inside the cabin?" Abom asked.

"No," Ford replied.

Abom asked whether it was fair to say that police vehicles had potentially driven over and destroyed evidence that may have been on the ground outside before police placed barricade tape. Ford admitted that vehicles had driven up close to the residence, but he did not know if they had driven over anything.

"At what point did you relinquish custody of the trailer?" Abom asked.

"I did not. The Huntingdon County District Attorney did that," Ford said, with seeming relief that it was not his carelessness being spotlighted.

"Were you able to establish, through the course of the investigation, who actually killed Carl Ryder?" Abom asked.

"Yes," Ford replied.

Abom asked if it was "through circumstantial evidence of other things, not as to specifically how it happened?"

"I don't know the exact definition of circumstantial evidence and what isn't. So, I can't really answer that question," Ford said.

The major drift of Abom's questioning ended, and Krom had no redirect. The Commonwealth rested.

I broke out in a sweat when I learned that latent prints from the cabin were still at the lab. That meant that they had just recently submitted evidence as basic as fingerprints almost two years into the case. And there was no reason police should not have had other forensic evidence that North had been in the cabin. I am sure DNA from North was on the backpacks he stole, the plate he ate from, and the bed he slept on.

There was no mention of the bloody tarp we had stored, the shotgun barrel police had left uncollected in the shed, the slug belatedly removed from the wall, the uncollected sabots, or the knife we had found beside a large drop of blood on the bathroom countertop. Nor did they mention all the times we had to call investigators back to the property to investigate, collect, or not collect. They did an abominable job of investigating and preparing for the hearing with no weapon or motive named, no plan to subpoena expert witnesses, and evidence still at the lab. They had initially taken a slight interest in the shotgun, tracing it through several owners to the dealer, but strangely abandoned it as evidence and neglected to send it to forensics. And it was pathetic that a state police lead investigator would claim he did not know the "exact definition" of circumstantial evidence.

REQUEST FOR DISMISSAL

In his legal comeback, Abom agreed that the Commonwealth had established most of the charges except for the two most substantial charges of burglary and homicide. "At best, there is some circumstantial evidence that, it seems to me, receipts that were established that Mr. North obtained in purchasing items on August 7 and 8 and were later found inside the trailer. There is no evidence that he was not authorized to be there, so that goes to the trespass, but ultimately, if Mr. North was there and went inside that trailer, he could have gone there and once inside, if he had formed an intent to take something, that wouldn't be a burglary, that would be a trespass and a later theft."

Abom contended that the Commonwealth needed to establish a break-in to establish a second-degree felony. "There is no evidence of any break-in at the trailer at all. I mean, a window was open in the back, but that could have been opened because it was too hot inside, but there is no evidence of a break-in.

"There is no evidence that he was inside the cabin, and I gather we heard that there are two fingerprints they are now sending off to the lab. And certainly, even if he was inside, it doesn't establish a burglary. At best, it's a trespass because you have to enter with the intent to commit a crime inside.

"And, finally, regarding the homicide itself. Cause of death was blunt force trauma, but the Commonwealth has not established how that happened, when that happened, and who caused that blunt force trauma. I can see there is circumstantial evidence that Mr. North came into possession of Mr. Ryder's belongings, and even including Mr. Ryder, himself, after he was deceased. However, to establish a homicide, the Commonwealth must establish that Mr. North intentionally, knowingly, recklessly, or negligently caused Mr. Ryder's death. They haven't established that at all, whatsoever."

Abom requested a dismissal of the homicide and burglary charges, insisting that they had not met a *prima facie* burden because they had not established that North killed Carl.

Krom argued that they established *prima facie* evidence, specifically circumstantial evidence. She said, "to determine what someone's intent is at the time they make the entry into the location that is burglarized, in this case, the trailer and the cabin, we have to look at the circumstantial evidence. Individual's intent is not necessarily painted on their face at the time they entered, so you must look at what they did at the time they entered.

"In this case with respect to entry into the cabin, did Mr. North enter—did he eat some food? Maybe he ate some food. Did he sleep on the bed? Maybe he slept on the bed, but what he did do was place his prison ID in a backpack that was viewed by Diana Hennessy on either the fourth or fifth of August of 2006, and then he took that backpack out of the residence. So, we have been able to establish through Diana Hennessy's observation of her child's backpack having Mr. North's prison identification in it that he removed that backpack because it was later found in Mr. Ryder's trailer. So, through that circumstantial evidence, the Commonwealth can establish his intent at the time was to commit a theft.

"Moving onto the trailer, burglary does not require that an individual forcefully enter into a residence. They don't have to break locks; they don't have to break windows. If they enter through a window, that is still a burglary, and when Mr. North entered Mr. Ryder's cabin (she meant trailer), he used then his driver's license to falsely represent himself to the Pennsylvania State Police, he used his credit cards to obtain goods, personal items. He used the coins—he took the coins out of the residence. We have receipts showing that he used those coins at various locations to convert them to paper currency. Each of those things would support Mr. North's intent to commit a crime inside the trailer of Mr. Ryder. Not only that, but at the time that Mr. North was stopped and apprehended by Trooper Rhyner, he admitted that he had been staying at Ryder's cabin (trailer), and at that time had Mr. Ryder's phone, Mr. Ryder's car, Mr. Ryder's credit cards, Mr. Ryder's driver's license, all those things taken from the residence (Carl's phone, license, and credit cards were taken from his person after he was murdered).

"With respect to the charge of criminal homicide, the Commonwealth has established through circumstantial evidence that Mr. North had—was in possession of Mr. Ryder's vehicle. Inside Mr. Ryder's vehicle was an address book, Mr. North's address book that contained Mr. North's prison identification. On that address book was blood positively identified by the Pennsylvania State Police crime lab as a DNA match to Mr. Ryder.

"So, we have got Mr. North driving Mr. Ryder's vehicle," Krom continued, "with an address book, with Mr. North's prison identification in it with Mr. Ryder's blood on it. The police then obtained the trunk liner from the trunk of Mr. Ryder's vehicle. According to Trooper Butler, that liner had a substantial quantity of blood in the trunk. That's why the trunk liner was obtained. It was processed, and it was determined that the blood in the trunk was Mr. Ryder's blood.

"The state police also obtained a soil sample from outside of Mr. Ryder's residence, just outside of Mr. Ryder's residence. That soil contained Mr. Ryder's blood. All of these things, circumstantially, along with the fact that Mr. North has admitted being at Mr. Ryder's residence, is in possession of Mr. Ryder's belongings, and when questioned, indicated that he had, in fact, placed Mr. Ryder's body at the location where it was found in Tell Township, Allison Road, Tell Township in Huntingdon, produced sufficient evidence for this court to determine that there is *prima facie* evidence of criminal homicide," she finished.

It was up to Judge Knepper. Shabby as some of the forensics was, at that point, would the judge consider the "circumstantial evidence" substantial enough to continue to trial, or would she dismiss it? Strong components were missing that could easily have been established early on. We sat tensely in our seats, scarcely drawing breath as if doing so might jinx the outcome for which we so desperately hoped. It was only a few seconds but seemed an eternity before she spoke.

"This case will go to the Franklin County Common Pleas Court. Your next court date will be July 30 for mandatory arraignment, and your bail will remain the same," Judge Knepper announced.

The heavy air lightened some. It was up to Nelson and Krom to try North on criminal homicide, escape, burglary, and the lesser charges.

The prosecution was inept, but Krom's characterization of burglary was accurate. Intent is not "painted" on a perpetrator's face. North did all those things, including murder. Even with important evidence not yet forensically processed by the time of the hearing nearly two years after the crimes, and some not yet used or discovered, the judge found sufficient evidence for trial.

It was a relief when Krom called us to the back of the courtroom. No one had communicated with us about the case, except more than a year earlier in May 2007 when Nelson forbade contact with the media, but we should have guessed what she would say.

"Don't talk to anyone about this case," Krom warned.

"Will this be prosecuted as a first-degree murder?" I asked, trying to hide my disappointment that her only concern was that we keep our mouths shut. "He said he was going to kill Carl and did it as an escapee during the commission of a burglary. He stole his car and other things."

"Well, I guess you must've read up on things, and that's how you know about court procedures," she remarked.

"Well, *you* put someone like Scott North out there, and look what happened," I said, barely containing my anger at her condescending response to a reasonable question.

She had nothing to offer but an insult and a command to keep quiet. Our first impression was confirmed. We felt Krom and Nelson were not really interested in prosecution and preferred that we dumb country rubes stay uninvolved and keep our mouths shut. Yet, we knew much more about the details of the compromised case than they ever realized. Our relief that the judge had ordered the case to trial was quickly dissipated by Krom's arrogance.

Though the judge had ordered the case to trial, that in no way meant it would make it that far. It was up to them, and we knew we would never have a say in it. We still felt they would seize any means to make it go away, as they had from the beginning.

It was June 24, Carl's birthday, and five miserable days since the preliminary hearing. We met at Mom's for dinner and discussed whether it would be in our best interest to attempt to have Krom removed from the case since, in a roundabout way, she had had a hand in North's release before he killed Carl. We didn't want Nelson on the case either.

But we lacked the mental and emotional stamina to put up a fight. Under extreme stress, some of us had experienced subtle personality changes, detachment from who we had known ourselves to be, and disorienting moments of not knowing who we were. They were episodes triggered by severe stress that psychologists would call derealization. It was a bewildering feeling.

A surprise call from Ford later that week clued us that they might be examining evidence. Ford and Trooper Frampton were at Carl's place to retrieve the tarp that Clint and I had stowed away almost two years earlier. "Where's that rubber tarp?" he asked.

"It's in the barn, folded and to the right—just inside the door," I said.

"Where on it is the handprint and sneaker print?" he asked upon retrieving it from the barn.

"Unfold about half of it, and you'll see a large pool of dried blood, and beside it, you'll see a bloody sneaker print and a palm print," I instructed. The tarp was black, and after two years, I suspected blood would be difficult to see without knowing exactly how it had been partially unfolded when Clint and I had first examined it. "What are you doing with it?" I asked.

"We're taking it with us. Do you still have those socks?" Ford asked, referring to the jail-issued socks we had discovered in August 2006.

"No, Clint got rid of them a year ago," I said. "We asked. You didn't want them."

CHAPTER 20

"IF YOU SEE ONE OF US LAUGHING . . ."

Who led thee through that great and terrible wilderness, wherein were fiery serpents . . . ? —Moses

Six weeks after the hearing, we received a call to meet with Jack Nelson and Angela Krom on July 17, 2008. As we stepped off the elevator, Nelson exited the restroom and walked by without acknowledging us. We met up with our victim/witness coordinator and Ford and wordlessly situated ourselves around an ugly, faux woodgrain conference table. Nelson entered and eyed each of us. We stared back as Krom slid into a chair.

"Just because it seems like nothing is going on doesn't mean we're not working on the case," he began. "Now, if you see one of us laughing, that doesn't mean we're not taking this serious."

We were unsure whether Nelson referred to Wetzel's inappropriate chuckles or Krom's giggles in the courtroom at the hearing six weeks earlier. Since he mentioned it, we later speculated that someone besides ourselves had found their lack of decorum offensive and wondered if the judge had dealt a private reprimand over the unprofessional display. It certainly was a jarring experience.

"Are you planning to file a notice of aggravating circumstance?" I asked, aware of the limited amount of time they had after filing murder charges to announce their intention to pursue a death penalty case. Receiving no reply, I asked, "Who's the judge on this case?"

"Judge Herman," Krom said as she lounged sideways along the edge of the table, head in hand.

I had expected it to be John Walker, the presiding judge whose court the gun charge had been dropped against North just days before his escape and murder. We learned little from the meeting. They ignored most of our questions and presented no outline of prosecution or length of time it might require. We confronted a wall of prosecutorial secrecy, unable to get answers, even with several of us attending, and they did not volunteer information. Even though we had a right to know at least some of what was going on, we learned only that they were working on the case, the name of the assigned judge, and that if we saw one of them laughing, it didn't mean they weren't "taking this serious."

"Keep this under your hat," Ford reminded us as we left the meeting.

What's to keep under our hat? I wondered. They had denied the crime scene for almost two years, shoved the case around, and belatedly sent evidence to the lab—some they never sent at all and some we discovered and stored ourselves.

Later that week, Ford interviewed two inmates at the Franklin County Jail. The minimal information I squeezed from him was that one interview backed up another, indicating North was lying. Disturbed by the amount of evidence that had not been processed, we contacted Dr. Symes at Mercyhurst College and discovered he still had Carl's clothing. The state police had led us to believe they had it, as also documented on Dr. Kamerow's autopsy report. Instead, Carl's T-shirt, right shoe, and denim shorts had remained in Erie, which meant the state police had never forensically analyzed the items.

Furthermore, Dr. Symes imparted that he was not pleased with the quality of the photos taken during the 2006 autopsy. After we forcefully complained to Krom that Carl's clothing was still with the anthropologist, the state police collected it in mid-July 2008. We couldn't help but think they had no intention of sending his clothing to the lab.

That month, a rumor rumbled through the valley that Scott North had escaped, and police were hunting him in an unmarked car. Why unmarked, I don't know. Phones were ringing, and people were riled up and armed, ready to take on this killer should he come their way. A retired state police member from the valley said it was a different Scott North. That was hard to believe, especially since we learned that a guard had "lost" a handcuff key that was later found on North during a strip search.

After the escape mystery, family and friends requested leave to attend the July 30, 2008, mandatory arraignment, but someone had failed to issue a transport order to move North from Greensburg State Prison to the Franklin County Jail. We received an exasperating call from the coordinator the afternoon before, telling us *not* to show up at court. We still had a lingering suspicion that North had escaped from an earlier transport. The court rescheduled the arraignment for August 6, 2008, two years and one day since the murder.

Sleep had been hit or miss since the meeting and the escape rumor. In fact, lack of sleep had been the norm for a long time, but any dealings with the officials always made it worse. One night, seesawing between wakefulness and weariness, I saw Carl sitting on the stone wall behind my house. He had no shirt on, a rarity since he considered it rude to be shirtless in front of people. He favored colorful T-shirts in the summer and flannel button-down shirts in the winter, but he had neither during this visit.

I went straight to him and laid my hands on his shoulder and arm. "I haven't seen you for so long!" I exclaimed. I awoke the moment I touched him, and my hands felt as if they were on fire. I stuffed them under my pillow, thinking to smother it, but it grew worse, so I flicked on the light and saw raised, burning welts on my palms. Thinking I had a bad case of poison oak, I ran downstairs to find something to put on the welts, but they disappeared as quickly as they had materialized. By touching Carl, I had regrettably ended our happy but brief reunion in the spirit. I quickly landed back in our grim reality, but his visit fortified my belief in the eternal soul, thankfully something Scott North could never destroy.

Clint had a similar experience the same night. He was asleep when he saw Carl without a shirt and noticed scars on his shoulder and arm. Carl turned to him and said, "He got me under the lungs."

It was no coincidence that Carl visited us both. It was strange that he visited without a shirt and that I laid my hands where Clint saw scars. Carl mentioned the location of the first wound that had ripped through him from the side. He seemingly knew what was brewing at the courthouse and how badly they had botched the case. He was entitled to justice, but it might not be forthcoming.

The scars stirred thoughts of Blairs Mills, where North had pulled Carl from the car's trunk. A body roughly dragged across the asphalt and stony berm would receive abrasions and cuts. The autopsy report noted torn clothes, likely the result of being loaded and unloaded. The brutal handling could have been the cause of the hip dislocation that police had mentioned initially.

Meanwhile, Krom requested additional time to determine whether she would file a notice of aggravating circumstances, normally done by the time of the mandatory arraignment. She had to wait for DNA results from items that police failed to send to the lab two years earlier. According to Pennsylvania Rules of Criminal Procedure, North's defense team was required to file an answer to the petition within ten days.

In response, North's attorneys referred to the case Commonwealth vs. Wesley: "Trial courts must not permit the Commonwealth to amend a rule when the effect will be to prejudice the defendant's ability to defend against the aggravating circumstance and when the prosecution was aware of the aggravating circumstance before arraignment and offered no good cause for its untimely notification."

While Krom awaited DNA testing results, North's attorneys argued that it was not possible to effectively answer the petition because of lack of specificity or even determine whether good cause had been shown. Moreover, they had not received discovery, were unaware of when the Commonwealth first received the DNA, or when Krom requested additional testing, and what if anything it might reveal as it related to the Commonwealth's ability to prove that North murdered during the perpetration of a felony.

The court authorized spending up to $5000 for forensic pathologist services for the defense and transported North from Greensburg State Prison to Franklin County, where on August 6, he waived his arraignment and entered a not guilty plea. The court set a November trial date.

Ford called us a few days later. "Is there anything that you want tested that could have been used as a weapon?"

Since he had told us "the slug is clean, it isn't what killed Carl," and they refused to talk about the shotgun, I reluctantly suggested a splitting maul that had been near the deck when the killing occurred. I didn't believe that was the weapon, but according to Ford, a murder weapon did not exist.

In the meantime, North's attorneys filed motions for more time to prepare a defense. The court rescheduled the trial term to the January 2009 trial term. I tried to contact Nelson several times following the July meeting, but he never returned my calls. I commented to the coordinator that it seemed as if a plea bargain was in the works; otherwise, at the least, prosecutors would delve into a motive. The theft of Carl's guns and North's subsequent firing were the catalyst for vengeance and should have been an integral part of the investigation in establishing a motive. No one was interested in the fact that North had said he would kill Carl and throw his body somewhere.

In September 2008, North requested a copy of the autopsy report and photographs "to be used to help build a defense." A short time later, Ford enthusiastically revealed that an inmate acquainted with North had sent a letter to the courthouse. "It's good information about a struggle, and it's up to Angela Krom to decide if she wants to divulge the contents to you," Ford said.

What's good about it? I wondered. It felt like the makings of a self-defense claim. North had seized on the prosecution's supposed ignorance of the cause of death and then concocted a new scenario to share with his jail buddy, defense, and prosecution. It was troubling how eagerly the police and prosecution were to accept lies as if they lacked solid evidence to the contrary. Nevertheless, we grew a little hopeful when the court permitted the prosecution more time to file a notice of aggravating circumstances, which might open the door to a death penalty case.

～～

In the meantime, our attorneys, AWI attorneys, and Judge Van Horn held a hearing on the survivor suit on October 2, 2008. We felt Van Horn should have recused herself since she had granted North the opportunity for work release that led to the escape and murder in the first place. According to the Pennsylvania Code of Judicial Conduct, "judges should disqualify themselves in a proceeding in which their impartiality might reasonably be questioned."

Our attorneys argued in court that North's escape was foreseeable because of his history and because the employer chose not to supervise him. In addition, stressors such as having no home address, no money, no car, and being wanted, could prompt a felon on the run to become more dangerous, especially one who is prone to violence.

The company's attorneys argued that his escape was not foreseeable because the county is not supposed to put violent criminals on work release.

Judge Van Horn would rule within thirty days. We were sure it would be politically expedient—in favor of the company, which would also relieve the county and state of any embarrassing publicity. We held little hope for victory in an uphill battle because of the ramifications of opening the way for liability or punitive damages. It would be easier to just quickly close the can of worms.

Our attorneys felt it would be challenging yet possible, to find a third party negligent for what an individual did because the third party was extremely negligent.

By the end of the month, Van Horn ruled, "[N]o special relationship existed between [North] and [AWI]. The fact that North was permitted to participate in the Franklin County work release program indicates that he was not suspected to be a highly dangerous person; therefore, [AWI] would have no duty to protect [Carl] from [North's] actions."

She said work release provides a service of "social utility" to the county, as well as to the inmates who are permitted to participate in the program, and it was not reasonably foreseeable that North would walk off the job after being cleared to participate in the work release program and "allegedly kill Carl."

Van Horn ruled that imposing a duty to supervise inmates would place additional burdens and costs on employers, and providing "security guards" would not serve the public interest but instead would "discourage participation in an integral component of the criminal justice system in Franklin County."

She granted AWI's preliminary objections and dismissed our case, with prejudice which meant we wouldn't be allowed to refile. We felt her ruling was a brush-off, and her reasons vague with underlying bias. The issue was whether the company was legally responsible under common law negligence. Pennsylvania law on joint liability holds that if one party is 1 percent liable and the other 99 percent liable, the entire liability falls to the one who can compensate. The company could be held liable only if North was considered likely to hurt others or act violently or if the company had personal knowledge, North could be dangerous.

We felt the duty created by the contract between Franklin County and the company as a work-release participant had been breached; however, the judge cleared the company and county of liability. The county would have been liable only if we could establish that they knew North was violent and still put him in the work-release program. It is difficult to believe they were not aware of his violent propensities and executing escapes with his history.

Our attorneys regarded Van Horn's ruling as an attempt to quash the suit. We felt we were right in viewing the county and AWI as negligent; both had carelessly set this ugly tragedy in motion. Van Horn denied our right to a discovery that would have allowed us to perhaps uncover damning material regarding North's murderous intentions, for instance, the details of the "you're done" writings allegedly directed at Carl, which were found in North's Franklin County Jail cell after his escape. Ford now said they were just "dark poems."

During the murder "investigation," a story surfaced that North had left the worksite because he received a phone call that one of his kids was sick, although inmates on work duty are not permitted private calls. True to form, he blamed someone else for his actions, even if the call he received could be construed as abetting an escape. Krom told us the story had been verified, although details remain under wraps. Our requests to see investigative reports have consistently been denied. There are two kids and two mothers connected with North; coincidently, one mother is the daughter of a retired state trooper.

Since Van Horn had dismissed our case against AWI, our attorneys proceeded with the suit against North only for the time being. They had stipulated all the facts, so there would be no reason for the judge to dismiss the case against him. Once the criminal trial was complete, if ever, then the lower court would allow our attorneys to appeal our civil case against North to the Superior Court.

The miserable year of 2008 was nearing a close when Krom called a meeting. Nelson sat at the ugly round table that morning shaking and stinking of alcohol. "I have Lyme disease. That's why my hands shake," he mumbled. "I probably won't file a first-degree murder charge because there are no aggravating circumstances. We can't prove burglary," he said while I eyed his hands.

"Stewart told us 'Franklin County couldn't wait to hand over this case,'" I said matter-of-factly.

Nelson's thick mustache stood on end over pursed lips as he stared at me. Still glowering, he said—contrary to the "strong evidence" he had mentioned for the newspaper—"This case stayed in Huntingdon because there was no evidence that showed it happened in Franklin County."

"With all the blood on everything, this case should never have gone to Huntingdon," I said, staring back.

How long does it take to form an intent to kill, from a legal standpoint?" I asked.

"It only takes a second to form intent," he replied, shifting nervously in his chair.

It was the only thing we ever agreed upon, although the prosecution was not interested in trying to establish North's intent.

"Were pictures even taken of the crime scene at Carl's?" I asked.

"I had the slug sent to the lab. It has Carl's DNA on it," Krom piped up.

"What? I thought they sent it!" I said incredulously. "I can't believe it! Ford told us there wasn't any blood on that slug a couple of years ago! He said it wasn't what killed Carl! He said the slug was 'clean!'" I gaped as she averted her eyes.

"I believe Carl walked into his place that night with the shotgun intact. Did he travel around with guns?" Nelson asked.

"No!" I said firmly, floored at the absurd insinuation that Carl had a shotgun with him on vacation. By "intact," he meant the barrel had *not* been sawed off.

"Carl was accidentally shot in a struggle. The investigators re-enacted the scenario and said it was possible," Krom said, buying into the concocted story in North's scheming letter. "Oh, and they checked again—there *was* blood on the floor tiles," she added almost as an afterthought.

"Ford told us there wasn't any blood on those tiles two years ago!" I said angrily as Krom and Nelson stared in silence. I was outraged that they finally admitted the presence of blood on the slug and floor tiles but now characterized the shooting that they initially insisted had never happened as a struggle and accident.

Excited over the newly acquired "struggle" letter, Krom insisted this "good information" told the whole truth about how North had not meant to shoot Carl. A struggle ensued when Carl walked through the door with the gun, North fell, and it went off. I have never known Carl to vacation with a gun, let alone be so weak that someone like Scott North would be able to wrestle *anything* away from him to start with.

Nelson and Krom claimed that Carl walked into his place with the gun intact, yet the letter mentioned a "sawed-off shotgun." The same sawed-off gun for which I had found the barrel and the shavings; the same gun discovered in Carl's car when the state police apprehended North. It was disturbing they plucked whatever parts of North's self-defense/accident story they wanted and incorporated it into their impossible scenario.

The letter was nothing but a self-defense claim in the making; a way for North to reduce culpability—to get away with murder. Carl did not vacation with a shotgun. It was stolen from his home while he was away, the lock to the shed cut, the gun barrel sawed off with an electric hacksaw, and the altered gun loaded and used against him. Afterward, North carried it with him everywhere he went until it was discovered by police, contrary to his first claim that the "shotgun found in the car was not mine or associated with me at all. It was in there when I gained access to the car." The grammar of his written statement, simple as it was, has never failed to strike me as incongruent with a man with an eighth-grade education and atrocious spelling. If the sawed-off gun was in the car when North gained access to it, as he claimed, how was it that Carl carried an intact shotgun in the door with him? In other words, North and the prosecutors claimed that after North wrestled the "intact" gun from Carl and accidentally shot him, Carl then sawed off the gun barrel and returned the gun to the car. Since there was evidence of more than one attack, that means Carl did this while North had been attacking him again to make sure he was dead. Their stories were beyond ridiculous. Carl never laid a hand on that gun.

North shot him from the right as he came through the front door. Carl was not even facing the gun. The autopsy supports it. There was no exit wound in his back. Blood spatter evidence supports it.

To enhance his story, North claimed he was drunk on sake (rice wine) when he accidentally shot Carl. Carl didn't drink, and there was no booze on the premises. If North had alcohol, he had taken what little was in Hennessy's cabin, which affirms that part of his crime spree was burglary. I had cleaned the cabin for Hennessy two months before the murder while Carl swept the garage. The only sake in that place was a small swill in the bottom of an old bottle with a dog-eared label; not nearly enough to cause impairment.

I reminded Jack Nelson of North's plan to kill Carl and his actions to make it happen; he decided to murder Carl two years beforehand, going so far as to share his plan with his cousin. North headed directly to Amberson the day he escaped. He broke into Carl's place after burglarizing the cabin and then wrote a letter to a former jail buddy stating that he needed money and a car and was just "sitting around waiting." He carried out his plan when he sawed off and loaded a shotgun, positioned himself to the right of the front door, and pulled the trigger.

Nelson's mustache went inert as he stared. Krom had nothing more to say other than touting the phony "struggle" re-enactment. "I have an appointment," she said, rising from her chair. She stopped at the doorway and turned. "Mr. Stewart was here last month and asked how his case was going," she said with a hint of indignation. I stared coolly. At one time, it was his case, transferred to him without justification, and he had let it sit for a year and a half before his replacement sent it back.

"I prosecuted a case in 2001," Nelson said. "There was a lot of circumstantial evidence."

I knew which case he casually referred to because it had recently resurfaced in an appeal and made the papers. The Harshman case, consisting of a triangle relationship and a spent shell casing found with a metal detector fifteen years after an alleged murder. A shell casing discovered on the property of the accused matched one supposedly found in the barn of a neighbor man who had disappeared in 1985. Nelson had used jailhouse informants, and the defendant's attorneys now alleged that Nelson traded lighter sentences for false testimony. I don't know if Harshman is truly guilty or not. There were whispers that the shell casing exhibited in court was shiny, which would have been impossible after tarnishing in the ground for fifteen years.

"What does that have to do with our case?" I asked. "You have tons of evidence."

"You're not a trooper, and you're not an attorney," he said.

"I'm also not an idiot," I shot back, realizing that that was the first time anyone had ever told me what I was not.

"Is your father still living?" he asked.

"Yes, but what's that have to do with our case?" I asked, feeling as though he spent more time sizing us up—considering how much fuss we might kick up and who might do it—than he spent building a good case. "If you're planning a plea bargain, we're not going to be happy about it," I said.

"Well, you're not going to be happy with anything," he snapped.

That certainly was true as far as never being able to change what had happened to Carl, but it sure would have helped to have a prosecutor who was interested in prosecuting and investigators who would have immediately processed the gun, slug, and other evidence. The way things stood, it was going to take work to try an inexcusably delayed, although salvageable case, and he didn't want to do it. Hoping for justice to prevail through Nelson was courting deep disappointment.

"Just because you and North want a plea bargain doesn't mean we do," I said as the meeting abruptly ended.

Nelson ignored me as he headed toward the restroom. The jack of all plea bargainers had made up his mind, probably months earlier, that there would not be a trial.

The next day, Krom sent an email to me expressing how "horrible" she felt that we had gotten the impression the DA's office couldn't wait to get rid of our case. Hopefully, we now knew that it "couldn't be further from the truth."

On the contrary, their ridiculous "struggle" story only reinforced what Stewart had told us initially. I replied to Krom's email, reiterating the absurdity that no one had sent the slug to the crime lab in the beginning, yet relieved that DNA tests finally confirmed our suspicions beyond a doubt that the initial attack on Carl had been with a gun. I noticed she had carbon copied Ford on my incredulous reaction to the mishandled slug in a future email.

～～

A Thanksgiving fire led to a bloody discovery of more evidence on January 19, 2009, almost two months after my losing battle with Nelson. Pat Hennessy had permitted Clint and his wife Leah, for Leah's mother Sherry, Sherry's mother Marlene, and Marlene's sister-in-law Ruth, to make use of his cabin over the holidays while they visited.

Pat had used the cabin very little since North's brief unwelcome occupancy and the murder nearby. Leah's relatives planned to stay a couple of nights. Clint and Leah built a fire in the fireplace, got them settled, and went home. As the fire burned down, the women went to bed. It was a windy night that stirred the trees and inconspicuously stirred a spark from the chimney that somehow made its way inside the wall. By midnight, the fire was roaring through the cathedral ceiling. Ruth stirred awake to the smell of smoke and a glow around the top of the fireplace. She woke the others. Sherry called Clint and Leah, who dialed 911 as they hurriedly dressed.

Clint grabbed a garden hose, and they raced to the burning cabin, where Leah positioned herself against a wall and sprayed the ceiling while Clint tried to get to the fire through the metal roof, to no avail. Despite their effort, flames engulfed the wall around the fireplace, and the ceiling glowed, burning from the inside. A fire truck eventually arrived and saved most of the cabin. After the fire, they shut off the furnace and drained the water pipes because there was a huge hole in the roof.

Carpenters later replaced the roof, but some of the pipes still held water that had frozen and burst while the heat was off. Clint noticed it, so he and our cousin Roy set about repairing the copper pipes for Pat. Upon removing a register cover in the bathroom by the shower, they discovered dried blood on the back of it. A lot of dried blood. Distraught at this unexpected discovery, Clint called me at work. "Hey, we took a register cover off at the cabin, and there's a lot of blood on the back of it."

I drove over after work. There was much more than just a couple of bloody smudges, as if someone had nicked their finger while installing the register cover. There were thick clumps of coagulated blood that had dripped from above and dried on the back of the cover. There were also barely visible blood spatters on the front of the cover and, on closer inspection, some on the bathroom wall.

Clint called Ford, who sent Trooper Dick to collect the cover the next day. It tested positive for blood protein, but forensics never performed a DNA test. Even so, we know it was Carl's blood, and we know how it got there. We believe North retreated to the cabin to clean the blood off himself just in case someone would show up at Carl's place. He hung his clothes, bloody from the attack and murder, on the towel rack above the register, so saturated that blood dripped off in thick globs through the register slot at the top and onto the back of it. It would have indicated what North did immediately after he murdered Carl had they bothered to perform further tests. I was surprised investigators returned it after the court proceedings were over, which indicated they had not logged it as part of the state's evidence.

An interesting side note raises the question: Do we ever really know someone? Ruth, who had been staying at the cabin the night it caught on fire—her sister Delores—had been married to the notorious John List, the New Jersey man who had murdered his family in 1971, then promptly disappeared. He became Bob Clark and married Delores, who, of course, had no idea that he was a killer. A fugitive from justice for eighteen years, he was discovered through *America's Most Wanted*, arrested in 1989 in Virginia, and sentenced to life in prison in 1990. There are several books about John List, alias Bob Clark, who died in prison in 2008, as we continued to suffer through our case.

CHAPTER 21

TOBACCO JUICE AND BERRY JUICE

Behold, I send you forth as sheep in the midst of wolves . . .
—*The Apostle Matthew*

In December 2008, North's attorneys filed a motion to suppress evidence, claiming biased search warrants, an illegal stop, publicity issues, and the right to a speedy trial. The court rescheduled the February 2009 hearing for March, when the judge would determine the admissibility of evidence that could be introduced during a trial.

Over a year had passed since the case landed back in Franklin County. Despite our fear that it would be disposed of through a plea deal, we still dared to hope that Franklin County's prosecutors would diligently pursue the case because it was the right thing to do. But the right thing to do doesn't always dictate what will actually be done, especially when politics have dogged the situation from the start. After trying to get rid of the case for, what we believed were personal and political reasons, prosecutors belatedly revived it only because they had to. That is how we saw it.

We smelled a plea deal. On a cold, windy day in March 2009, our suspicions were confirmed when the *Public Opinion* published an article about the county budget. According to Nelson's latest interview with the local paper, they had three potential death penalty cases that were not likely to materialize. One killer pleaded, a second was likely to plead, and the third case was unlikely to reach trial that year. Being familiar with all three, we knew he was referring to ours as the case likely to end in a plea deal. The commissioners anticipated saving $100,000 on each case not tried. We knew they intended to dump our case. We had been naïve to think that the district attorney would surely meet with us before corroboration from the paper. (*Public Opinion*, www.publicopiniononline.com, March 19, 2009, "Franklin County Budget Proposals Hit the Mark.")

I wasn't able to get any information from anyone at the courthouse the following day, but two days later, Nelson sent a request to meet with us. We arrived at his office as he slowly ambled across the waiting area to the restroom. At that moment, a victim/witness coordinator called us into the conference room to sit around the same ugly table as before. We knew Nelson had called us there to tell us his plan to offer a plea bargain.

Nelson came in with troopers Ford and Carter. As he glanced at each of us, an odor of alcohol wafted through the room. As we expected, Nelson began by telling us how all the evidence was just no good. "There were things that should have been done in the beginning that weren't. We're looking at a plea bargain," he said, as if he, himself, had not been involved at the start.

Everything we expected from Franklin County was coming true. There was something wrong with every point we made and every piece of evidence.

"The burglary is an aggravating circumstance," I insisted, fighting off a familiar panic.

"We can't consider that a burglary," he said.

"Why isn't it a burglary? He's charged with burglary. He stole money and things from inside both places. It's on the bill of particulars that the state intended to prove burglary. It was a burglary at the preliminary hearing in front of Judge Knepper."

"The most North could be charged with is breaking and entering. As a district attorney, I must consider what is best for the state as far as public safety, and this way North can't file an appeal after he's sentenced," he argued.

"Too bad no one was concerned about public safety when he was put out there," I said.

"Then we'll be rid of it," Nelson said, reiterating what we knew all along. They had been trying to get "rid of it" from day one. We argued with everything Nelson said. He became short with us, sighed, and nodded at the investigators, signaling them why a plea bargain was the best option.

"So is North's address book with his thumbprint on it in Carl's blood not good evidence either?" I asked, directing the question toward Ford.

"We just thought it was a bloody print. That turned out to be tobacco juice," he lied shamelessly while looking at Nelson.

"What about the blood on the back bumper of Carl's car?" I persisted.

"That was berry juice," he lied again.

Forensics had already established the facts. There is nothing more incriminating than a killer's print in the victim's blood; it is the best physical evidence in the world, but he likened it to nothing but innocuous tobacco juice.

They were against us. Toward the end of the meeting, we could only stare at them. Arguing was pointless. They had outrageously mishandled a textbook first-degree murder case that could have put North in prison for life as he deserved.

Police and prosecutors had disregarded blood evidence at the crime scene, setting the stage for dispensing with the unwanted case. Police undermined the autopsy in the beginning by failure to forensically test the slug, relegating the cause of death to nothing more than a guess. The infuriating thing was, there was no excuse in the world they could not have built a good solid case if someone would have just done it instead of shoving it somewhere else. It was a mishmash of horrendous mismanagement, wasted time, lies, and indifference, but evidence is still evidence, and there is no statute of limitations on an act of murder.

An unjustified plea deal would allow Carl's killer to plead *nolle contendre* (no contest) to third-degree murder. Nelson told us he would drop the other charges. The meeting ended abruptly, and he hurried out the door to the restroom. As we left, Ford uttered his catchphrase, "Keep this under your hat. Don't be talking."

Following the meeting, Krom tried to make a plea bargain sound appealing. "North could get thirty years with this deal," she said.

But we knew that was misleading. Thirty years was likely the max, with the minimum being much less. After almost three years of pure hell, it was boiling down to a lame plea bargain for a murderous crime spree. With all the evidence, the viciousness of the crime, the premeditation, burglary, stolen car, occupancy of Carl's residence, and the murderer's remorseless behavior capped with jailhouse bragging about the killing, this was a miscarriage of justice, far out of proportion to what Carl had suffered.

"What about the 'sitting around waiting' letter," I asked, referring to the full page of writings I had gathered off the floor that first day at Carl's. "The letter is enough to show a progressive intent to carry through with a plan to kill Carl, a strong premeditation."

"It wasn't enough for a handwriting analysis," Krom claimed. "You can have Carl back if you agree," she added, aware that we had periodically requested the return of his remains with a nagging fear they might be misplaced.

I couldn't believe it. They had done little but waste time, and it was unfair that during all that time, they had refused to return Carl's remains, but Krom's attempt to use that prospect as an inducement for us to cooperate was inexcusable.

"Maybe we'll contact the attorney general's office after all," I said as I left. One of the reasons, besides our weariness, that we had not filed an official complaint by then was that the prosecutors held the power to manipulate the case any way they wanted. We lived in fear that they would retaliate with a slap on the wrist for North. We didn't trust them or anyone connected with them. Attorney General Tom Corbett and Huntingdon County District Attorney Robert Stewart were well acquainted, and we figured Nelson was too. We saw how the system had been manipulated thus far and feared Corbett would dismiss us as "just looking for someone to blame" as Warden John Wetzel had.

I was still mulling over the meeting several days later when Mom got a call from Nelson. "I'm calling to let you know that North accepted the plea agreement. I just wanted your thoughts on this issue," he said.

"My feelings about it are still the same, Jack," Mom responded, feeling less than amenable to the expected news. "I haven't changed my mind. I'm sure he did accept it. That convinces me even more that you have plenty of evidence, and if this went to trial, North knows he would get life. He should never have the chance to get out of prison. What he did with Carl after he killed him is a heinous crime itself. He just threw Carl away like a bag of garbage. It's not right that he could have the chance to get out someday to do this again to someone else. How much change does the county have left over from North's paycheck for his two-and-a-half days' work? Does it cover the expense it's costing the county now? If North isn't put away for life, you know he'll have a chance to get out and ruin more lives."

"Well, I just wanted your view on the matter," Nelson said to bow out gracefully.

Mom offered her view, but it would never go any further than deaf ears. We suspected Nelson no more wanted views than he wanted to prosecute but instead was fishing to see whether we might follow through with our threat to complain to the attorney general.

They set a hearing to pound out an agreement for the plea bargain. The only ones it seemed to please were North and the prosecutors. We heard it put a gleam in North's eye. A jail employee reported to us that North was bragging about the deal he was getting.

There was nothing left to do. On March 16, 2009, half an hour before the scheduled morning hearing, I went to the courthouse's second floor and delivered a letter addressed to Judge Herman. It was a desperate last-ditch effort to stop the deal.

We asked in the name of decent and fair justice for Carl that he not accept the plea deal. We found it unacceptable that Dr. Kamerow had not reassessed his autopsy report after forensics had proven Carl's DNA on the slug. We also challenged the prosecution's reliance on the bogus letter North wrote after discovering at the preliminary hearing that they were ignorant of, or had failed to use, evidence proving how he carried out the murder. North had seized the opportunity to make up the story about a "struggle" leading to Carl's death.

In our letter to the judge, we noted that Stewart had intended to file a second-degree murder charge and had guaranteed us that North would "never see the light of day." Yet the case languished in Huntingdon, and upon its return to Franklin County, it deteriorated even more as they dragged their feet on prosecuting it. We made clear our opposition to the plea bargain and warned of the possible destruction of another life and family should officials set North free in the future.

We had been waiting in the courtroom for an agonizing hour when the court apologized for North's late arrival. The sheriff's office had been inadvertently notified not to transport North, and they had to go get him when the mistake was realized. We nervously settled in to endure a hearing for a plea deal that we did not want.

"SUBSTANTIAL ADDITIONAL INFORMATION"

Ruddy complexioned and white-haired, Judge Herman was difficult to read by his expressions. North's attorney had alerted the court earlier that they had prepared a proposal to set aside the pretrial hearing, and instead to "go down perhaps a different path, and if that path proves unsuccessful . . . come back to this point and embark on having a hearing."

To our relief, Herman was not eager to push the hearing through without knowing the details "because of the nature of the case, the seriousness of the charges." He requested "substantial additional information," claiming that he knew little about the case, other than what he learned from reviewing the pleadings and charging documents.

"I understand that you have been discussing plea negotiations," Herman said.

Nelson concurred that they were "very close" to a plea deal.

To our surprise, Judge Herman suggested a separate hearing. He wanted the exact terms and conditions of the agreement placed on record so that he could "know as much information about the reasons for the plea . . . some development of the Commonwealth's evidence, or lack of evidence so that the court can know whether or not the plea would be acceptable."

He also wanted a "pre-sentence report . . . the impact that this agreement might have on those areas that the court is required to consider under the sentencing code such as the victims, the defendant, the people of Franklin County, and so forth . . ."

He further directed officers from the investigation division of the Franklin County Probation Department to be "present and prepared with a special report along with the already developed reports of the abundant information" on North from other cases and to develop information from the community.

Herman acknowledged that our family was "definitely in opposition to any plea agreement that would be considered in this case" and included our letter as part of the report so it could be considered along with all the other evidence developed from the probation department. The court scheduled an April 6 hearing to consider whether there should be a plea agreement.

It was over in half an hour, and we left the courtroom satisfied that, at least for now, the plea bargain appeared stymied, or at the least, someone showed some interest in what we wanted. At her invitation, we trailed Krom to her office. Pointing to two cardboard boxes sitting on the floor, she commented, "These are the same two boxes of evidence that we sent to Huntingdon in the beginning. That's all they sent back."

In other words, no one had gathered additional evidence for the year and a half the case was in Huntingdon. We stood before her desk without comment, anticipating her pitch for the plea deal and listening as she read parts of North's "struggle" letter. She had the letter clamped in her fingers when Loree asked, "Why do you say Carl walked through the door with the shotgun intact when the letter calls it a 'sawed-off shotgun'?"

"Oh," she said, staring at the letter, speechless that she had been called on such a blunder. That is not exactly a small detail, easily overlooked. The description of the gun as "sawed-off" had slipped through as an inadvertent truth among the lies. But how could she contradict their re-enactment of Carl walking through the door with an "intact" shotgun?

A trial meant a possible life sentence but pushing for prosecution was not getting us anywhere. We feared we were about to get the short end of the stick, just like the rest of Scott North's victims, so as we left, we brainstormed about how we could gather additional support against the plea deal. We needed a way to share the story more widely in hopes of building public opposition to a plea bargain for such an atrocious crime. Our niece, Carrie, suggested a petition, and despite Krom's warning that it "could hurt the case," we embraced the idea with renewed hope.

The probation department had provided us with victim impact forms, but we wanted something that went beyond just a few words on paper. A petition and letters representing the public's perception would supplement our grief-on-paper forms, although I never filled mine out because it seemed pitifully insufficient. Judge Herman had given us ten days to have materials submitted, so we had to get busy right away.

Loree got it started, and social media support snowballed into a mountain of signatures. After hearing the story and learning of the probable plea bargain, one young man, a customer in Mom's shop, literally shook in his shoes as he signed the petition.

The following Saturday, gathering one last handful of signatures, I stopped at a public auction where I knew several people. As they waited in line to sign the petition, an Amberson resident observed, "Carl was a big man. I don't see how Scott North could have killed him with blunt-force trauma." Despite Ford's reminder to "keep this under your hat," I finally told the truth. "It wasn't blunt force," I replied, "North shot him with a shotgun, and not only that, they never sent the slug or the gun to the lab, and they ignored all kinds of evidence that showed Carl was killed right there at his own home."

Keeping my mouth shut, being party to their secrets was not serving anyone but Nelson and those working for him. He obviously had no plans to prosecute, and I refused to continue covering for the district attorneys and the investigators who failed us. Silence certainly did nothing to protect any evidence because every piece of it supposedly was no good anyway.

This newly revealed bit of information spread like wildfire. Once the truth was out, a young man came forward and shared an encounter with North in the Franklin County Jail. Upon learning Carl had been shot, this man's mother contacted us and shared the details of her son's exchange with North. She said they had not told anyone sooner because they heard Carl had died from "blunt-force trauma."

While serving a short sentence in the county jail, this young man had a run-in with North and declared he hated him for killing Carl. North responded menacingly, "Yeah, I killed Carl, and I'll wait on you and shoot you too." If true, it was a statement straight from the source betraying his murderous mindset: He was not done killing. I shared the story with Ford, who then taped an interview with the man North had threatened.

By our deadline of March 26, 2009, we had a petition with over one thousand signatures from three counties and two states, letters from friends in Jerusalem, a soldier in Iraq, past victims, relatives, and friends, all packed in a cardboard box and submitted to the Department of Probation and Parole. It was the department's responsibility to prepare the submissions for court. We heard that a letter also arrived at the probation office from a close relative of North's, declaring him a serial killer who should never be released.

Something caused him to suddenly cease bragging, perhaps a rumor that his deal might be in jeopardy. His arrogance subsided, and he blamed us, asking an employee at the jail why we were doing this to him. Apparently, he fully expected to serve only four years, as he had told his grandmother he would.

That month, a work-release inmate jailed for simple assault failed to return from an assigned worksite, indicating that escapes were still occurring. Clearly, the work release program's flaws had not been corrected.

The absurdities kept coming. Since prosecutors were not interested in uncovering the truth, I contacted Kamerow in April 2009 and asked him to re-evaluate his autopsy report because of the DNA on the slug. But even after the bloodied slug had tested positive for Carl's DNA, he refused to change his report, implausibly claiming, "DNA could have come from sweat from Carl touching his own bullets."

Even if Carl had somehow touched the lead beforehand, heated gases would have burned away touch DNA as the slug traveled through the gun barrel when it was fired and then through Carl's body. The genetic information forensics retrieved from the slug was Carl's blood DNA.

Two years and eight months into it, police claimed they recently sent the gun, gun barrel, metal shavings, and hacksaw North had used to cut the gun barrel and padlocks to the lab for forensic testing. That was not true; they had never gathered the metal shavings, and we still had the hacksaw. They did have Carl's shirt and photos of the shirt transported from the Mercyhurst College Anthropology Department to the

Chambersburg State Police barracks because of the ruckus we raised, but we didn't believe they were at the state police forensics lab.

～～

Early spring 2009 embroidered the countryside with new green foliage; farmers prepared their fields, and birds sang—but every miserable day seemed the same no matter what time of year it was. All was quiet from the nerve-wracking March hearing until May 11, when Nelson called us the day before an election for two county judge seats and magisterial judgeships. It was only the second time he had ever personally contacted me; the first was the day before the press conference for North's murder charge when he forbade me from speaking to the media. I was surprised he called, but what he said during our short conversation set me on edge for days.

"If you're going to campaign against the prosecutor, then I'll have to contact the attorney general, and it will take longer for the case to be over," he threatened.

Nelson was accusing me of campaigning against Angela Krom, who was running for judge of the county Court of Common Pleas. She had plastered slogans describing herself as "courtroom tested" around Franklin and Fulton counties. As her campaign manager, Nelson himself had placed campaign cards in all his favorite drinking haunts. I certainly did speak up about her campaign promises, and I told him so. She shamelessly asserted in her campaign that she never offered plea bargains to the accused unless the victims' families agreed to it. But in our case, she pushed a plea bargain despite our strong objections—and she tried to use the return of Carl's remains as a bargaining chip to get us to go along with it.

Nelson was unaware that after the last hearing, we had decided to share our concerns with Pennsylvania Attorney General Tom Corbett's office, although we stopped short of filing a formal complaint. The individual we spoke with (anonymously because we didn't pursue a complaint) was stunned at the handling of the case.

Had I really wanted to derail Krom's campaign, I would have started weeks before the election, canvassing Fulton County, which falls under

Franklin County's 39th Judicial District because the sparse population doesn't warrant its own court system. It is somewhat removed from the politics of Chambersburg. But sparse or not, Fulton County's collective vote can be potent. But I didn't have the energy for any strategy, political or personal. Still, I had a right to my opinion and a right to campaign or vote for whomever I wished.

Nelson shifted to another topic. "Scott North filed papers in federal court," he said.

That meant nothing to me, and as usual, he didn't explain it. I later learned North had filed a frivolous complaint, pro se, against Krom and his attorneys over some petty grievance.

More notably, Nelson claimed, "We now have some new detailed and reliable evidence that will be very helpful for prosecution. In fact, you'll probably hear something in the next few days that this case will proceed to trial. We never offered Scott North a plea bargain."

His accusation and threat to contact the attorney general were annoying, but it rattled me that he was claiming he had never offered North a plea bargain. It rose to the level of diabolical. It is a deceiver's nature to lie—but still. He had already informed Mom that North accepted the plea deal. It was the reason for our March meeting with Nelson, and the hearing that followed, at which time they were working out the details of the plea agreement between Nelson and North's attorneys. There was also Krom's assertion about the thirty years North could get, her bribery attempt with Carl's remains, North's jailhouse brags, and our petition.

Judge Herman's request for a separate hearing and more information before deciding whether to allow the plea deal provided a little hope. The court added Herman's hearing to the calendar, while we frantically gathered petition signatures against a deal. But a pretrial hearing was not going to happen with a plea deal still taking shape. No new evidence had materialized. There was the jailhouse interview and old evidence belatedly sent to forensics, but we held little hope it would change the prosecution's aim to "get rid of" the case—no matter how damning the evidence might be.

Nelson's claim of "new detailed and reliable evidence" was a smoke-screen, yet it sparked a small, reckless hope that the case really would "proceed to trial." With the benefit of hindsight, I can offer a bit of guidance to anyone unfortunate enough to be snowed with official lies: Ask for outside help, talk to the media, find an attorney, or contact a state representative—kick up a fuss in any constructive way possible. Unethical conduct from a prosecutor should not be part of your ordeal. Do not tolerate mistreatment in hopes that it will all work out in the end. That is if you can overcome your grief and horror to stand up for your human rights.

CHAPTER 22

THE WATCHER

When the waves of death compassed me, the floods of ungodly men made me afraid. —Samuel writing about King David.

We found ourselves at the mercy of the ways of this world, entangled in too much power and politics and fighting evil. I wondered where God's warring angels were and if they would fight for us. Our long rollercoaster ride of ever-changing news kept us on edge to the point that we almost lost our sanity. Even sleep couldn't quell the agony—and the predawn hours brought troublesome dreams that seemed premonitory and symbolic.

I had one in which a sick, skinny snake two feet long, dull black with a thin white stripe, lay stretched out and still. It had dents here and there. I knew it was not long for this world, and it, too, seemed resigned to its fate. Suddenly, it shriveled and dried up, becoming a dry keyboard of little curved bones—a little deceiver exposed and dead. The image stuck with me as a seeming omen.

Three miserable years had passed since the murder, our time sliced away piece by piece by incompetent officials. The April hearing had been rescheduled to September 2009 to allow North's attorneys time to complete a discovery and review the results of the additional laboratory testing that Krom had ordered. We had a faint hope that Nelson had told the truth about the case going to trial. My sisters in Florida had decided to skip the hearing, not wanting to risk another last-minute cancellation. Every time the court set a date; it suddenly would be pushed off. They intended to be at the trial, of course, and be there on the day of the sentencing to present their victim statements.

I should have known. The afternoon before the scheduled hearing, I received another distressing call. The plea deal was "back on the table." I shook so that I couldn't even pick up a pen and could barely walk. Unsure of my ability to drive, I hesitantly left work and contacted Loree on the way home. She didn't take the news any better. Fury finally broke through Clint's placid nature. This hearing could mark the end of our beleaguered case.

I had left Harrisburg and had been driving on Interstate 81 for forty-five minutes. I was almost home and beyond fury when my vision suddenly disappeared. Everything before me vanished into a dark blanket of nothing. I quickly wrenched my car to the berm and slammed on the brakes until my sight returned. It occurred to me that rage really can trigger a physiological blind madness.

Tripped up again, neither Chris nor Sarah had time to rearrange their school and work schedules to attend. Sarah had just relocated from Delaware to Florida, near Chris. Relatives and friends who had waited with us for more than three years to see the murder tried were not able to get off work on short notice.

That night brought bad dreams and prayers but no sleep for anyone. Now that the primary election was over, the plea bargain was back. I headed for the courthouse the next morning. Struggling for the courage to stand in court, I told myself that if Jesus could drag a heavy wooden cross slung over His shoulder through a crowd of jeering, spitting, name-calling persecutors while being whipped and pummeled, I could brave this latest affront. If He could carry the world's torment on his back while blood ran into his eyes from the crown of thorns they jammed onto His head, I could face this injustice. Even if I couldn't change what would happen, I could at least be there to speak for Carl.

Loree prayed before leaving home, asking God for strength to stand before Judge Herman—to find the right words to change his mind about the plea deal. After praying, she said she felt more at ease with, not so much a crystal-clear answer, as a feeling that what is meant to be will be. "What about Jack Nelson?" she prayed again. She later described the response she heard, clear as a bell: *I'll take care of him.*

Her anxiety fell away, but I still had mine, and I had no peace. The fate of the case seemed sealed.

Mom traveled to Chambersburg with Loree. Our friend Pam met us at the courthouse. Clint refused to come, so enraged, he was afraid he would end up in jail. Like me, he had had a dream. He saw a bird's nest built onto the wall the way swifts and swallows build nests. Thinking it held baby birds, he approached it, but instead of downy babies, he found the nest crawling with a brood of little vipers that began hanging out over the edge. The pretense of a trial had melted away and the plea bargain plot hatched.

Mom, Loree, Pam, and I were the only ones there because of the last-minute notification. It would have helped to have the company of more family and friends, but the surprise left us with minimal support. Carl's girlfriend Debbie was home, sick; so was Dad. Others just couldn't be there on short notice.

At 8:15 A.M. on September 17, 2009, three years and forty-three days after Carl's murder, we stood on the sidewalk at the courthouse entrance picketing with signs made from poster board and wooden paint stirrer handles. We had to do *something*. One side read JUSTICE FOR CARL; the flip side read NO PLEA BARGAIN. It was our last stand. Like sport wrestling, after all the struggling we had done, we still found ourselves caught in a full nelson hold.

We felt our mini protest would have little effect because the outcome was preordained, but it called attention to our opposition and prompted people to ask questions. It was our way of letting people know that an escaped felon, burglar, murderer, car thief, and body dumper who had gone shopping with Carl's cash and credit cards and continued to live in his home after killing him was getting a plea bargain. We met a woman who shared her own horror story about an unwanted Nelson plea deal during our quiet demonstration. We then discarded our signs and made our way to the fourth floor to wait outside his door.

As we watched him head to the restroom again, our victim/witness coordinator led us to the familiar table where we sat waiting for Nelson, who eventually entered along with investigators Ford and Sneath.

In the end, no prosecutor was going to step up to fight for Carl. North would plead guilty to escape and plead no contest to third-degree murder. Nelson told us, "hearsay statements can't be used in court," refer-ring to North's statement that he was going to kill Carl, ongoing state-ments from him while jailed, and Ford's latest witness interview after North's jailhouse death threat against a fellow inmate.

Contrary to Nelson's claim, however, a prosecutor certainly can in-troduce out-of-court statements, and they can have direct legal signifi-cance as long as the witness can be cross-examined. North's intent to kill Carl and admission to his murder, both expressed to others, constituted circumstantial evidence, which alone or added to other evidence could establish premeditation and guilt.

"What happened to the 'detailed and reliable evidence' that was good for the prosecution that you mentioned in May when you accused me of campaigning against Krom?" I asked.

"I don't know about that," he remarked as if it were a figment of my imagination.

I fully expected his denial and saw no benefit in arguing with him. Resigned, I said nothing more, but I suddenly felt an unseen presence as if some other power were watching and noting what was taking place. Something hung in the balance other than the plea bargain. But what could it possibly be?

Nelson's spiel was over in ten minutes. Then he dropped something unexpected. "North will probably be sentenced as part of the hearing."

Although the plea deal was made without our consent, we were still counting on the opportunity to make a victim impact statement. We never expected the sentence to come the same day as the hearing.

Disappointed and disgusted, we made our way to the second floor of the courthouse. The date—September 17, 2009, at 9:00 in the morning or 9, '09 at 9—felt like the flipside of 666 as they began the proceeding that would ultimately determine how many years Scott North would spend in prison for his "GREAT ESCAPE" and heinous murder.

A new letter from North, dated September 7, 2009, was the key. It was now in Krom's hands, and surprisingly, she allowed me to read it when we crossed paths before the hearing. I later obtained a copy from the courthouse records.

North wrote that he would "accept the plea for 3rd degree"—with conditions. He wanted to be finished with the court and returned to "my state prison by the end of October, begining [sic] of November." He wanted the pretrial hearing to be "turned into" a plea agreement hearing and to be sentenced the same day, all by teleconference.

The postmark showed that the prosecutors likely had had the letter for at least eight days. They had it when Nelson toyed with our hopes, asserting, "this case will proceed to trial. We never offered Scott North a plea bargain." Now we couldn't help but think this lie was a calculated ploy to prevent us from trying to stop the deal. Now his accommodation of the murderer over us had deprived some of us of the opportunity to give victim statements.

North's eagerness for a plea deal was a coward's way of avoiding a trial for murder and the commensurate sentence. At any rate, he must have felt our protest had threatened his deal. He hobbled into the courtroom in his prison garb, clapped in leg irons and a shock belt with cuff chains. His face bore the most hateful to-kill look I had ever seen. He looked both maniacal and angry. It was easy to imagine how he could easily fly off the handle and kill someone. I hoped he wanted to kill me. I fought off an urge to floor him and plant my foot on his neck until he was dead.

The court introduced Case #1224 of 2008, numbered according to the year police filed charges—not the year the crime occurred. Cheerless weeks had passed, then months, and finally years. Our life sentence had begun on August 5, 2006. We were about to hear what yawned ahead for Scott North. The following are the highlights of the hearing:

RID OF IT

Nelson and Krom represented the Commonwealth, eager to "be rid of it." Abom and Weitzman defended North.

We braced ourselves as Judge Herman announced that the district attorney and North's counsel had indicated that "they had, once again, reengaged plea negotiations and had arrived at a plea agreement for consideration by the court."

Nelson offered a proposal for North to enter a plea of "no contest or nolo contendere to third-degree murder with an agreed-upon sentence . . . of not less than 20 years, nor more than 40 years."

In addition, he would plead guilty to "a charge of escape, a felony of the third degree, with an agreed upon sentence of not less than two years, nor more than seven years, to be served at the expiration of the sentence for third-degree murder."

Nelson acknowledged, "I cannot tell the court that [the victim's family] are supportive of the plea." However, he said investigators "are one hundred percent supportive of the plea."

North wouldn't have to risk a trial that could result in a harsher sentence. Krom had told us earlier that the murder and escape sentences would run consecutively (one after the other). She also told us North would first finish serving his resentencing for old parole violations and a previous burglary.

We appreciated that Nelson mentioned our opposition to the deal. We had made it so apparent he could hardly lie about it, but the investigators' views were less wholehearted than Nelson had led the court to believe. When Nelson made his assertion, Loree and I noticed that one of the investigators appeared to be less than enthusiastic. His testimony did not exude confidence, and he occasionally held one wrist with his opposite hand. The subtleties of body language and lack of confidence do not lie.

Nelson said, "As the court well knows, criminal homicide can range anywhere from involuntary manslaughter to first-degree murder, and the key issue is the state of mind of the defendant at the time the crime was committed.

"In this particular case, we had received information that the defense, if the case goes to trial, would intend to introduce evidence that could go to a justification defense which could result in acquittal, and/or voluntary intoxication or ingestion of drugs that could support a verdict of third-degree murder."

I suspected the impairment defense was the rice wine lie North had told. Impairment is one of the oldest mitigating circumstances in the book. Still, I wondered how the defense could introduce evidence of intoxication when police didn't have him in custody until almost a week after he had murdered. Nelson had informed us beforehand that the burden falls to the state to prove otherwise. He wanted no part of prosecuting an escapee, burglar, killer, body dumper who claimed impairment by the ingestion of drugs or alcohol. I failed to see how a claim of diminished capacity could work anyway when substance use is a free choice. But it seems that lies hold a lot of weight in court unless a prosecutor is willing to tear them apart. Once again, North's habit of blaming someone or something else for his depraved actions would be to his benefit.

If tried, a jury could reduce first-degree murder to a second- or third-degree murder if they fell for his story. Then again, a trial by jury would decide North's culpability based on the evidence and quality of prosecution. We felt that a trial would not necessarily have gone North's way. If the case had not been stalled for such an exorbitant amount of time, North wouldn't have had as much time to try out multiple stories before finally hitting upon a usable one. Nelson's proposed plea bargain eliminated the chance of North getting a life sentence, as well as our chance of never having to deal with North again. In Pennsylvania, life is life.

Nelson explained that there were "viable suppression issues" and that several state troopers were there and prepared "to proceed to a lengthy suppression hearing involving various issues." He said the plea would be tantamount to "removal of those issues from the case and from any possible claims on appeal."

He mentioned that the deteriorated condition of Carl's body "hampered the determination of the cause of death and, also, resulted in the Huntingdon County District Attorney assuming jurisdiction over the case in as much as the law is that when presumptively a murder occurs in the jurisdiction in which the body was located."

Nelson nebulously claimed, "It was not until a year and a half later when the newly elected District Attorney of Huntingdon County contacted us. We were not involved with the case for a year and a half. He contacted us and advised us that there had, in fact, been a substantial amount of evidence uncovered indicating that this crime occurred in Franklin County.

"We sort of started behind the eight ball with the investigation. If the case went to trial, the focus of the trial would be what evidence the

Commonwealth could introduce with respect to the degree of criminal homicide we could prove beyond a reasonable doubt. It's a matter of evaluating the risk versus the reward. This is an appropriate plea agreement, and it's consistent with the interest of justice, and we would ask the court to accept the plea."

Suppression of evidence is a standard tactic in any murder case, lengthy or not, so I failed to see the concern. I later examined public records at the courthouse since they had not named the issues in court. I discovered a pretrial motion for relief contending that the court should dismiss the escape and fleeing and eluding charges because the Commonwealth had failed to exercise diligence in bringing the case to trial because more than three hundred and sixty-five days had elapsed since authorities had filed the original charges. His attorneys wanted a change of venue because they believed impaneling an impartial jury was not possible because of pretrial publicity. They claimed the stop police made the night they apprehended North was illegal because the tip from Whitsel's Bar was unreliable, and the description of the car had not been specific enough to raise reasonable suspicion to justify the stop. They alleged that North had never consented to a polygraph test, nor voluntarily, knowingly, or intelligently waived his Miranda rights, and police had illegally obtained statements and evidence, thus making information from interrogations inadmissible. Furthermore, they claimed the search warrants were biased and overly broad and used as an investigative tool to determine if a crime had been committed, based only on police suspicion.

Ford had told us months earlier that North had requested to take a "lie detector test." A polygraph measures the blood pressure, pulse, respiration, and galvanic skin response to questioning. Dishonest answers allegedly produce physiological reactions that indicate deception. The test doesn't measure arrogance, but regardless of how smart North thinks he is, the test clearly indicated deception, or he wouldn't have tried to suppress it.

Nelson neglected to reveal that he and the state police were the ones who claimed the murder never happened at Carl's place. He didn't explain why prime evidence was squandered at the crime scene, and evidence in possession from the beginning was belatedly sent to the lab at the eleventh hour, and in some instances, not submitted at all. He ignored the sneaker in the field and the extraordinary amount of blood visible indoors and outdoors. He certainly didn't mention that Stewart had divulged to us that Franklin County wanted to be "rid" of the case and that we kept finding important evidence on our own. So, no, the condition of Carl's body isn't what hampered the case.

Troopers told us the day of the transfer that Franklin County would still be involved, and Ford would remain on the case. We called Ford each time we found more evidence. The "substantial amount of evidence uncovered" was the same evidence that Franklin County had sent to Huntingdon initially, not counting the evidence we discovered on our own. Krom had implied the very same, the day she pointed out the only two boxes of evidence sitting in her office that had been returned from Huntingdon.

They were involved from the start, and they had put themselves "behind the eight ball" when they decided to play politics. The maneuver was not "consistent with the interest of justice" and had undercut a potentially strong case and our health. The plea deal was nothing more than a Band-Aid applied to cover incompetence and negligence—it had nothing to do with justice.

Judge Herman acknowledged that we opposed the plea agreement, that we felt there was sufficient evidence for a first-degree murder conviction, subjecting North to a sentence of life imprisonment. Ford flinched, and Nelson uncharacteristically shifted in his seat as Herman assured us, "I just want to let the Ryder family know to the extent that they're represented here today. I have the submissions that you gave to the probation department. They're in the file. There are writings there. They were extensive. I'm going to take [them] into account, but this is an additional opportunity if anybody would like to come forward."

Yes, we were represented, but only because we stood up for ourselves, gathering evidence, raising hell, and producing a petition along with letters and submissions from citizens who cared. Legal representation was next to nil. With three of our family and a friend present, we took the opportunity to speak again. Since we had fallen for Nelson's assurance that there was "detailed and reliable evidence" and that "this case will proceed to trial," the resurrected plea deal and sentencing surprise left us somewhat unprepared to give detailed statements. We didn't attempt to delve into our immense personal loss but instead focused all of our remaining strength on an earnest cry for justice.

TO ENSURE NO FUTURE POTENTIAL FOR HARM

I made my way from the gallery to the judge's bench, with each step drawing closer to the man whose decision would affect the rest of our lives. Throwing accusations would have hindered our cause. The only option left was to get as harsh a sentence as possible for North. My only recourse was to set the tone by showing respect toward the judge, mention the trail of suffering that North had created throughout his life, and clearly state that we'd rather see the case follow a different course. "Your honor, the decision you make today, we trust that it will be the right one, whatever that may be," I began. "I want to say that Scott North has left a string of victims for more than fifteen years, us being the worst. There is no describing what he has done to us." As my words trailed off, I felt North's stare from behind, and I turned to look at him. His eyes held a glint of something like satisfaction. At my unexpected glance, the glint vanished, and he looked down. I took it that he enjoyed hearing the fruits of his big deed—that people were still suffering from it—but it rattled him that I had seen the jubilation that he thought was hidden.

Judge Herman responded: "[You] hit on a point that over the years the court has been able to experience directly in that this is a unique situation for people who are affected by it. . . . It's a lifelong impact as opposed to maybe some other types of criminal conduct where victims heal over time or even recover losses," Judge Herman replied. "It's not possible for that to happen in most cases like this. There's no question about it."

"There is one thing we would rather see, and that would be a guilty plea to the murder charge," I said.

"I understand," he said. "Acceptance of responsibility is a major factor in the court's consideration as well. It's not often clear that you get that in some situations, but that's a factor that the court will take into account."

"Thank you, judge." I glanced again toward North as I returned to my seat. He now projected an air of contempt. He obviously had no intention of accepting any responsibility. He was just waiting for it to all be over.

Loree approached the bench. "I am the younger sister of Carl Ryder. There really isn't a punishment comparable to what we've lost. Life imprisonment is the best we could do in this realm, so the plea bargain is still something that we would rather not see. Mr. Nelson explained the risks of going to trial, not only this trial but any trial, in general. We understand that, but we still believe that this case is strong enough for a conviction of first-degree murder. We haven't changed that in any way, and I think I represent the entire family when I say that; however, you're in the position that you are in because of your expertise, and we believe in that and trust in that, and we trust that you will make the right decision because you've been in the courtroom a lot longer than we have."

Herman replied, "One of the things that the court looks at in these situations is that assuming an individual is liable to punishment for a certain degree of homicide, whatever it might be in addition to what you suggested, punishment certainly is a factor," Herman replied. "There's no doubt about it, but as you know, I think you've learned in watching this prosecution that there are other factors that are considered. One of the most important in a case like this is public safety. Can we arrive at an agreement that's going to ensure no future potential for harm? And that's one of the things that's going to be paramount in the court's consideration assuming Mr. North adequately accepts responsibility for it, so I just want to let you know that. And that's for the public in general and not just the victims."

I failed to see how the judge would ensure public safety with a plea bargain that almost certainly meant the system might someday set a killer free. Assuming North would accept responsibility for what he did is akin to believing a predator may someday lose its instinct to lie quietly in wait for its prey. Especially after he said he was going to kill Carl and did it.

Especially since he allegedly had made a comment in jail that he'll kill us all if he has to do time for something he didn't do. Believe me, we will never forget his propensity for vindictiveness.

Mom introduced herself at the bench. "I do not feel that the plea agreement is enough punishment for what we have lost. I will never be able to see or talk to my son again, and it's not fair. He had the right to go home—without fear of his life being taken away by someone who just thought that he had the right to go into his home and be there," she said through tears, prompting sympathetic tears from a probation employee who was present.

"Thank you, Mrs. Ryder. I appreciate your comments," Herman said, grappling for a reply to a mother who lost her oldest son to a work release inmate whom the courts knew well.

Pam, a family friend approached the bench last. She explained that she had seen our family "go through hell and back" and that she felt the case was strong enough for a conviction.

We did go through hell, but really, we never left it behind. It burned into our souls like hot coals through a snowbank. We expressed respect for the decision the judge was about to make, without delving deep into our own private hell. We reiterated our dissatisfaction with a plea deal after all the damage North had done, then held our breath, alternating between hope and fear for the remainder of the hearing.

CHAPTER 23

"... NOT AWARE OF THE SLUG"

None calleth for justice, nor any pleadeth for truth: they trust in vanity, and speak lies; they conceive mischief, and bring forth iniquity. —Isaiah

Breathing a sigh of relief after presenting our statements to the judge, we listened to Ford's awkward testimony. Fear temporarily overrode the bitterness that had settled in our hearts over the preceding three years.

THE PLEA DEAL

In contrast to our worries, Ford addressed the court confidently. "I believe based on everything that I have uncovered, what I've worked on for several years that I believe this is an outcome that I am completely comfortable with and I believe in this case that it's completely justifiable and a just outcome," he said.

"Have you been working on this case from the very beginning when Mr. Ryder . . ."

"Yes, I was there," Ford interrupted Judge Herman. "I wasn't the first policeman there, but I was the first criminal investigator at Carl's location the morning that Mr. North was caught in his car so, yes."

"And was there a break in your work, so to speak, because of—in other words, I assume from that point you pursued the investigation for a period of time?" Herman asked.

"I pursued the investigation from August 11, 06, until August 16, 06, when I did not become lead investigator anymore because Mr. Ryder was found in Huntingdon County," Ford explained awkwardly. "I did assist trooper—Corporal Sneath now, at the time Trooper Sneath, with the investigation. I wasn't with Huntingdon County, but I was no longer lead investigator in the case after that date until the case came back to Franklin County."

"Do you remember how long that was before you began working on it again?" Herman asked.

"Well, I became the lead again, I believe in 07," Ford said.

Herman asked Ford if, in addition to his own work and the other trooper's work, he had the benefit of information from laboratory work and forensic scientists.

"Yes," Ford said. "I was involved—myself and Corporal Sneath were in constant communication throughout the investigation. Most of the lab stuff that was done was based on the joint effort between me and Corporal Sneath throughout several years."

Do you have "as much information that is out there that's possible to get?" Herman asked.

"I believe at this point that we've done as much as we could possibly do in this case, very comfortable with it," Ford murmured.

Taking an unusual tack, Herman asked if there were "areas that you would like to see information on but for some reason it's not available or disappeared or it was lost due to the timing or anything of that nature?"

"Obviously, there's always—you have more evidence . . . it's my belief based on some circumstances that could not be controlled by anyone. There are things out there that will always be in question but there's no way of obtaining them," Ford stammered.

Ford took charge of the case again in 2008 when Huntingdon County DA George Zanic officially returned it to Franklin County, not 2007 as he testified. In the beginning, we were told he would remain on the case even though it went to Huntingdon. His disingenuous testimony on how thoroughly they investigated, and his comfort with it—the "constant communication" and "joint effort" meant nothing more than a standard line he offered the court. He seemed as misleading as Nelson had been when just minutes earlier, he claimed they had "no involvement in the case for a year and a half."

Lab work "throughout several years" could have been better described as sporadic, begrudging, and belated. While we searched for Carl, Ford told us we didn't need a body. He rejected the crime scene and the weapon, failed to investigate motive, and dismissed blood as berry juice and tobacco juice. Ignoring evidence, abandoning Carl's clothing in Erie at Mercyhurst College when the state forensics lab should have been analyzing it for gunpowder, blood, and damage was not diligent investigation. If Dr. Symes had not described and measured the hole in Carl's T-shirt and included it in his report, we would never have known it existed.

Corporal Sneath took the stand.

"How can you help us this morning Corporal?" Judge Herman asked.

Sneath testified that as lead investigator, while the case was in Huntingdon County, he was "involved in this investigation from the first day and continued through until today" and he believed it an "appropriate plea, a plea [deal] that given all the circumstances, serves justice in the Commonwealth of Pennsylvania and the people of the state fairly."

Sneath said that he "also had the benefit obviously of every detail in the investigation as lead investigator at one point what other troopers did, what work was done outside my own efforts as far as laboratory work and analysis, forensic applications, ballistics, all those things were available."

Huntingdon County had told us Trooper Sneath was off the case because of a promotion and transfer to Philadelphia, so it was confusing to hear him say that he was on it for its duration. To our knowledge they had no one assigned to the case for a long period, at least not actively.

The hearing shifted to the perpetrator. North agreed that he understood the nature of the charges to which he was pleading, that he had discussed the case and the elements of the crimes with his attorney and was presently not under the influence of drugs or alcohol, and that there had been no threats or promises made to persuade him to accept the plea.

"And is it correct that your understanding is that if the court accepts this plea you would receive a sentence of not less than twenty years nor more than forty years on third degree murder, and not less than two years nor more than seven years on the escape, and that those sentences would run consecutive; in other words, one after the other?" Nelson asked.

"Yes," North said.

"So that the total sentence, the total exposure that you would be looking at for these two offenses would be up to 47 years in jail and/or up to a $40,000 fine?" Nelson asked.

"Yes," he said, contorting to the limits of his constraints.

"And did anything happen to you while you were in jail that would cause you to enter this plea against your will or cause you to involuntarily enter this plea?" Judge Herman questioned.

"Nope," he mumbled.

"Do you have any questions you want to ask the court about this plea agreement?" Herman inquired.

"Nope," he said as he stared stonily at the judge.

We were right. North's minimum sentence of twenty-two years for escape and murder was far less than the thirty years Krom said he could get. We could never count on North serving the maximum of forty-seven years. That rarely happens. All the other charges fell by the wayside. Abuse of a corpse was the one charge I requested that Stewart consider adding to the initial charges, and he did. Only a second-degree misdemeanor, it wouldn't have netted more than a two-year sentence under Pennsylvania law, but we wanted that charge to remain. By dumping Carl in that rural location, North meant for him not to be found. It outraged our sensibilities, stole our right to a traditional viewing, prevented us from having Carl back for more than three years, and forced us to endure two heartbreaking services years apart. It was pure hatefulness and, as with many things North has done, he will not be held accountable for it.

Assistant District Attorney Angela Krom's summation covered several main facts, but with erroneous details. She recounted North's July 5, 2006, Franklin County Jail sentence and term of incarceration, and his failure to return to the jail three days into his work release employment on August 2, 2006. She declared those facts "sufficient for the jury to find Mr. North committed the crime of escape, graded a felony of the third degree" and mentioned the importance of "[incorporating] those facts into the facts of the third-degree murder."

Krom briefly described the August 10, 2006, apprehension of North by Trooper Warren Rhyner of the state police in Huntingdon County, after a high-speed chase. Rhyner found North with Carl's vehicle, driver's license, cellphone and credit card, and North identified himself as Carl Ryder. When police failed to locate Carl regarding his vehicle and personal property, further investigation revealed that "Mr. Ryder had been in the Outer Banks area of North Carolina since at least July 29, 2006, but had returned to Franklin County, Pennsylvania on August 5, 2006. Credit card receipts put Mr. Ryder in Newport News, Virginia on August 5 at 1:03 P.M. Surveillance from the Sheetz on Wayne Avenue in Chambersburg put Mr. Ryder in Chambersburg around 9:00 P.M. A woman (Carl's girlfriend Debbie) the police interviewed contacted Mr. Ryder by telephone at approximately 9:30 later that night. After that there is no further evidence of Mr. Ryder having contact with anyone."

A search warrant executed on Carl's vehicle on August 11, 2006 revealed "a significant quantity of blood" in the trunk. Also found in the vehicle was "an address book that appeared to have blood on it." The address book held North's prison ID.

Krom recounted that on August 16, 2006, "a decomposed body was located along Allison Road in Huntingdon County, Pennsylvania. The body was found approximately one hundred yards off the side of the roadway down an embankment." Dr. Harry Kamerow ruled the cause of death to be "blunt force trauma."

Continuing her summation, Krom said that forensic dentist Dr. Richard Scanlon positively identified Carl. At the time he was discovered, "the deceased was wearing only one Skecher shoe. The mate to that shoe had been found days earlier in a grassy field close to Ryder's residence by the state police who had searched Mr. Ryder's home." After recovery of a shotgun slug from the wall of Carl's residence on August 16, they took samples of "blood spatter in the area of the doorway." A soil sample from Carl's front yard was taken by the state police on August 18, 2006, because it appeared that a "quantity of blood had dried on the grass." The Pennsylvania State Police Crime Lab revealed that the DNA from "the blood in the trunk, on the address book, in the front yard, around the doorway as well as on the shotgun slug was Carl Ryder's blood."

Krom remarked that North had formerly been employed by Carl in his fencing business, describing it as a "kind of an on again, off again relationship, a friendship that was often very stormy."

Momentarily transposing names, Krom wrapped up her statement to the court by saying that between August 6 and August 11, 2006, "Mr. Ryder had—Mr. North had cashed in a quantity of wrapped change stolen from Mr. Ryder's home as well as used Ryder's credit card to make several purchases. In various statements the defendant has admitted to shooting Carl Ryder and disposing of his body."

"Based on the evidence the Commonwealth would argue to a jury that the defendant had caused the death of Carl Ryder by shooting him with a shotgun inside Ryder's residence, fatally wounded, Mr. Ryder bled out on his front yard. Rather than summoning emergency assistance or providing any type of medical care to Mr. Ryder, North loaded Mr. Ryder's body into his vehicle and drove the body to Huntingdon County where he dumped the body where it was later found, all of which would lead a jury to find that Mr. North maliciously caused the death of Carl Ryder."

It was vexing the way officials repeatedly misconstrued North's three-week employment as a friendship between Carl and North. There was no relationship beyond North's employment, and certainly not a friendship, yet that irritant remained threaded into this ordeal as if factual. Krom's "stormy" depiction implied a long relationship fraught with ongoing problems when the whole thing was a hire-gone-bad, a fatal mistake that cost Carl his life. Investigators had admitted to us they had proven North's statements during interviews to be lies, yet it appeared they all accepted them. It seemed like an attempt to make their work release program seem less risky for potential employers, as if killing a "friend" was a step better than killing your former employer.

We knew Carl better than anyone did, and had the two been friends, I would say so. Carl was friendly to almost anyone but considered only a select few as friends just like most people do, and we know who they are.

One of Carl's old schoolmates from thirty-four years earlier had passed through the area in August 2015. He decided to look Carl up, only to discover to his horror that Carl's life had violently ended nine years earlier. He listened to the story in disbelief. To this day, friends faithful to his memory occasionally wander in, still feeling the loss and emptiness left by this murder. They reminisce, pouring out stories of the "old days" but tinged with sadness. We love those visits because they remind us that Carl kept company with people of real character and real feelings—real friends!

I believe Krom's inaccurate information about the distance from the roadway where Angel found Carl's body originated with investigators. Carl was approximately sixty-six feet from the berm (I measured it myself), which would be twenty-two yards, not one hundred yards. One hundred yards is the actual playing field of a one hundred and twenty-yard NFL football field. North did not drag Carl's body the length of a football field. Krom also seemed a little unclear as to where police had apprehended North. It was in Mifflin County that the car chase ended, not Huntingdon County. The errors were troubling because it showed a lack of familiarity with details—indispensable knowledge in a murder case. It showed how disinterested prosecution was. We wondered how many more specifics they had overlooked, ignored, or misconceived.

As for the DNA, it really was Carl's blood, not tobacco juice or berry juice as Ford had insisted months earlier in March. Nor did transmission oil kill the grass in the front yard as police had suggested.

Abom's final statement to the court pointed to two justifications. He said that "had this case gone to trial, the defense would have presented evidence in the form of justification, specifically self-defense, regarding an altercation between Mr. North and Mr. Ryder that began as an argument and then as a physical altercation that if believed would have provided . . . justification in this particular matter regarding the killing of Mr. Ryder.

"In addition, Mr. North was aware that we could present evidence of voluntary intoxication or voluntary drugged condition as a defense would—it wouldn't be a complete justification, but it was a reduction and he's aware—reduction of the grading of a homicide offense."

Oh yes, the timeless self-defense strategy almost every killer turns to, and if believed, would be the "justification" for killing Carl. On the contrary, North sought out and unlawfully entered Carl's home, then lay in wait behind the door in a cowardly ambush. It was not an act of impulse or self-defense; North was prepared to kill and accomplished it in several attacks. There was no argument or physical altercation. It happened quickly. There was no way to justify any of it. The truth *would* eventually come out.

Lucky for North, he didn't have to defend his lies. If this case had gone to trial, the bulk of defense would have come from any testimony North or his attorneys might present. North's weak self-defense and impairment excuses would have been his only two justifications against a battery of evidence that was haltingly, and at times, unenthusiastically assembled or processed—but it was damning evidence all the same. He had shared a murder plan beforehand. DNA, latent prints, a bloody print, stolen items, money and car, taped interviews and shopping sprees, receipts, statements the night of arrest, boasts and writings in jail are just some of the available evidence of a willful murder. An involvement in a true accidental death would have brought with it feelings of remorse. I can tell you, there was no remorse and never will be. The police claimed they had between four hundred and fifty and five hundred pieces of evidence, so why didn't the District Attorney use it?

Judge Herman asked Krom a surprisingly astute question in view of their closemouthed investigation. Was there a "definitive cause of death that was arrived at or was it a question of two possible means of killing?"

"At the time the autopsy was completed by Dr. Kamerow, the state police and the Commonwealth were not in possession of the slugs that had been—or were not aware of the slug, had not had it tested for the presence of DNA," Krom claimed deceptively. "Dr. Kamerow's finding at that point was blunt force trauma and based on my conversations with him after the finding of the slug he was reluctant to change that, thus I believe we're left with blunt force trauma. Although we do have—Mr. North had made statements of various types indicating that he shot Mr. Ryder."

Krom's false claim that the state police and the Commonwealth were not in possession of or aware of the slug was astounding. It's a fact that police had removed the slug from the wall the same day they recovered Carl's body, and the pathologist autopsied Carl the next day. Kamerow didn't generate his report until a year later. Shocking as it is, it appears that no one bothered to mention the slug at the autopsy. Also, her reference to "slugs" made us wonder if there was additional evidence, we were not aware of, or was it just another misstatement.

The Commonwealth had nothing else to add, and Judge Herman called a recess. After lunch, he would announce whether the plea was acceptable, and if so, he would pronounce the sentence.

CHAPTER 24

THE PALE RIDER

And I looked, and behold a pale horse: and his name that sat on him was Death . . . —The Apostle John

We met Vicky Taylor for lunch. We had little appetite and our discussions revolved around North's infuriating presence, and how much time we hoped he would get. We discussed the cruel way Nelson played on our hopes for a trial, only to reveal the day after the election and day before the pretrial hearing that the plea deal was "back on the table." With heavy hearts we returned to the courtroom to hear the final word on our mishandled and misconstrued case.

We waited for near strangers to pronounce a reckoning for a very personal catastrophe, our hearts and souls at the indeterminate mercy of those whom we felt did not really care. To what extent would they represent us according to the guidelines for third-degree murder and escape?

THE SENTENCE

Judge Herman resumed, "It's a difficult and disturbing issue for the court because as soon as we received [input from victims and the community] back in the early part of the year, we began to move through these comments and statements from people affected by this crime, but it not only illuminated the incident from the standpoint of what possible sanctions would be appropriate in the case in terms of the degree of the offense and type of sentences that would be imposed, but it also helped the court understand how the investigation developed, and the victim's viewpoint of it, and why there is such a strong belief in the community that the ultimate penalty in this case—this is not a death penalty case, but the ultimate penalty, the highest penalty in this case would be life imprisonment without parole."

Herman said it was "clearly evident without little more than examination of [North's] history . . . through the pre-sentence reports that the expressions of Mr. North's conduct as being remorseless and showing no compassion for what he's done. . . . [T]he fact that he has been in the criminal justice system in similar circumstances on at least three other occasions. There had been previous probation and parole violations."

He acknowledged that North had "continued in the same conduct . . . which was well recognized by the people in the community that he committed additional burglaries that resulted—in some cases, more than one case—either firearms being in his possession, of firearms stolen, indicating a willingness to engage in highly dangerous behavior."

Herman said that people who had provided input described North as "coldhearted, calculating, and it appears the record bears this out, and . . . the killing that took place in the present case, it follows in that same pattern . . . all the letters and statements from the community indicated that Mr. Ryder was never shown any mercy or displayed any opportunity to avoid the death that befell him . . . and now Mr. North is not entitled to that consideration either, and while we may agree with that, that this is a case that certainly the conduct rises to the level of life imprisonment, first-degree murder, we have to take a cold hard look at how we would get there, and . . . it may well be true that this was—these were all intentional acts on the part of Mr. North, an intentional killing, premeditated, planned, and that there is substantial evidence of that killing, a specific intent."

Herman went on to explain that specific intent is what separates first-degree murder from third-degree murder, the "conscious intentional knowing objective that causes the death of another person" clarifying that third-degree murder is the "intent to do harm . . . but it lacks the fully formed intent to cause the end of a person's life even though the actions and the conduct of that person resulted in the death of another person."

Herman was right. North's criminal history bore out in the same pattern of calculation and cold-heartedness. Why then, with outstanding probation and parole violations, did Judge Walker drop a gun charge and Judge Van Horn grant work release?

Developing a motive was essential to the case, but no one applied any real effort, and as Herman said, "intent is what separates first-degree murder from third-degree murder." North said he was going to kill Carl, and the "sitting around waiting" letter I had discovered on the floor indicated he had no intention of leaving without obtaining whatever it was that he was waiting for, whether a car, money, revenge, or all three.

Herman continued, "It is believed that Mr. North waited—lying in wait for Carl Ryder, set up a plan to take his automobile and part of that plan was to kill him to do these things. And, again, this may be a correct assessment of the circumstances, but it's the burden of the Commonwealth to deliver that evidence to a jury so that they can conclude beyond a reasonable doubt that that in fact is what happened."

Herman mentioned that there was "somewhat of a gap in the evidence that the Commonwealth has available to it which would cause a jury to conclude beyond a reasonable doubt there is a specific intent to kill even though there were statements made by Mr. North . . . and as [Carl's family] refuse to go along with Scott North's lie about a struggle over a gun. . . ."

Herman said, "The Commonwealth, even if as [Carl's family] said, a jury would not believe Mr. North's testimony about what happened. . . . [T]he jury is going to look to the Commonwealth and say we don't believe Mr. North's testimony, but you have to tell us what evidence you have that supports a verdict of first-degree murder. . . . [B]ut at the time of trial that evidence will be in the hands of the defendant, Mr. North. He's the only one that was there.

"The Commonwealth would be at the mercy of whatever Mr. North chooses to describe the events and actions that took place between him and Mr. Ryder and, as I said, it may well be as the family described, but unfortunately the Commonwealth doesn't exactly have that particular evidence even though perhaps members of the Ryder family are convinced in their mind and, as I say, who knows, they may be right, that this is what happened. That nonetheless requires evidence, and we believe that there's a high likelihood that in this case the jury would find that this is a case of third-degree murder or perhaps even less, and we think that it's appropriate under the circumstances of this case that the court attempt to gain whatever public safety measures we can that are offered by the plea agreement in this case, and we intend to accept the plea agreement."

Herman said that given North's past "the history that Mr. North presents, his conduct, his attitude in this case certainly will justify that in a life sentence in the first-degree murder case, but the prerequisite for that simply would be a necessary conviction of first-degree murder, and we're afraid that the jury might be left speculating about the specific intent to kill because of the state of the evidence, so in that sense the court will accept the plea, and in terms of the sentence agreement itself he is to receive the maximum penalty for the charge of third-degree murder. The court cannot give him anymore penalty because that's the maximum penalty authorized by the legislature in this case."

This was why we so desperately needed an involved prosecutor who cared about "the state of the evidence" instead of one who, in our opinion, hurriedly pushed it off to another county, only to unenthusiastically mop it up when it was returned. Prosecution could have been so much more.

Herman said he intended to add an appropriate penalty for escape to the penalty for third degree murder, and he would consider North's prior record score. Abom declined the opportunity to provide any additional information on behalf of North, and North had no wish to address the court himself. For one who apparently cannot see clearly through the darkness of his own soul, he would never offer an apology. Nelson indicated that he had only some restitution figures to present.

Judge Herman pronounced Nelson's intended minimum of 22 years up to as many as 53 years including time North still had on the sentence he was serving before his escape. He said the prison board "cannot exercise its discretion to make any kind of release in that period of time before the minimum sentence, but even after the minimum sentence cannot do that without consulting with the victims."

Herman asked if a representative of the Ryder family had anything final to say. I thanked him for taking the time to look at everything—even though the decision was not what we wanted.

Herman replied that he had "the same feeling of disappointment. . . . [A]nd wish the results were different. . . ."

Herman completed the sentence orders. "Mr. North, even though that was the sentence that had been agreed upon in your case with your attorney and the district attorney, do you have any questions about the terms and conditions?

"No," he snapped.

The case that kept our lives swirling around the edge of a black hole for years was over by 1:37 P.M. North had the right to challenge his sentence by filing a motion for modification or reconsideration within ten days or file an appeal to the next higher court within thirty days. After he serves his minimum sentence, any further prison time will lie in the hands of the Pennsylvania Board of Probation and Parole. According to law, we have the right to submit a protest before they take any action to release him. The violent inmate who, as Herman put it, "continued in the same conduct" for years, with "a willingness to engage in highly dangerous behavior," will likely be free someday. Weighing continued punishment against an inmate's acceptance of responsibility is dubious. Blaming the victim and pleading no contest to murder is not accepting responsibility; it's just admitting that abundant evidence exists that can prove he did the heinous crime. I feel it fair to say that North acted true to his nature, and he only regrets getting caught.

The judge left the courtroom. Maybe he did the best he could, but justice fell far short. There would be no proportional judgment according to the damage North had inflicted upon Carl. Deputies huddled near the judge's bench talking among themselves instead of whisking North from the defendant's table like most courts do. My thoughts went directly to how easy it would be to step over the railing from the gallery and wring his murderous neck. I weighed the worth, breaking into a sweat, glancing back and forth several times from him to the police. They finally shuffled over and took him away when they heard me tell North to get back in his cage as I approached. There is just something idiotic about the way they handle things at that courthouse.

Krom approached us. "I'll release Carl's remains to you now," she said with a toss of her hair.

"If anything, further should come up concerning appeals or other issues with this case, will we be notified?" I asked.

"Yes," she said tersely. "I admire the way you fought for justice for Carl," she added.

I'm glad we did fight against such travesty. We did the best we could despite the crippling effects of official incompetence that we felt helpless to counter. I was told by an individual closely connected with the courthouse that had we not persisted and argued the way we did, based on the outcome of past cases, we would have been lucky to see North serve eight years.

This crime that caused so much suffering was so needless and preventable. Our hearts were heavy with the realization that North got his way. There would never be a trial. For all the fuss we kicked up, we were not able to impress upon the prosecutors that he did not deserve a bargain. Then again, this world isn't about who deserves what. For all our effort, we still carried in our hearts nothing but sorrow, ever-present grief, and the devastation all victims and survivors of violent crime live with. Before leaving the courtroom, we calculated 2030 as the year he would finish serving his minimum sentence, and the year we would have to deal with the parole board. A victim's advocate later said North's eligibility for parole would be 2029. They start the year prior to the date of the minimum sentence.

Vicky's September 18, 2009, article in the *Public Opinion* hinted at what was in store with the burglary sentence Krom had said North would first serve before starting his murder sentence.

RYDER'S KILLER GETS 22 TO 47 YEARS IN PRISON The Franklin County jail escapee who killed Amberson businessman Carl Ryder more than three years ago was sentenced Thursday to 22 to 47 years in state prison.

The sentence was part of a plea agreement in which north, 29, pleaded no contest to third-degree murder and guilty to escape.

North's sentence on the escape and murder charges will begin when his current burglary sentence ends. He still has six years to serve on that sentence, but he has already served the minimum. His attorney, John Abom, said after the hearing that if a state parole board chose to cut that sentence short, the newest sentence would begin at that time.

Herman said during the sentence hearing that with Thursday's sentence added to North's current sentence, he could be in state prison for about 53 years.

Several weeks after the hearing, we learned that North had begun serving his murder sentence immediately, instead of continuing to serve time for his burglary and the resentencing for parole violations as Krom and Herman had said was possible. We were not surprised.

I had devoted a good deal of time, up to that point, analyzing high-profile murder cases, and I had not run across any in which the murderer had claimed so many different scenarios. It was like a hit and miss to see which would work the best. They fed into his stories without scrutiny, each warring with the last. I had not found a case that held so much evidence yet languished for almost two years without so much as a murder charge. There were no complicated layers to peel back. It was neither a question of solvability nor a baffling cold case. The case seemed riddled with mismanagement, incompetence, and dishonesty. I never found an instance in which a prosecutor showed so little interest, claiming there was no murder scene, and pushing the case to another jurisdiction, only to suddenly acknowledge a murder scene existed upon its return.

We did what we could, short of filing a formal complaint with the Attorney General. The bungled case had lashed us to a seesaw of hope and despair, false hopes raised then dashed with deceit. We were slowly worn down by disinterest, obfuscation, and incompetence. It was difficult to accept that the case went the way *they* intended it to go. As Carl had said to me in my dream, ". . . they put me under the earth."

Krom refused my request to see the police reports and other documents concerning the case, claiming that they contained personal information they could not allow us to see. It was unreasonable that someone could not have redacted certain information so that we could have at least read copies of the reports. We knew that prosecutors had permitted other families to view documents at the courthouse after a closed case. Instead, she suggested I file a formal request under the Right-to-Know Law. I never bothered because police reports are not obtainable under that law. Months later, I requested a copy of the records from the State Police Commissioner, on the chance that they might relent. Not surprisingly, they denied my request.

Following the exhausting hearing and sentencing, an alarming vision or dream intruded into my sporadic and weary sleep one night. I saw Carl in his green field coat without his hands. I couldn't shake the disturbing image. It seemed to burn into my memory just because it was unpleasant and unwanted.

Krom had released Carl's skeletal remains to us after the sentencing, but they were still in Erie at Mercyhurst College. We would have to retrieve them ourselves. A family member happened to be near Erie on a job-related excursion. On his way home, he made a detour to meet with Dr. Symes to pick up the box that held Carl's remains.

On September 24, 2009, three years and fifty days after the murder, we held a second service in Carl's memory. As we removed a sealed white cardboard box from the back of the SUV, I hesitantly read the label: MISSING PHALANGES FROM RIGHT HAND. Finger bones were missing! I recalled the disturbing dream that I had tried so hard to forget. It was like a hellish nightmare. "Don't tell Mom," I said. "Not here anyway."

Carl's girlfriend, Debbie, commented to Vicky Taylor, who attended the service, "It's comforting to know where he's at, and to be able to visit his gravesite, but it still doesn't make his death any easier to accept."

Debbie was right. The familiar feeling of walking through deep water, which had plagued from the beginning, returned as we placed the white box into the oak casket that had been stored for three years. We added the green urn and covered both containers with a white linen cloth, then closed it. I forced myself to reason that Heaven has healed those missing finger bones and it no longer mattered. Considering the horrendous things that happened to him, I should have been thankful we had at least most of him back.

The men in the family carried him to the grave, this funeral no easier than the first. Minds under duress will alight on the most mundane surroundings and thoughts, seeking relief. We focused on the field as we sat in chairs by his casket.

"Look at the oats rolling," Clint said as we tried to fend off the stabbing grief by staring at the golden waves rolling with the breeze. It was as if an unseen free spirit brushed its hand across the grain before a backdrop of blue mountains and blue sky—the beautiful place from where Carl was untimely cut off.

Reverend Meagan Boozer recalled the first funeral in 2006, saying, "The shock of that moment was so very great." Acknowledging our ordeal and fight for justice, she said, "Carl was freed from the world the moment he took his last breath more than three years ago, but the family has been enslaved by the judicial process. It has been hard not to be overwhelmed in your fight for justice."

She cited the suffering of Job and his unwavering faith. It was our book of comfort. She prayed that we could find a way to let go of our hurt and anger and look to God for peace.

That's the key, finding a way through the darkest paths of atrocity to a sense of peace. A psychologist familiar with the case described this murder, our prolonged fight for justice, and the residual damage as akin to a psychological trauma borne from fighting ferocious bloody battles in war—fear rising and guts flying. A persistent trauma forever sticks with one's soul.

The week following the funeral, I spoke with a former employee of the Huntingdon County Courthouse to let her know we finally got Carl back. The conversation quickly turned to the handling of the case. She shared with me that of all the rumors heard pertaining to this case, there was always the comment that Franklin County did *not* want it. It had been an ordeal from beginning to end, but in the end, it caged North for at least a couple of decades in what he referred to as "my state prison."

Things still had not really settled down. On a restless night of October 5, 2009, I dreamed of death on a pale horse. The rider was a skull with big hollow eyes morphed with a horse skeleton as a single figure of otherworldly bones, all the same shade of ashen white. Nothing else existed around it as it came chasing in from the darkness, sliding by on a mission without so much as a glance toward me.

Clint called me at work three days later, on October 8, exactly three weeks to the day since the plea deal and sentencing. "Hey," he said. "I heard that Jack Nelson died."

I immediately thought of the watchful presence at our meeting three weeks earlier, the skeletal rider just three nights before, and the premonitory curved snake bones six months before the lie about there being no plea deal. The presence, watcher, or reaper had returned three weeks to the day and time of the unwanted plea deal. The rumor was that he bled out from an ulcer and died around 9:00 A.M. I can imagine it would be a bloody way to go, although not nearly as terrifying as bleeding out from a shotgun blast across the midriff. I heard that he had written a goodbye letter to his family, something Carl never got to do.

His family held a service, and he was praised by all his drinking buddies and venerated by courthouse colleagues. They said great things about him and laid him to rest.

We spoke to Nelson's replacement, District Attorney Matt Fogal, about our ordeal. He commented that he wished he had had the case. We would have welcomed that, had he proven himself a warrior of justice.

CHAPTER 25

LOOSE ENDS

And judgment is turned away backward, and justice standeth afar off: for truth is fallen in the street, and equity cannot enter. —The Prophet Isaiah

In November 2009, North filed a motion contesting the restitution he owed us for theft and damaged property. To my dismay, the court subpoenaed me as a defendant. I refused and suggested to Krom that she deal with North's attorney herself and whittle restitution down to an agreeable and decent amount that would compensate us for North's shopping spree, the loss of the car, damage to the truck, and the cost of the grave marker. The damage to other miscellaneous property and our lives could fall by the wayside.

I should have known better. Krom allowed the car to be removed from the list because "it would still be runnable." Really now, who in their right mind would want to replace the tires that had been destroyed by stop sticks and drive it as an ever-present reminder of where Carl had spent his last dying moment's locked in darkness? She worked out an agreement that held North liable for only the grave marker. Even though restitution is doubtful since he owes thousands of dollars to courts and previous victims, Krom should have strived to hold him accountable for purchases and things he destroyed during his crime spree.

That month, I arranged to have the vehicles moved by rollback from the Chambersburg barracks impound lot. They had been sitting so long that each tire had sunk into the asphalt in shallow dips. An empty bird's nest rested on the rear left tire of the truck. An officer pointed out that both vehicles had been full of bees the summer before. He also mentioned Nelson's "untimely death," which I ignored without comment.

Denver's CDC Repair & Towing removed the vehicles to their Shippensburg garage. With the car still on the rollback, I climbed a stepladder at the rear. I wanted to see whether the police really did remove the trunk liner. Hesitantly, I popped the trunk and saw that it was gone. A neatly wound one-hundred-foot extension cord lay on the back ledge of the trunk. It was empty of any other items. I slammed the lid shut within seconds of opening it and descended the ladder feeling very ill. I would never reopen it.

Inside the car, mouse nests filled the glovebox. I slammed it shut too. Some of Carl's clothing was still in the car. I removed a pair of jeans with a leather belt still in them, shorts, and other articles of clothing. They were dirty clothes from the Outer Banks. Cement trowels lay on the back floorboard, indication of the stonework that he had done while on vacation. There were maps; Carl always had those.

North had removed the factory license plate holder from the front bumper. We knew by credit card statements that he had bought a new one, apparently to change the look of the car, but he had never installed it. Two six-packs of Budweiser, bought at Whitsel's Pub the night police caught him, still sat on the back floorboard along with a Sony CD player and a scattered assortment of rap and head-banging heavy metal CDs. They didn't belong to Carl. Besides the "Freebird" song, Carl liked Creedence Clearwater Revival, and that type of music. Besides, he never bought CDs. He listened to the radio.

I fished out Carl's pocket Bible, the New Testament with Psalms and Proverbs, from among the CDs that North had played as he partied, shopped, and showed off his joyride to impressionable women as he finally made his own, brief place in the world by taking Carl's.

We had already decided against parking the car out of sight on Carl's property to sit and rust, which would have meant likely having to deal with it again. We certainly didn't want to run it ourselves or sell it and risk seeing it on the road as a reminder of the crime, knowing that Carl had been hauled in the trunk. I knew I would never be able to see it driven without the urge to chase it down, expecting to see North behind the wheel. Denver stashed the car out of sight in another town until a junkyard could destroy it. Carl's truck went into the garage to have the damaged ignition replaced, and many other things repaired because it had sat for so long.

I wanted to know the music genre that North's killer mindset enjoyed. On my way to work one day, I played parts of the heavy metal CDs that I had discovered in Carl's car. They were horrible lyrics that chilled the morning drive; songs about killing, slitting throats, missing souls, and being a killer.

What kind of junk is this? I wondered aloud. Freedom of expression is still alive, so far, but to me the words were alarming. They were a reminder that true evil is not just a fable about a horned devil with a pitchfork. Evil exists here as a real presence that latches onto anything keen to oblige it. I felt sick and engulfed in trash by the time I arrived at work. I still had no answer for where God had been on that night when evil had assailed Carl—why goodness lost out to such hate, where the saving angels had been. And I could only skate the surface in imagining what he must have felt as he was being murdered with no one to help him. Carl did nothing to provoke it but come home tired, only to be attacked by a hateful demon set on murder. It's likely that his family flashed through his mind in pictures and moments. He might have thought of Debbie, or a friend, or he might have had time to recall a special moment in his life, but one thing I know he did not have was mercy or help. I'm heartsick I was not there to save him, or to die trying.

The decent man died that night, and I have never understood why it had to be that way. Carl was privately close to God, said prayers; he was grateful for things. I even found a couple of short thank you notes to God among his many doodles, scribbles of appreciation when he received a divine lift or a lead in the right direction. He wrote whatever he was thinking when he had a pencil. I kept the notes. Carl knew about humility, hardships, and burdens of the heart. He knew about God.

At our request in December 2009, the police released items to us that had no or little significance to the case. They told us evidentiary items will remain in storage for fifty years, but with each person I asked,

I received a different answer. The one surprising item I signed for was a small magnetic tack hammer no longer than my hand. I'm sure using it in an attack could put a knot on someone's head, but it certainly didn't fit with the immensity of the injuries Carl had suffered. I was shocked that investigators had collected such a piddling item when they had left significant evidence untouched. They returned an answering machine and a few coins that North had not had time to spend. Police returned the splitting maul and two axes that we provided after being falsely informed that the slug was "clean" of DNA.

We requested a meeting with the investigators who had been involved, demanding an answer to why they sent the case away. As expected, they pointed out the county line on a map and stuck to their claim that there was no evidence of a crime scene, although amid the meeting Ford dropped a blatant contradiction when he stated, "it was political." The meeting was worthless.

In February 2010, our attorneys for the survivor suit executed a default judgment on the claim, suing Scott North and Showbest/AWI for Carl's pain and suffering between the time of his injuries to the moment of death, and loss of future earnings. An actuary calculated Carl's total estimated earning power based on his life expectancy, loss of retirement, loss of Social Security income, other financial losses, and loss of enjoyment of life. A jury assessed the facts and awarded damage. The established amount, along with a final order on litigation, allowed our attorneys to appeal to Superior Court to reinstate a claim against the company, and it was on notice to participate at trial if they wanted.

Showbest/AWI declared that they had no standing and could not intervene because Judge Van Horn had dismissed the case. Even though she had issued a final order dismissing the case, the Superior Court said we had a right to develop facts.

North admitted to our private attorneys that he shot Carl from the right, and "witnessed Carl Ryder die at his home," that it was the result of a "gunshot wound, which entered under his ribs on the right side of his body (just like we said it happened)." Carl lived a short time after North shot him, during which he "walked approximately ten feet, from inside his home to his outside deck, where he collapsed, and blood pooled around his body." North piously claimed that he "knelt" to determine if Carl was dead.

This partially true story established Carl's conscious pain and suffering, and supported the avulsion noted in the autopsy that indicated North shot Carl from the side, although it was a much-sanitized account, as we expected. There was no indication that blood had pooled on the deck. Blood would have stained old wood, making it very visible. The blood pooled and soaked into the soil approximately sixteen feet from Carl's front door. I doubt instinct would have allowed Carl to walk while trying to save his own life; he would hurriedly stumble if possible. Furthermore, the autopsy provided a very strong indication of additional attacks, not to mention the existence of two sabots, a sharpened metal post, and a bloody knife. North didn't kneel; he pursued to make sure he accomplished what he set out to do. If he was that concerned, he had Carl's cellphone and could have dialed 911 instead of inflicting more wounds and dumping him in the wilderness. North's half-truths and blood evidence proved he shot Carl inside his front door, contrary to Nelson, Stewart, and the police initially insisting nothing happened there, and then belatedly re-enacting a "struggle" story. Despite political whims and lies distorting the case, we knew the truth from the beginning.

The justice system did not serve us well, but the courts were done with our case for the most part, and despite the risk of yet another inmate escaping on work release, we were finally feeling a bit of a reprieve when another senseless tragedy hit us. Murder and evil come in many forms and from any direction, and at times, strangely intertwine in eerie coincidences. In late July 2010, a nine-year-old girl at a babysitter's house near Shippensburg shook Uncle Terry's grandson, ten-month-old Heath Ryder, and slammed him into a crib. Heath's parents, Mark and Shelly, begged the doctors at Milton S. Hershey Medical Center to give him a chance, and they did, but after three days, they determined he had suffered severe and irreparable brain trauma. On August 2, the doctors removed Heath from life support. It was the same day as North's birthday escape four years earlier.

In the fall of 2010, I found a smidgeon of hope, or rescue, or maybe purpose, at the possibility of helping others who live with grief, while searching for a way to help myself. I discovered the PA Speaker's Bureau; a program for victims of crime who are interested in helping other crime victims. An application must be submitted, and the applicant is required to go through a screening process to determine if they are psychologically ready to contribute to the program. The successful applicant then attends a weekend training course to prepare for speaking to other crime victims in a group setting. I had a lot to say about grief, so I figured I had a lot to offer.

Over the months, I requested an application three times by phone, but never received one. In July 2011, I made my fourth request in writing. I asked if the bureau still existed, and if it did, why I could not seem to obtain an application. Someone finally contacted me and advised that it did indeed exist, renamed Crime Victims Alliance of PA, and assured me I would soon receive an application. It never came. I made this book my purpose and contribution to victims instead.

Our attorneys were surprised to find Judge Herman presiding in December 2010 for the pretrial conference in the ongoing survivor suit. Twenty minutes into the hearing, Herman suddenly and somewhat abashedly admitted that he was not sure why he was assigned to the hearing. It was Judge Van Horn's case, but she had failed to note she was recusing herself, *if* that was her intent. We had no objections since we didn't trust her either, but it raised the question of why she did not remove herself at the start before doing damage to our suit by dismissing it with prejudice.

Herman was satisfied with our attorney's preparation. They submitted the stipulations and admissions, and the expert report became part of court record to use in later proceedings. We were going to trial unopposed against North only, but before we could continue, the court needed to determine which judge was supposed to be on the case. If Van Horn still had the case, it would be up to her if she wanted to set a new pretrial hearing. A trial date was set for March.

Van Horn apparently no longer wanted involved after she did her part dismissing the suit against the company, and in January 2011, jury selection took place in Herman's court where twelve jurors and two alternates received instructions to not look into or discuss the case. A trial was set for March 2011.

In March, I testified about Carl's business, the type of work he did, his private contract work, contract with Lowe's, and his plans to expand his business to the Outer Banks area for part of the year. Without opposition, the trial was over by noon. The jury calculated damages and awarded $1.1 million in compensation against North. We never expected to get it, nor cared. Carl, the direct victim of this heinous crime, cannot be compensated, and no atonement on this earth can be made to us—we cannot have Carl back. What we really wanted was to expose the irresponsibility of the county and employer, but we didn't get that either.

Our attorneys then filed to hold AWI/Showbest accountable for the compensation. In turn, Judge Herman denied our motion to reverse Van Horn's decision to dismiss our suit against the company. "[Persons] approved for the work release program in Franklin County do undergo screening, both in terms of their potential for violence and their likelihood of flight."

Herman ruled that the company had a named manager in charge of general supervision, complying with the Probation Department's rules. He said that in "discussing the ruling with the Honorable Carol L. Van Horn, it is clear that . . . our colleague had no specific recollection of any facts relating personally to North and did not at the time recall approving him for work release two years before."

Judge Herman—who had sentenced North for murder, had spoken of North's demonstration of "a willingness to engage in highly dangerous behavior," and had also mentioned "previous probation and parole violations"—now ruled there was no evidence that North "was known, or should have been known, as a person with a 'peculiar tendency'" toward dangerous acts. He claimed North had "no history of violent behavior" and "it was not foreseeable he would elect to leave the job site."

Herman said that imposing a duty upon an employer would make companies reluctant to participate in the vital program. It would result in "high cost" to participating employers to provide "security guards" or "high fencing" and it would lead to "high consequences" of reduced participation in work release programs. He concluded there was no duty of care owed to Carl "who had the misfortune to cross North's path."

What about the high cost of Carl's life? The ruling meant the court viewed a gun-toting felon known to attack people and animals as non-violent, and the county, regardless of consequence, can freely hire out any violence-prone inmate to a company for which it has outdated and incorrect records and which provides no tangible supervision. The mention of guards and fencing took it to the level of absurdity. No one expects employers to provide that level of security. The public just expects legitimate employers and responsible supervision as a deterrent to escape. Furthermore, Carl did not "cross North's path," nor was he at the wrong place at the wrong time. He entered his own home to go to bed. We appealed our case to the Pennsylvania Superior Court.

CHAPTER 26

THE LORD ALSO SAID

Such as sit in darkness and in the shadow of death, being bound in affliction and iron. —*King David*

Scott North, inmate HJ7560, was transported to Camp Hill State Prison, classified, and assigned to the medium-security Greensburg State Correctional Institution near Pittsburgh. With several misconducts so far during his latest prison stay, he will be eligible for parole in November 2029, although the court said we would have our say each time a parole hearing comes up. Even though Franklin County got "rid of it," we never will. Carl was murdered in 2006 and his murder case was wrapped up in 2009. He doesn't get a second chance at life.

Behind bars, the system makes choices for him. He has a job assignment, whether he wants one or not, but we are not permitted to know what it is. Wages range between 19 and 51 cents an hour with a thirty-hour workweek depending on ranking, performance, and time on the job. He pays a few cents at a time toward the thousands of dollars in fines, court costs, and restitution he owes to prior victims dating back years. We are last on a long list, and don't expect to ever be compensated. It's an insult anyway, when the thing he really owes us is his life. Restitution is court-ordered compensation that victims of serious crime rarely see.

We know that releasing North would endanger society, but in the year 2029, the state parole board will have the authority to grant or deny parole after he has served his minimum sentence. A 2018 Special Report on recidivism from the U.S. Department of Justice shows an estimated

68 percent of released prisoners in thirty states were arrested within three years, 79 percent within six years, and 83 percent within nine years. Even without proof of statistics, I believe it is highly likely that he will resume victimizing people if released, for there is no pill to change his nature.

If paroled, he would be required to submit a home plan to the parole office and list his intended address. Guidelines require that field agents interview the permanent resident at the address before approval or disapproval of the home plan. If he is released, I suggest that the judge who initially granted him work release, or the employer who left him on his own, or the plea-dealing prosecutor readily offer their home as part of his home plan, since they felt he was not enough of a threat to keep in jail, keep supervised, or put away for life. They can sleep well knowing they are safe as he transitions from prison to society.

We registered with the state's Office of Victim Advocate, established in 1995 to represent crime victim rights before the parole board. We worried about having to provide written or recorded statements to the board rather than face-to-face testimony. Then new legislation provided victims with a crucial right. Susan Hooper, whose brother was poisoned to death by his wife, crusaded to change that antiquated representation. Her own tragedy prompted her to lobby endlessly for the right to testify in person at parole hearings. Senator Lisa Baker was chief sponsor of Senate Bill 508, which allows crime victims and their families to address the parole board directly, face to face, without relying on written or taped communication or the Office of Victim Advocate to represent them. We are relieved at this new bill and will be at every parole hearing that may occur in the future, no matter how difficult it will be.

Bad dreams are always the most persistent of dreams, especially after a traumatic experience. On August 5, 2010, exactly four years after the murder, a writhing nest of snakes tormented my sleep. One, a partial skeleton, repeatedly struck at me. The dream led me to expect something troubling somewhere, most likely court. That would turn out to be true.

Angela Krom never notified us of appeals as she had promised. Through an article in the paper, we learned that North had filed an appeal under the Post-Conviction Relief Act, claiming that he was eligible for relief because the plea deal, he had agreed to was involuntary and coerced. As if he were the victim of a punishment and bribe scheme, he blamed the jail for confining him to the restrictive housing unit prior to his plea, and afterward permitting re-entry into the more privileged general jail population. He requested a withdrawal of the plea and a move to trial "as if this did not happen."

North's appointed attorney filed an amended petition based on North's claim that his attorneys told him they would not work very hard on his case because he wasn't paying them. In addition, he claimed that the court didn't grant a request for new counsel, prosecutors didn't have a cause of death or the ability to prove North guilty of murder and he had learned that information through letters instead of from his attorneys. The petition argued that North's attorneys failed to adequately research the issues of cause of death, intent to commit burglary, and intent to kill, which forced him into a plea agreement. North placed further blame on the Greensburg State Prison deputy superintendent for discussing the case with Krom, claiming that it resulted in harassment by people at the prison, making his situation "uncomfortable." He requested a transport for a hearing on the matter so the court could withdraw the allegedly coerced plea.

North's claim that his attorneys never informed him that prosecutors had no cause of death was baseless. He had been present at the preliminary hearing when Krom drew attention to their failure. He had soaked up that information like a sponge and delighted in their lack of specificity. Furthermore, he had signed a paper at his sentencing, *and* verbally agreed that his plea was voluntary.

Judge Herman heard North's appeal at a hearing by teleconference in 2011, all but five years after Carl's death. The hearing was over by the time we learned of it, again, through the local paper.

North failed to show that his plea had been involuntary or that his attorneys never advised him of available defenses, or that they had provided erroneous advice regarding his sentence. He did not get the trial he wanted to avoid at first, and we had so badly wanted. He is stuck with his plea bargain.

As for politics. Krom had won her election for judge for Fulton-Franklin County Court of Common Pleas back in May 2009, although not with votes from her home county. Nelson's campaign management had pulled it off thanks to Fulton County's vote. Krom spent over $44,000 to fund her campaign, compared to an opponent who spent merely $11,000 yet received more Franklin County votes than Krom. Even so, she had advanced from prosecutor to the bench as a Franklin County Judge in January 2010.

In January 2011, Attorney General Tom Corbett took office as Pennsylvania Governor. He nominated Franklin County Warden John Wetzel as state Secretary of Corrections. The State Senate Judiciary Committee briefly suspended the confirmation hearing at the request of the Democratic caucus concerning an issue over a new multimillion-dollar state prison. The committee later lifted the postponement and Wetzel received his appointment.

Wetzel also serves on the Board of Directors for the Council of State Governments' Justice Center with legislators and other officials to guide projects for the Justice Center such as the National Reentry Resource Center and Justice Reinvestment Initiative. They grapple with skyrocketing costs of corrections, sentencing policy revisions, and transition issues from prison to community—including *public safety*.

In early 2013, the Senate Judiciary Committee revealed a plan to close Cresson and Greensburg state prisons and farm out the prisoners to other prisons. Somehow, the Department of Corrections failed to notify eight hundred prison employees that they could lose their jobs, even though the plan to close the prisons had been in the works during all of 2012. In defense of the indifference, Secretary Wetzel said, "We did not do [notification] well. I take sole responsibility for that. There is no playbook for this."

How hard is it to notify employees that their jobs are in jeopardy? Some were offended that he didn't bother to stay for the remainder of the hearing to hear the union's testimony.

In early summer of 2013, officials transferred Scott North from Greensburg state prison to a new, state-of-the-art 200-million-dollar facility in Bellefonte, Pennsylvania, less than two hours north of the scene of the murder. In his dedication speech for the new prison, Wetzel said he was confident "the operation of this prison will further the Department of Corrections' mission of public safety and offender rehabilitation."

In November 2013, Huntingdon County District Attorney George Zanic, who had sent our case back to Franklin County where it belonged, was elected as judge. He began his tenure as Huntingdon County President Judge in January 2014.

Governor Tom Corbett left office in January 2015 after losing his bid for a second term to Tom Wolf, marking the first time ever in Pennsylvania that an incumbent governor lost a re-election since the state allowed second terms under the 1968 Constitution. Some political observers believed Penn State's scandalous Jerry Sandusky case, in which Corbett had been involved while previously serving as attorney general, had doomed a second term as governor. In Franklin County, retiring President Judge Herman administered the oath to Judge Van Horn in January, as she assumed the role of the new President Judge of the 39th Judicial District of the Court of Common Pleas in Franklin and Fulton Counties.

A year later, Wetzel and new Governor Tom Wolf announced that the Department of Corrections had reduced the state inmate population by 1,598 over the preceding two years. Wetzel said they were "expecting reductions of equal or greater amounts in future years." That sounded analogous to the inmate population reduction at the Franklin County Jail that he had also boasted about not long after Carl's murder: "We don't control the front door. We don't control the back door. This isn't a 100 percent success type business, but we're headed in the right direction."

They should always have 100 percent control over their doors. Murder by their escaped inmate did not seem like the "right direction" to us. Despite Wetzel's claims, the number of employed inmates at the Franklin County Jail dropped to about 40 percent two years after Carl's murder (*Public Opinion* newspaper, www.publicopiniononline.com, Chambersburg, PA. June 1, 2009, "Franklin County Jail Inmates Having a Tougher Time Finding Jobs for Work Release Opportunities".) Some of the decrease can be attributed to a downturn in the economy, but we had been told by several local business owners their reason for not hiring inmates was because of the murder. They grew leery of the work program. With plenty of other applicants available, employing inmates was not worth the risk.

Of further concern, budget woes drove the Department of Corrections and Governor Wolf to close Cresson and Graterford prisons in 2013 and 2018. They are now considering additional prison closings, which would ultimately increase the parolee population. Doing this would be gambling with public safety, like the county-level "reform" that led to our tragedy.

Concerning ongoing efforts to reduce the state's prison population by increasing parolee numbers, my view remains the same as when Wetzel chuckled in court at our hearing. Overzealous plans are never compatible with public safety, and I would not trust him or the state with my life or with my family's life.

In 2018, there were ninety-three murders committed by Pennsylvania state parolees. Department of Corrections Secretary, Wetzel, and Governor Wolf's 2016 expectations of "reductions of equal or greater amounts [of incarcerated] in future years" is in full swing. The overhaul of the parole system had made Wetzel overseer of parole agents who say they have been stripped of discretion in their ability to remove potentially dangerous parolees from the street. Six homicides committed within two months' time during the summer of 2019, prompted public outrage.

One parolee beat a two-year-old to death. One shot a police officer three times in the back. Another strangled his girlfriend's mother, after which he set fire to her home. Another parolee stabbed his own sister and niece to death and stabbed his nephew who survived. He had three parole violations between the time of his release and the killings. Another parolee who stabbed an eight-year-old boy to death was under maximum supervision after serving twenty years for third-degree murder. His twenty-seven misconducts during his prison stay included breaking another inmate's jaw and stabbing his cellmate in the eye. No time was added to his sentence for the incidents. According to Pennlive, state Secretary of Corrections, Wetzel, told the Associated Press that the parolee's record was clean for seven years prior to his release. Whether it really was or not, he obviously is a violent man and should not have been released. Wetzel stated publicly that "his agency will review the parolees' history in prison . . . and try to determine if something should have been done differently."

Blackwell, president of Pennsylvania State Corrections Officers Association called for an independent review by state lawmakers because Wetzel's agency "already had a chance to study the system that it helped create." He said he does not trust the Department of Corrections to identify its own problems, which are "rooted in a disregard for the opinions of prison guards who interact with inmates day in and day out" and their "mechanical checklist" doesn't work.

Because of these latest crimes by parolees, Representative Aaron Bernstine introduced legislation that would preclude the parole board from prematurely releasing an inmate at the expiration of minimum sentence if the inmate was convicted of a violent offense while incarcerated. In September 2019, The House of Representatives passed House Bill 1855 called Markie's Law after the eight-year-old boy who was stabbed to death. It was tabled in the Senate in June 2020 with no action taken since then.

Concerning the closing of prisons, Governor Wolf removed Wetzel from participating in the process after a public hearing in October 2019, on whether to close a state prison in Luzerne County, because he inadvertently commented into a hot mike, "This does suck. I wish I didn't have to close this fucking facility." He added, "It is what it is." After those remarks he leaned toward executive deputy secretary George Little who was seated beside him and was heard saying, "Honestly, we're just making it look like I'm paying attention. I just want people to think that I'm paying attention."

As I said earlier, I would not trust Wetzel or the state with my life or my family's life.

———~⁓—

As for our survivor suit, our attorneys had filed a Brief for Appellant (notice of appeal to higher court), requesting a review of the case. Two Pennsylvania Superior Court judges ruled against us; a third found the case troubling. The court ultimately upheld the rulings of Judges Van Horn and Herman letting North's employer off the hook.

In our argument that the lower court should have permitted us to conduct a discovery to determine if AWI might have known of North's propensity for violence, Superior Court ruled that that determination had been already made by the county, and AWI had no duty to Carl because Franklin County Probation cleared North for work release. The court said he was acceptable for the work release program because "he would not harm or injure others and was not a flight risk."

The Superior Court ruled that the employer had a named manager in charge of general supervision of the worksite and properly complied with Franklin County Probation's *Rules for Employees of Pre-Release Inmates* handbook. Shockingly, the court claimed that the record showed a prompt notification by the employer to the authorities within ten to fifteen minutes of learning of North's escape. Furthermore, the court claimed that North was not an employee of AWI when he killed Carl, and that he had been temporarily released from custody of the Franklin County Jail because there was no reason to believe he would escape or injure others. The court asserted that an "alleged temporary lack of direct supervision" did not breach a duty owed to a third person such as Carl.

The Superior Court described Franklin County's work release program as "vital" to the community, and as having "great social utility" to help rehabilitate prisoners and smooth their return to society. The court claimed that imposing a duty would be the "death knell of the work release program if employers were to serve as jailers."

The Superior Court denied our motion requesting that it rehear the case *en banc* (with the entire nine-judge bench). The court's final ruling has ramifications for the entire state. It means the state doesn't consider felons with a long criminal history, violent propensities, and work release violations a risk and they are still acceptable for work release if their county says so. The employer can leave an inmate on his own if there is a designated supervisor, whether present or not. There is no consequence for breach of supervision; the employer has zero liability for failing to oversee the inmate, and it doesn't matter that the company approved to participate in the work program isn't the same company the county has listed on their records. An unsupervised inmate can be absent for an extended period, yet the state and county can claim the employer promptly notified officials no matter how much time passed before the discovery of the escape or the length of time it took to look for the inmate before reporting the escape. Should an inmate commit murder after walking off from his place of employment, the state doesn't consider the escapee to be an employee of the place from which he escaped. The ruling creates a conflict when the "social utility" of a poorly run work program has become more important than the government's own mission of protecting public safety. Our fight was over. We had little chance in either court to hold anyone accountable for the flawed work program.

It's nearly impossible to wring good from evil but striving to overcome the damage evil creates can lead to something good. Our cousin Mark Ryder had also felt the sting of injustice after the horrific July 2010 death of his infant son Heath at the hands of a nine-year-old girl under the neglectful watch of a "trusted" babysitter. The light penalties for those involved drove Mark to seek justice for future victims. With the assistance of Franklin County District Attorney Matt Fogal, who described the case as the most disturbing he ever handled, House Bill 217, Act 12 sponsored by state Representative Rob Kauffman, passed the Pennsylvania Senate in June 2017. Signed by Governor Wolf, it provides for harsher penalties for endangering the welfare of a child or creating a substantial risk of death or bodily injury of a child. Mark said, "It won't bring back our son, but we can hope it will make a difference for someone else."

As for our experience, we had struggled through a never-ending swamp of injustice, hoping in vain for justice. It was a relief when the courts finally were finished with Carl's case.

However, many of those who played a role ultimately answered to a higher court. An unusually large number of people directly or indirectly related to the case have since died.

Lieutenant Governor and President of State Board of Pardons, Catherine Baker Knoll, who never acknowledged our letter of complaint about Franklin County's work release program, died on Wednesday, November 12, 2008, from neuroendocrine cancer at the age of seventy-eight.

Franklin County District Attorney John "Jack" Nelson fell ill on October 5, 2009 and died three days later. At fifty-eight years old, he

bled out from an ulcer three weeks to the day North received his plea
bargain and sentence. County employees claimed that when they cleared
out Nelson's office, they discovered so many empty whiskey bottles it
looked like a barroom. The 2001 Harshman murder case is like a bad
penny that keeps turning up. It resurfaced again in May 2015, when a
key witness pleaded the fifth (refused to divulge self-incriminating information) about an alleged deal with Nelson for testimony and early
parole. In 2019, a federal judge overturned Harshman's conviction and
ordered a retrial or set free. Certain Franklin County judges recused
themselves from the case. In 2020, Harshman chose the lesser of two
evils; he pleaded no contest over a retrial, making him eligible for parole
because of the time he had already served.

State Senator Terry Punt, who did acknowledge our complaint, sadly
died of heart complications at fifty-nine on Monday, December 27,
2009. He faithfully served the 33rd Senatorial District for thirty years.

Huntingdon County Coroner Ron Morder, who was present the day
police recovered Carl's body, was killed along with a passenger on Monday, February 24, 2011, when the garbage truck he was driving hit a tree.
They were both forty-four.

Ralph "Scotty" North, former cop and father of the killer, died of a
brain tumor on Thursday, January 24, 2013. He was sixty-four.

Attorney Rick Bushman, who strangely recommended that we dis-
pose of Carl's property through sale soon after his murder, died of brain
cancer on November 3, 2015, at age sixty-eight.

———～———

Our family, from the oldest member to the youngest, and those not
yet born, lives with an emptiness that cannot be filled. The young girls
who so admired and loved Uncle Carl saw murder touch their lives before they even understood it. It broke our hearts and still plays havoc as
we live knowing the terror that Carl must have felt.

We dread the coming of dates, year after year. Summer creeps up,
descending moodily into August, and by the fifth, that tormenting night
is upon us again to reopen the wounds. There is no joy without thoughts
of Carl not being here with us. The good times are fragile; a constantly
mended thin veneer over a deep wound. Clint's birthday is marred by the

murder of his brother. It doesn't matter that it's a different year. It weighs on our souls as if there is not enough air to breathe. Old nightmares revisit and the miserable nights slip into days of fresh pain. Still, we value the rare moments of repose, and the importance of friends and family; we have a heightened awareness of evil.

Carl never got to be Clint's best man at his wedding. Leah missed out on a brother-in-law whom she would have adored. He never got to see his nieces Stacey and Jordyn marry, nor his sisters and nieces earn their degrees. He never saw Madi grow up; only three when she lost her Uncle Carl, she mentioned him for several years after he was gone. He never met baby Savannah. Scott North robbed those little girls of experiences, memories, and love. Carl's older nieces have fond memories of him and still mention the things they did together. That's all there is now—those happy memories of yesterday that intensify today's longing for things that should be but are not.

A state police employee, not comprehending our ordeal, suggested that we find a "new normal." Normal is gone, obliterated. The suggestion is akin to implying that because the killer is behind bars, we now have closure. Closure is not even a miserable comfort, let alone a finality. It's a relief he's imprisoned, but there will never be closure because there's no way to fix atrocity, and he will always be trying to get out. There is no way to satisfy the debt with a few years behind bars. It's not even an empty victory. Nothing marks the end.

Only one person, either brave or naïve, suggested that it might be beneficial to forgive Scott North for killing Carl. Perhaps from a religious or maybe a philosophical point of view, the person meant well. But I can't excuse a murderer on a crime spree, who made many choices along the way. Forgiveness is a godly virtue, and I have extended it a few times in my life, but I feel no moral imperative to pardon, no spiritual obliga-tion, and no duty to shower my brother's killer with any goodness I may still have in my heart. Pardon can be a tonic to some, but I would better serve myself by gathering the remnants of my shattered life, wiser to the evil that lurks in every corner of this world. I would be better off accept-ing that the Almighty doesn't stop evil for us mortals.

North showed no remorse, and remorseless people don't seek forgive-ness—they seek more victims. It's unlikely he will ever change his twisted way of thinking. Some people are just outside the bounds of humanity. The black heart who took my brother is still here—a counterweight to anything good—and I don't like it. I bear no shame in feeling that a special spot in the circles of hell would not be hell enough for his murderous soul.

In my opinion, he is more than capable of killing again, and it's doubtful any amount of prison time will change him. I wasn't opposed to witnessing his execution—but since that will never be, I will be here to slam shut and hold fast any door to freedom that may crack open for him, should he come up for parole.

We must take the hits and try to live on the best we can. There is one small bright spot— the cabin where North holed up before he murdered Carl was eventually sold to a dear relative, Sally McVitty. It never sits empty now. The shadow that had clung to it has vanished.

We have tried to move forward with our lives. Loree earned her NMD degree from Southwest College of Naturopathic Medicine in Tempe, Arizona. She views the handling of the case as politically motivated. Sarah owns a skincare practice in Winter Gardens, Florida. She took Carl's death very hard but refuses to slip into the pit of grievance and says little about the treatment we suffered. Chris works for a heart specialist in Florida and carries her sadness close to her heart. Clint runs his dump truck at construction sites. It takes too much out of him to rehash the horrendous experience. Mom closed her shop, sold her place, and moved into an addition that Clint had built onto his house. She has always felt that those responsible cared little because our family had little political influence. Natalie worked at a theological seminary at the time, and thought of Carl often, her life was indelibly changed. She passed away in January of 2020. I left the Pennsylvania State Police for employment with another state agency. Any positive notions I had about law and politics have been replaced by a hard-edged awareness that both can be readily twisted. I cannot help but hold a grudge against those who exacerbated our pain by ignoring their responsibility. Carl's girlfriend Debbie mourns him daily, and I doubt that her grief will ever diminish. She has remained single. Nieces have grown up, and work and attend college. Carrie works for a hospital. She would love to know Carl, now, the way she knew him then as a young girl who adored him. Stacey married and works for a heart specialist in Florida. She becomes uncharacteristically reticent at the mention of Carl's murder. Gayle moved to Arizona and attends grad law school. Jordyn moved to Florida, near Sarah and Chris. Little Madi is not so little anymore. The A's she worked for in high school payed off and she left her volleyball tournaments behind to attend Arizona State University. Jordan Hennessy, the young boy who built the memorial out of boards, sticks, and stones in Carl's field, worked as an executive legislative assistant to North Carolina State Senator Bill Cook until his term ended in 2019. He attends a university and owns his own cleaning business. He will never forget his pal Carl. Dad became ill not long after Carl was murdered and slowly declined, succumbing on Father's Day 2013. He felt that North should be shot and thrown into the wilderness for the animals and worms to consume. Dad's brother, our Uncle Terry, who lost both his nephew, Carl and baby grandson, Heath to homicide, passed away the following year—2014—also on Father's Day. He often spoke of Carl and the things they had done together. We all feel profoundly betrayed, and those whom the prosecutors robbed of a victim statement at the close of the case will never forget it.

Not long after the case closed, Loree dreamed that Carl was standing in the company of twin fawns in a beautiful place of mountains, streams, and fields. "I made it!" he said. We know he did, and God has not forgotten that horrible summer night that took Carl from us, just a few feet from the special maple tree that he often prayed beneath.

Therefore, I leave it to God because I believe He also misses seeing Carl live the life He gave him. God did not mean for this to happen. I have come to realize that this murder not only hurt us, but it also hurt God. "'For I know the thoughts that I think toward you, saith the Lord, thoughts of peace, and not of evil, to give you an expected end' (KJV, Jer. 29:11)."

The Lord also said, "Vengeance is mine."

CHRONOLOGY OF EVENTS

July 20, 2006 – Carl Ryder leaves his home in Amberson, Franklin County, for a vacation in the Outer Banks.

Aug. 2, 2006 – Scott North, serving time in Franklin County Jail for burglary, flees his work release assignment in Shippensburg and heads for Amberson and Carl Ryder's residence. It is his 26th birthday.

Aug. 4, 2006 – Diana Hennessy, owner of a cabin next to Carl's place, finds that someone has been in the cabin and left items behind. She senses the person is still around and leaves hurriedly.

Aug. 5, 2006 – On his way home from the Outer Banks, Carl stops at a friend's house, and talks by phone with his girlfriend Debbie at 9:29 P.M. It is the last time that anyone close to Carl speaks with him. Carl arrives home at about 10 P.M., where he is ambushed by Scott North and murdered with Carl's shotgun.

Aug. 7, 2006 – North shows up looking "crazy" at an ex-girlfriend's workplace in Chambersburg. Frightened, she calls state police, and they tell her to call back if he returns. North goes on a shopping spree with Carl's credit cards and money.

Aug. 11, 2006 – State police contact Ryder's family to ask if they've heard from him. Police say they caught Scott North in Ryder's car. Family gathers at Carl's place where police are conducting a desultory search. There is considerable blood around the residence.

Aug. 12, 2006 – Family members find two sabots, or parts of fired shotgun shells on the property, but police are not interested in them.

Family begins searching the mountains for Carl. They continue for five days.

Aug. 16, 2006 – Carl's body is found off Allison Road, Tell Township in Huntingdon County after a passer-by reports suspicions.

While Carl's body is being recovered Franklin County District Attorney Jack Nelson hands off the case to Huntingdon County.

Ryder's family begins searching his property, finding a piece of a gun barrel that had been sawed off a shotgun with a hacksaw in Carl's shed.

Dr. Harry Kamerow conducts an autopsy at J.C. Blair Hospital in Huntingdon. Some of the remains are cremated and will be returned to the family; the rest is held as evidence.

Aug. 18, 2006 – Dr. Steven Symes of Mercyhurst College in Erie arrives to examine the Blairs Mills crime scene. He takes Carl's skeleton and clothing for further study.

Due to a seeming lack of interest by state police, family members continue to search Carl's property, finding a rug thrown outside the home and patch of grass and clover that has turned black, indicating blood. They contact state police, who eventually collect samples.

The family also finds a bloody tarp containing a sneaker print and handprint, but police are not interested, so they store the tarp in the barn.

Aug. 26, 2006 – Family holds first of two services for Carl.

Aug. 31, 2006 – North pleads not guilty to car chase charges at a preliminary hearing in Huntingdon County.

Sept. 11, 2006 – Family is astonished when the Huntingdon District Attorney releases Carl's trailer home.

Upon entering the home, family members find evidence overlooked or ignored by police: a drop of blood and an opened penknife on the bathroom counter; the words "fucking hostile" spelled out with the stamp set Carl used for his fencing business; blood on the door and on a picture on the wall; jail-issued socks with North's name on them.

Nov. 17, 2006 – North is transported from Huntingdon County to Franklin, where he pleads not guilty to escape from work release.

May 2007 – Huntingdon County's DA tells the family he is getting ready to charge North with criminal homicide. The DA, Robert Stewart, also is running for re-election.

Later this month, Stewart loses the primary election. There will be a new DA handling the murder case in January 2008.

June 2007 – Family sends letters to several state officials complaining about the lax Franklin County work release program.

Nov 2007 – Family files a civil suit (survivor claim) against North and his work release employer Showbest/AWI.

July 2007 – Dr. Symes in Erie files his report.
Huntingdon County pathologist Dr. Kamerow files an autopsy report listing the cause of death as "blunt force trauma," a nonspecific catchall term.

December 2007 – The district attorney-elect in Huntingdon County, George Zanic, decides to send the case back to Franklin County when he takes office in January 2008, due to the crime scene evidence (blood) at Carl's residence.

January 2008 – North files a Post-Conviction Relief petition, arguing against his October 2007 resentencing for old probation violations. It is dismissed.

Jan. 10, 2008 – Huntingdon DA Zanic meets with Franklin County DA Nelson and investigators to transfer the case back to Franklin.

Mid-Feb. 2008 – In a phone call with a family member seeking information on the case, Nelson claims to be unaware of the case, then says he hasn't looked at it yet. The family requests a meeting, and he says someone will call.

May 7, 2008 – Family gets a call from Trooper Ford saying he plans to charge North with criminal homicide.

May 8, 2008 – Nelson tells the family that prosecutors will be holding a news conference on the case the next day.

May 9, 2008 – Assistant DA Angela Krom approves a criminal complaint against North and police issue an arrest warrant, one year and nine months after Carl's murder. North is taken to a district justice in Pleasant Hall and charged with criminal homicide.

At a press conference, Krom defends the delayed charges, saying the investigation took time because it spanned two counties. Police at the news conference cited strong evidence including blood samples.

May 13, 2008 – Krom dismisses the escape charge and canceled jury selection on that charge, a formality.

June 2, 2008 – Krom refiles for escape, plus the dropped charges from Huntingdon County: false ID, fleeing or eluding, burglary, criminal trespass, theft, access device fraud, forgery, and abuse of a corpse.

June 2008 – North admits during a police interview that he dumped Carl's body. He claims Carl was already dead when he found him.

June 10, 2008 – Family received a receipt noting that their civil action against AWI and North had been served. The receipt had been delivered to a family member's home by North's uncle, who worked for the Franklin County Sheriff's office.

June 19, 2008 – North has a preliminary hearing before a district judge, who finds sufficient evidence to send the case to trial. She sets a date of July 30, 2008, for mandatory arraignment.

June 2008 – Trooper Ford contacts the family to ask where the bloody tarp with the sneaker and handprints is, plus the prison-issue socks that North had left at Carl's.

July 17, 2008 – Family meets with DA staff and investigators on the progress of the case but are given no information except the name of the judge.

Aug. 6, 2008 – North waives arraignment, which had been rescheduled to this date after a screw-up in orders to transfer him from Greensburg state prison to Franklin County Jail.

Krom requested time to get DNA results from items the police had just sent to the lab, after failing to do so for two years.

August 2008 – The court sets a November trial date, which it then reschedules to the January 2009 trial term.

Family contacts the DA's office several times but doesn't get a reply.

September 2008 – North requests a copy of the autopsy report and photos.

Oct. 2, 2008 – A hearing is held before Judge Carol Van Horn on the family's civil suit. Less than thirty days later, she dismisses the claim against AWI with prejudice, meaning that it can't be refiled. Family will appeal and proceed with the case against North after his criminal trial.

December 2008 – Krom and Nelson meet with family. They discuss a letter North has written claiming he killed Carl in self-defense. They indicate they want to pursue a plea bargain with North.

North files a motion to suppress evidence, claiming biased search warrants, an illegal stop, publicity issues, and right to a speedy trial.

Court reschedules pre-trial hearing to March 2009.

Jan. 19, 2009 – Family discovers more blood evidence in a bathroom radiator at the Hennessy cabin, where North likely went to clean up after the murder. State police collect the evidence. It is confirmed as blood but isn't DNA tested to determine whose blood.

March 2009 – Nelson and state troopers meet with family to pitch a plea deal, in which North would plead no contest to third-degree murder and other charges would be dropped. Ford claims blood evidence was really tobacco juice and berry juice.

March 16, 2009 – A pretrial hearing is refocused on the issue of a plea bargain. Just before it starts, the family delivers a letter to Judge Herman opposing a plea deal. North arrives late due to a transport screwup. Herman requests more information about the case and North's criminal history and schedules a separate hearing for April 6 to rule on the plea agreement (this is delayed).

March 2009 – Family circulates a petition against the plea deal. By March 26, they have over 1,000 signatures.
    Krom runs for Franklin County judge.

May 11, 2009 – Two days before the election, Nelson calls the family and warns them against campaigning against Krom (although they have done nothing of the kind).

May 13, 2009 – Krom wins the election for judge. She had asserted during her campaign that as a prosecutor she had never approved a plea bargain without the victims' consent.
    In a phone conversation with the family, Nelson claims to have new evidence, but this appears to be a smokescreen as he continues pushing the plea bargain.

Sept. 17, 2009 – Hearing is held before Judge Herman on the plea bargain, three years and forty-three days after Carl's murder. Before it begins the family pickets outside the courthouse. Herman accepts the deal, and North is sentenced to 22-47 years the same day.

Sept. 24, 2009 – Three years and fifty days after his murder, Carl's final remains are released to his family, and they hold a second service.

Oct. 8, 2009 – District Attorney Jack Nelson dies of a hemorrhage.

November 2009 – North contests the restitution owed for theft and property damage.

December 2009 – Police release items to the family that have little or no significance to the case. Family members meet with investigators to ask (again) why the case was transferred to Huntingdon County. Ford says it was "political."

January 2010 – Krom is seated as a Franklin County judge.

February 2010 – The family's attorney's request a default judgment in their civil case against North. North admitted to the family's attorneys that he had shot Carl and watched him die, although North lied about other things.

December 2010 – Pretrial conference in the civil case.

January 2011 – Jury awards 1.1 million in civil suit, unlikely to ever be paid.

March 2011 – Civil trial. Judge Herman denies motion to reinstate AWI in the case. Family appeals this decision to Superior Court, but it is denied by a three-judge panel.

July 2011 – North appeals in Franklin County court for Post-Conviction Relief. His various claims were rejected via teleconference.

July 2013 – North is transferred from Greensburg State Prison, which later closed, to a new facility in Bellefonte, less than two hours north of Franklin County.

Nov 6, 2029 – The state parole board will have authority to grant or deny parole after North has served his minimum sentence of 22 for murder and escape.

ABOUT THE AUTHOR

C. Lee Ryder was born and raised in rural southcentral Pennsylvania next to the Tuscarora State Forest in the Ridge and Valley region of the Appalachian Mountain chain. She spent seasons exploring the mountainsides, valley, and banks of the West Branch of the Conococheague Creek that wends its way many miles to the Potomac River. She loved art class, played on the basketball team, graduated from Fannett-Metal High School in Franklin County, Pennsylvania in 1978, and was later inducted into the Fannett-Metal Hall of Fame.

Ryder attended Athens State College in Huntsville, Alabama, studied Computer Graphics, Art, and Religion with a concentration in Jewish History and the Old Testament. She earned Collegiate Awards and Academic Scholarships, became a Phi Theta Kappa colleague, and graduated Summa Cum Laude. She was a recipient of the 1998 Tennessee Valley Advertising Federation Addy Award. Ryder's employment spans the Pennsylvania Game Commission, State Police, Labor and Industry, and currently the Pennsylvania State System of Higher Education.

Ryder's first book *Black Clover* is about the heart-wrenching murder of her brother in August of 2006 and the ensuing murder case. Disinterest from state and county officials caused her and her family great anguish that the killer may go unpunished. This book grew from her unstoppable determination to expose the truth and to wring a personal measure of justice from the ordeal her brother and family suffered at the hands of the killer and judicial system. Learn more at cleeryder.com.